LIVING
an idea

Empowerment and
the evolution of an
alternative high school

Edison J. Trickett
University of Maryland

BROOKLINE
BOOKS

© 1991 by Brookline Books

Library of Congress Cataloging-in-Publication Data

Trickett, Edison J.
    Living an idea: empowerment and the evolution of an alternative
    high school/Edison J. Trickett.
        p.   cm.
    Includes bibliographical references.
    ISBN 0-914797-68-9
    1. High School in the Community (New Haven, Conn.) 2. Community and
school—Connecticut—New Haven—Case studies. 3. Educational innovations—
Connecticut—New Haven—Case studies. I. Title.
LD7501.N374T73   1991
373'.042—dc20   90-32660
                                                                CIP

This book is dedicated to
Sara, George, Ed, and Alice

Table of Contents

Preface

This book is unusual in several respects. First, it describes what may be the "oldest" alternative high school in the country. As a result of the turmoil of the sixties, alternative schools became fashionable. It was not that their numbers were ever frequent. They were a most self-conscious way to addressing the failures of urban school systems to address the needs and abilities of students and the dissatisfactions of teachers with the stifling consequences of rigid adherence to an insensitive, bureaucratic, traditional style of organization. If my experience is not atypical, these alternative schools were not enthusiastically endorsed and promoted by educational policy makers and administrators, but rather "allowed" as a kind of last resort to quiet unrest both within and outside the system. Although among those who spearheaded these efforts were some administrators, small clusters of teachers in these school systems carried the ball of innovation. That is the case for the alternative school Professor Trickett describes.

The second way in which this book is distinctive is that almost from its inception Professor Trickett and his colleagues set out to describe and evaluate what was happening. And that description and evaluation continues to today. In the educational literature there are precious few examples of the creation of a new school comparable in descriptive detail, clear conceptualization, and salient evaluation procedures to what we are given in this book. I must emphasize that this book represents a creative integration of fascinating narrative and systematic evaluation.

The third way in which this book is unusual is that although this alternative high school is by any criterion successful — not only in terms of longevity but in terms of being consistent with original purposes, the fostering of student and teacher growth, and maintaining its autonomy and organizational style — Professor Trickett is clear that he is describing a "relative" success. He does not gloss over problems, inadequacies, disappointments, and even failures. Even so, by the end of the story this "relative" success stands out as a tribute to what a truly dedicated, creative, overworked, overburdened group of teachers were *and* continue to be able to do. I am amazed by what these people did in the face of limited resources, problems new and thorny to them, and the knowledge that they were a lonely oasis embedded in an uncomprehending larger system. I am no less amazed by the commitment Professor Trickett made to this project, i.e., his willingness over years to observe and evaluate and to write this unusual book in a style both personal and objective. Longitudinal studies of any kind are infrequent because they require an unusual commitment that may be aborted for reasons beyond the researcher's control, or because the findings turn out to be very unclear or "too soft," or because the pressures in academia to publish are too strong to permit the young researcher to wait years before he or she finds out if they have anything worthwhile to write up. Fortunately for us, Professor Trickett stayed the course. For those interested in the natural history of educational innovations, this book will be most interesting and instructive and, I predict, that like the school he describes this book will have a long life.

Summer, 1990
Seymour B. Sarason
Professor of Psychology Emeritus
Yale University

Public Policy and Public Commitments to Enable School Restructuring: Lessons from the High School in the Community

by Willis D. Hawley[1]
Peabody College
Vanderbilt University

The Misguided Search for Simple Remedies in School Reform

In 1990, *the* magic pill being most widely prescribed to cure the ills of America's schools was "restructuring." Our attraction for this remedy was that it could include almost any proposal different from common practices. But, at the heart of almost all restructuring proposals were two changes in the way most public schools have been organized. The first, usually called site-based management, was to decentralize key decisions — about curriculum, teaching strategies, and the organization of the school day, among other things — from school districts to individual schools. The second change proposed by most advocates of restructuring was to provide teachers with a greater role in decision-making within schools.

In seeking solutions to complex problems, American reformers of education and other social services often seek answers in seemingly successful practices in different fields or in exceptions to the rule. An example of the former is the proposal to model teacher education after preparation strategies in other professions. An example of building reforms around exceptions to the rule is the effort to justify voucher plans that would give parents the choice of schools their children might

---

[1] Willis Hawley is Director of the Center for Education and Human Development Policy at the Vanderbilt Institute for Public Studies.

attend by pointing to the success of some parochial schools serving poor children.

The interest in restructuring schools, in order to radically decentralize decision-making to the school level and politically empower teachers, embodies both these reform impulses. It draws on practices in *some* private businesses and it points to the success of a very limited number of schools where, for various reasons, teachers and administrators have seized initiatives and accomplished great things where others serving similar students have usually failed.

There are at least two problems with these reform strategies. First, they decontextualize the examples they draw on. That is, they fail to recognize that the conditions that apply to the models they draw upon may not apply generally or that the success of the activity serving as a model may have negative side effects when implemented elsewhere. Second, they often discount the possibility that the success of a program is due more to the extraordinary people or conditions involved than to the program's characteristics. And, even when program characteristics both attract and enable extraordinary people, it may be that there is a limited supply of such people.

Not only do reformers often decontextualize analogies and overgeneralize from exceptional successes, they often fail to ask whether the proposals they are making have been tried before. History is often a wet blanket, and when we face trouble we don't want to know about the limitations on the options we seem to have.

The High School in the Community (HSC) is a rather pure case of the types of organizational changes being urged by most advocates of restructuring. Fortunately, Edison Trickett has given reformers an unusually elegant and comprehensive analysis of what must surely be one of the longest-running plays on the restructuring stage.

In his story they will find both reasons for optimism and reasons for concern about the prospects of decentralization and teacher empowerment. While there is much to learn from Trickett's analyses, in this brief commentary I will focus on what policy makers and advocates of fundamental restructuring might learn from HSC's history about how to foster and sustain the organizational innovations that HSC incorporates.

The Essentials of Successful Restructuring

It is not hard to identify the virtues of schools like HSC. Their strengths derive from the sense of sharing and caring they foster and their capacity to integrate students' learning and developmental experiences that enhance both cognitive and social capabilities. The hard question to answer is: Why is it so difficult to secure these virtues?

Trickett makes clear that HSC persisted and succeeded for two basic reasons. First, it attracted, motivated, and retained teachers who seem to be unusually imaginative, and competent, and who are committed to facilitating the learning of students — all students (almost). Second, the characteristics of HSC allowed these teachers, most of the time, to be as good as they could be. There is more to this than organizational arrangements. The structures that characterized HSC are both the product and the sources of a set of beliefs — a culture, if you will — that gave life to organizational forms and provided sufficient cohesion and resilience to weather the continuing challenges that elsewhere have led to a return to bureaucratic and hierarchial school structures. HSC developed from the ground up. Its culture, at least in large part, preceded its organizational forms and has been stronger than the forms themselves. Whether the system of beliefs necessary to invigorate and sustain restructuring can be nurtured by policy and thus implemented widely, remains to be seen.

Public Policy and Really Basic Restructuring

Trickett's study is a rich resource for those who seek to create organizational structures and cultures that facilitate the intelligent use of professional discretion on behalf of students. I will not try to capsulate those lessons here. As noted, I want to suggest some lessons for educational policy makers and other would-be reformers that might be used to create the possibility of the types of restructuring that HSC, at its best, exemplifies.

Lesson 1: Rules and regulations that seek to give direction to schools undermine the possibilities of reform. This lesson seems obvious enough, though the distrust of teachers and the concern for school quality that has driven much of the reform movement make it difficult for policy makers to re-examine the procedures they have put in place to ensure quality.

There are three basic reasons usually given for restructuring: it is motivating, it facilitates responsiveness to local conditions and needs, and it permits invention where the relationship between cause and effect are unclear. The first two of these reasons have dominated the justifications given for restructuring. The third is a powerful reason to seek relief from overregulation and bureaucratization.

Examples of the types of regulations and rules that constrain restructuring are:
 • statewide or nationally normed tests (about which I will say more below),

- detailed curricular guidelines,
- detailed rules and "standards" governing the certification and recertification of teachers,
- union rules related to teacher workloads and time commitments,
- rules specifying minimum class size, the length of the school day or class periods, and
- tests that require retention when student progress does not meet specific standards.

This list is not exhaustive and I have intentionally picked examples which have their virtues. The point is, of course, that we have built over time, for both good and not-so-good reasons, an elaborate structure of constraints on fundamental change which, if left in place, will trivialize "restructuring."

Lesson 2: The search for public accountability of education and the search for innovation and local responsiveness are incompatible. Virtually all calls for school-based management and teacher empowerment are accompanied by the call for accountability for outcomes. There can be little debate about the logic of this; the problem is in the implementation. While efforts are underway to develop alternatives to conventional standardized tests, the measures we now use to hold teachers and schools accountable tend to discourage innovation and risk-taking and to reward mechanistic teaching. It makes no sense to decentralize and yet measure performance as though the product we expect will be the same, regardless of curricula or teaching strategies.

Generally speaking, standardized tests understate the positive effects of innovations because they do not align well with what is being taught. Moveover, the less we rely on bureaucratic rules and roles for controlling organizations, the more we need to depend on information to shape behavior. And, of course, the information must relate to the goals being pursued.

Lesson 3: School District-level office procedures need to adapt to nonbureaucratic units. Central offices can complicate progress toward teacher empowerment and shared decision-making if they do not put aside conventional images of organizations and authority relationships. The one-leader, administrator-dominant image of schools is so pervasive that central offices may find it difficult to relate to different structures. Whether this is manifest unintentionally or with purpose, it can communicate a lack of commitment to restructuring. For example, awards may be given to individuals to recognize the success of the innovation, communication may be expected to go to and come from a single individual, and, when meetings are called, the school-level administrator may be the one invited to represent the teachers and may be expected to make decisions on their behalf.

Lesson 4: Efforts to flatten organizational authority relationships and redistribute responsibilities within schools are facilitated by creating small units for decision-making. Problems of communication and consensus building grow exponentially with the number of people involved. The larger the school the greater the likelihood that administrative structures will be needed and with such structures may come efforts to stratify authority and differences in status derived from differences in position. There is no agreed-upon formula for determining the optimal size of a school — or a "school within a school" — though it seems safe to say that most schools are too large to maximize opportunities for participation in the making of important decisions. It seems likely that the optimal size of a decision-making unit depends on such things as the history of the school, the characteristics of its students, and the nature of the decisions that have been granted to schools. Thus, experimentation with organizational arrangements like "schools within schools" and grade-level or departmental teams should be undertaken and studied.

Lesson 5: When schools are debureaucratized and responsibility is diffused, the teachers and administrators involved are likely to need support of various kinds that exceed the levels and types of assistance typically available to them. Genuine restructuring can be motivating and exhilarating, but it often increases group and individual expectations, makes greater demands on capabilities, and introduces ambiguity and uncertainty. These possible consequences of restructuring schools need to be anticipated and "managed" or they may result in goal displacement, excessive stress, withdrawal, and a failure to use the opportunities the changes provide. The best way to deal with these potentially negative outcomes is to increase the level of information teachers and administrators have about what they are accomplishing on behalf of students, how this compares with what happened in the absence of the troubling changes, and what everyone else in the organization is doing (one common assumption when one is experiencing unusual stress is to assume that others are not doing their share). But enriching the information about needs and outcomes without providing support to address the problems that information inevitably uncovers will result in frustration and further stress. This is not only a condition which could lead to a retreat from responsibility, it is a moment when the opportunities to facilitate professional development are great. Few school systems have the capabilities to respond in a timely and appropriate manner to such opportunities and challenges.

Lesson 6: Movement toward restructuring in a given state, school system, and school should be facilitated and encouraged rather than required. For reasons noted above, the motivations and capability to engage in the process of restructuring will differ from school to school within a school system. It follows that the implementation of restructuring plans should focus on those schools where the prospects of success are greatest. Allowing schools to enter the restructuring process when their administrators and teachers' faculties are ready allows school systems and states to allocate resources judiciously. Further, the successful implementation of major changes in some parts of a school system is likely to facilitate overall change both because this allows problems to be solved where they are most solvable and provides examples of the positive consequences of change to be developed where they will be most motivating and reassuring.

A school-by-school approach to restructuring also allows for some resolution of the difficulty of reconciling the need for accountability with the decentralization of authority. When schools enter a restructuring plan on their own initiative (more or less), specific goals can be established in which teachers are invested and agreements can be reached about the ways attainment of these goals can be assessed.

The Foundations of Fundamental Reform

One might interpret some proposals for school reform as calling for all or almost all schools to have the essential characteristics of HSC. Whether this is a good idea is, however, a moot question. All schools cannot be like HSC — at least not soon. Not only would substantial changes in public policies of the sort noted above have to occur, two even more fundamental changes would have to take place. First, we would have to change and clarify our conceptions of what and how we want youngsters to learn. And second, we would have to increase the rewards of teaching.

Conceptions of teaching and learning in America have been dominated by what Carl Rogers called "the jug-and-mug theory." Teachers and texts pour information into children's heads and levels of achievement are reflected in how much information the mugs hold and how much can be poured out again in the form of answers to common tests. It is increasingly clear that this conception of learning does not fit what is known about how children actually learn and that the results of teaching and curricula which derive from this conception do not meet the needs of the individual children or society. Schools like HSC should not be expected to "do well" when their efficacy is measured in ways we now measure the performance of most schools. HSC represents the wholesale repudiation of the jug-and-mug theory, and the narrowness of the goals are implicitly embedded in the conception of learning.

It follows then, that really basic restructuring of schools is unlikely unless there is greater understanding of how children learn and that the future well-being of both individuals and the nation depends on how able and how motivated children are to use knowledge and theory to solve complex problems, to continue to learn new things, to deal with change and uncertainty, to work well and learn from others, and to act intelligently in accord with a well developed sense of social responsibility.

Schools like HSC place extraordinary demands on teachers. These demands include emotional commitments to students and peers; the ability to teach across subjects; the capacity to learn new things and adapt accordingly; and to learn from each other. It is not clear that we can find enough teachers with these values and strengths unless the benefits of being a teacher are substantially increased. These benefits include salaries and working conditions which will attract and retain people who now pursue other professions and the status society accords persons whose work we believe is both complex and essential to maintaining our quality of life. The open distrust of teachers' motivation and capabilities that is reflected in a host of policies enacted during the 1980s that sought to assess competency and regulate behavior is a shaky foundation upon which to build new structures whose effectiveness will depend on those who work in them.

***

The story Edison Trickett tells about HSC should be required reading for advocates of restructuring. It provides unique and compelling insights to the promise, problems, and prospects of fundamental school reform. And it suggests that such changes will be very difficult to bring about.

CHAPTER 1

Creating Social Settings: Empowerment and the Alternative School Movement

How do we create new settings? Why do they often fail? Why, if they survive, do they frequently end up resembling the settings that they were originally a protest against? In this time of educational reform and innovations in service delivery to various groups in our society, such questions emerge as critical guides to our behavior. When new programs or schools are begun, when self-help groups organize, and when alternative settings for providing psychological or medical services are contemplated, those involved in their creation must grapple with how to translate their social values and social vision into social structure.

The purpose of this book is to aid our understanding of how complex and challenging this process can be. It is the story of the creation and 14-year evolution of a public alternative inner-city high school: New Haven, Connecticut's High School in the Community (HSC). The story describes its guiding assumptions, its planning, its struggles in putting its ideology into practice, and ultimately, its survival. It is a success story but not a smooth ride. Like most newly created settings, those who created the school had times of grave self-doubt, crises of direction, and concerns about its ultimate viability. Their efforts to deal with these and other issues are instructive to all who care about doing good through creating new programs or organizations.

Further, it is a story of a school that lived an idea. The idea was **empowerment**. Students would be encouraged to participate in shaping many aspects of their education, teachers would be responsible for running the school, and parents would be invited to help govern. The empowerment ideology pervaded the curriculum, the organizational structures and processes of the school, the relationships among students, teachers, and parents, and, indeed, the relationship between the author and the school. The present story serves as a hopeful yet sobering example of the kinds of commitments and contradictions that an empowerment ideology entails.

The focus of the book, then, is on the creation of a school setting intended to empower its participants. The school began with a focus on what Watzlawick, Weakland, and Fisch (1974) call "second-order change", or change in the deep structure or core assumptions governing interpersonal and organizational life. Few persons energized by a cause view their mission as minor tinkering with a system that is basically functioning well. Rather, as was the case in the school described herein, the desire to create a new structure was fueled by a deeply held set of social values involving fundamental differences with existing institutions.

The task facing the educators who started the school has been described by Sarason (1972) as "the creation of a setting", which he defines as "any instance in which two or more people come together in new relationships over a sustained period of time in order to achieve certain goals" (1972, p.1). This definition subsumes a wide range of seemingly disparate occurrences, from the creation of a marriage to the creation of a new social order through revolution. Sarason's purpose is not to minimize the very real distinctions between the wedding day and Bastille Day. Rather, it is to highlight the potential commonalities and generic concerns that underlie the creation of settings across a wide variety of events and levels of analysis.

One generic aspect of the creation of settings, for example, involves the notion that settings are profoundly influenced by the frequently unarticulated assumptions of their creators. Thus, states Sarason, "the creation of the marriage setting usually proceeds on the assumption that agreement on values as well as strength of motivation to succeed are the necessary and sufficient conditions to achieve the stated objectives" (1972, p.12). Only over time do the adequacy and implications of such assumptions become clear. In like manner, social innovators also bring to their task many kinds of assumptions which guide their work. These include assumptions not only about anticipated goals, but about processes of how to achieve these goals. From marriage to social innovation, these assumptions influence the course of the newly created setting.

While the present study involves but a single school, the general kinds of issues facing those who created this particular setting are of broad relevance today. Once again, public schools have emerged as a battleground for the social values and priorities debated in the broader culture. Recent books describing and deploring the current structure of public schools (e.g. Goodlad, 1983; Sizer, 1984; Powell, Farrar, and Cohen, 1985; Hampel, 1987) and accounts of exemplary schools (Boyer, 1983) have ignited debate about the restructuring of fundamental aspects of U.S. education. Ongoing concerns about merit pay, autonomy of building principals to use their budget as they choose, and the recent influx of school-age students from all parts of the globe suggest that new settings within the public school system are needed and are near at hand. How these inevitable innovations are conceptualized, and how the values underlying them are translated into social programs and social policy will affect not only students but the very definition of an education. The current story, though limited to a single school, is thus timely as metaphor for today's concern with how to create new structures in public education.

THE RESEARCH RELATIONSHIP:
COLLABORATIVE LEARNING OVER TIME

The present study covers a 14-year period in the evolution of a single school, a time span unusual in the available literature on the creation of settings (e.g. Perkins, Nieva, and Lawler, 1983; Smith and Keith, 1970; Goldenberg, 1971). Not only does such a length of time allow a much-needed longitudinal look at the evolution of this setting; it underscores the importance of the research relationship which was maintained over that period. In general, the relationship of the researcher to those providing data is minimized in social science reports. Its importance to the story that follows, however, mandates a brief discussion, for the nature of my relationship to the school carries important implications for the reader's understanding of the story and for the epistemology of social science community-based research more generally. Equally important are the kinds of biases I brought to the story.

Research Relationships:
Trust, Validity, and Access to Understanding

During the first four years of the school, a team of Yale-based political scientists and psychologists spent considerable time seeing how the school went from an idea to an institution. As a member of that team, I attended meetings, gathered both qualitative and quantitative data, and spent many hours discussing the data and the school with teachers. From 1974 to 1977 I kept in touch with the school both informally and by supervising graduate students who were serving as psychological consultants to the school. Leaving New Haven in 1977, I had minimal contact until the 1983-84 academic year when I returned to Yale for a sabbatical whose purpose was to discover how the school had changed over time. Several of the teachers were still at the school or in the area, and I re-established contact with them.

While my relationship to the school varied considerably during these 14 years, there was a core of teachers and local administrators who remained colleagues and friends to the present time. In addition to our more formal contacts, we sometimes shared life stories and served as sounding boards for one another across a wide variety of professional and personal issues. I was asked to deliver the school's commencement address in 1984 (see Chapter 10), and subsequently did a benefit concert of folk music for the school. Clearly the research took place within a wider set of commitments and relationships.

These relationships brought personal rewards and experiences that will linger. However, they also had direct implications for the range, quality, and believability of the data on which the story is based. A primary aspect of this relationship was its collaborative nature. The spirit of collaboration began with the very first efforts of the evaluation team in 1970 to design an evaluation process that was responsive to the school's concerns. These meetings between the evaluation team and the teachers, held in the summer of 1970, were not always smooth. School personnel were adamantly against standardized testing and had more goals than the evaluation team had resources to evaluate. Candid discussions were held about how much we on the evaluation team could accomplish with our limited resources. We argued about the relative merits of known versus unknown evaluation instruments, particularly as it might affect the external credibility of the school. But, importantly, we shared a concern for the welfare of the school and the empowerment of teachers in deciding on evaluation strategies. In the final analysis, it was their school.

This collaboration continued through the four years of the evaluation (1970-74), not only in selecting goals and instrumentation but in making sense of the results. At least once each year the evaluation team would provide feedback on some aspect of the school for internal discussion. In addition, we circulated the yearly evaluation reports among the teachers, who used them as one source of data in planning for the following year. As this story attests, the teachers were very reflective about their school and sought out many different data sources in their efforts to increase their effectiveness. That they did not always agree with our conclusions is testimony to their commitment to the process. That we sought out discussions about the goals and adequacy of the evaluation demonstrated our belief in the collaboration.

The spirit of this relationship was maintained over the 14-year period described herein. It promoted a depth and breadth of disclosure that helped clarify bedrock issues and potential discrepancies in individual recall of events or interpretations of "what really happened." In addition, teachers would often be reminded during our interviews of other sources of information that I should consult. One teacher remembered that a few years prior to our discussion teachers had tape recorded a discussion about how the school had changed since it opened. Geoff Smith, then a teacher at HSC, had transcribed the tape, and I was able to find the transcription (see Chapter 8).

In the preparation of this book, early interviews with teachers served as a basis for subsequent discussions and checks for accuracy. When initial chapters were written, I circulated them among several teachers for comment, and the three teachers who served as heads of the school during the 14 years as well as the Director of Special Projects and Program Planning in the school system were given copies of the final manuscript for review.

Through this process some differences in emphasis emerged. Alice Mick, for example, the third head of the school, expressed the belief that the book understates the degree of self-examination present in the school, even though the manuscript did include many of the school's planning and self-scrutiny efforts. Sam Nash, then Director of Special Projects and Program Planning, commented that the issue of school size was underplayed, noting that the school's small size allowed a number of processes to occur that would have been impossible in a large school. Through sharing the manuscript with individuals who participated in the creation of the school, however, some degree of "constituent validity," or credibility in the eyes of research participants has, I believe, been achieved.

Additional efforts were made to create occasions in which data relevant to the story could be presented in a forum of accountability to school members. For example, in 1989 I was invited to give a public lecture at Yale. The topic was an overview of what I had learned about how we create social settings, using the story of the school as data. Several teachers from the school were invited to serve as discussants of the presentation, both in terms of its accuracy and its implications for educational innovation. "It made me wince to relive some of those early days," said one, "but it's the way it was." Through such processes, efforts were made to remain accountable to those who had lived the story. While differences of opinion and emphasis certainly remain, the chance of the story being reasonably valid with respect to themes, events, and dynamics has been enhanced through these collaborative processes.

The implications of this for conceptualizing and designing community-based research cannot be overemphasized. It would have been impossible to construct the social reality of individuals who created the school without some degree of trust on their part that the relationship was a serious one dedicated to telling the story of an important undertaking. The validity of data was inevitably enhanced by seeking out multiple sources of confirmation or dis-confirmation and creating a process for correcting or amplifying basic understandings. Access to shared understanding enriched the story in a way impossible to glean from short-term asymmetrical research processes.

Bias, Values, and the Place of the Researcher in the Social Order

The foregoing should not be taken to mean that this author denies bias in the following account. From the earliest days of the school, I believed in the importance of the social experiment the school represented and the values on which it was based. I have, however, attempted to capture the difficulties and down-sides of the school. To ignore or gloss over difficulties would have been to betray the learning which is important for future innovators and scholars. It is hoped that sufficient data have been made available that the reader can form alternative hypotheses about the meaning of events and the salience of themes that recur. Quotes have been selected to amplify themes, not force them in the absence of corroborating understandings. Just as the school engaged in ongoing self-scrutiny, so I have tried to piece together the story in a way that makes sense of the data and validates the experience of the participants.

There are other sources of potential bias, however, that inevitably have resulted in underplaying some themes and exaggerating others. Though perhaps more subtle, they are for that very reason important to discuss. They stem from the observation that psychologists themselves reflect certain aspects of the social order which may inadvertently influence their understanding of social reality. The author, for example, is a white male, reasonably well off financially and working out of an academic setting. How these characteristics and institutional affiliations affected access to, and interpretation of, data must, to some degree, be a matter of speculation.

There are, however, some areas of inquiry where a white male researcher's access to and interpretation of data may require special scrutiny. One example involves the presentation of race dynamics in the book. In arriving at the portrait of racial issues and the differential experiences of white and black students and teachers in the school, I relied on both qualitative and quantitative data. Almost all of it, however, was gathered by whites. The evaluation team was white, including both males and females. The one account gathered by a black graduate student, Winston Gooden, provided both a richer and more complex picture of the experience of both black students and teachers than was previously available. It did not contradict other sources; rather, its context and the manner of Gooden's presentation deepened our understanding of the cultural differences brought to the school by black and white teachers and students.

How widely or seriously such sources of bias compromise the story is probably related to the specific area of concern. As the preceding comments suggest, the area of race dynamics is perhaps less fully portrayed than others. The story would have been more complete if, in the early years of the evaluation, we had acknowledged the conceptual importance of cultural diversity for our work. This is not to assert that the story which follows is necessarily told from a white point of view. The data are too varied and the sources too interracial to suggest that. Rather, the caution is one voiced long ago by Sarason; namely, that we cannot in a convincing way separate our world views from our place in the social order. While considerable efforts have been made to develop a valid story, one simply cannot be sure of when and how these biases intrude into the narrative.

In sum, the development of a long-standing research relationship with individuals at the school and the school itself allowed several important understandings for the book and for such research more generally. First is the positive value of creating ongoing, sustained, collaborative relationships and mechanisms for accountability when attempting to understand real life behavior in real life settings. This effort was respected by the school; it allowed access to a range and depth of information which more superficial approaches would have denied; and it provided a means of verifying hunches and elaborating on ideas which would not have been possible under other conditions. The extensive length of time permitted the author to follow the unfolding of various processes in the school over time. This time period was critical in distinguishing fundamental continuities of the school from transitory reactions in its long-term development.

This lengthy relationship, however, also brought into focus the importance of understanding how characteristics of the researcher can influence what data are accessible and how available data are interpreted. While not prescribing a solution for these issues, it is hoped that the present work forces on the reader what it eventually forced on the author; namely, that the nature of the research relationship is central to an understanding of community settings, and that the relationship takes place within a social context where scholar and citizen often occupy very different niches. The reader is urged to reflect on these issues while reading what follows.

THE CREATION OF SETTINGS AND THE ALTERNATIVE SCHOOL MOVEMENT

In order to provide a conceptual background and a frame of reference for the story, two literatures will be briefly reviewed. The first, on the creation of settings, reviews the concepts which previous authors have found useful in conceptualizing this process. The second literature involves the alternative school movement which blossomed in the late 1960's. Its assumptions, values, and goals represent important ecological influences on the school about which this story is written.

The Creation of Settings: Ecological Context, Internal Assumptions, and Stages of Development

While others have written narratives about the creation of settings in education (e.g. Smith and Keith, 1970) and industry (e.g. Boguslaw, 1965), Sarason's 1972 book *The Creation of Settings and the Future Societies* is often credited with highlighting the creation of settings as a complex yet under-conceptualized problem. His analysis includes attention to the internal assumptions of setting creators and the ecological context within which they are created. In Sarason's view, settings, like people, develop their own distinctive character. That character, however, does not artise in vacuo, but reflects and responds to larger cultural influences. Sarason's general framework has not been seriously altered by subsequent work. Thus, his perspective underlies the current study.

While Sarason's work focuses primarily on the early history of newly created settings, other theorists, predominantly in industrial/ organizational psychology, have sharpened the notion that new settings go through predictable stages as they develop (e.g. Van de Ven, Hudson, and Schroeder, 1984; Greiner, 1972; Bartunek and Betters-Reed, 1987). This stage emphasis represents a more longitudinal perspective for the present study. Because of its comprehensiveness and its relevance to participatory organizations such as the school to be described, the stage theory described by Perkins, Nieva, and Lawler (1983) will be used.

A. SARASON'S PERSPECTIVE: ECOLOGICAL CONTEXT AND INTERNAL ASSUMPTIONS

1. The ecological context within which the setting is created: Ecology, broadly defined, refers to the study of the interdependence of people and their environment (see Barker, 1968; Moos, 1974, 1979; Bronfenbrenner, 1978; Kelly, 1970, 1979, 1986; Trickett, 1984; Trickett, Kelly and Todd, 1972; Trickett, Kelly, and Vincent 1985). An ecological approach stresses the notion that behavior is context-bound and can best be understood through attention to the nature of the context in which it occurs. This general perspective is useful in understanding the creation of settings, for settings are not created in vacuo. Rather, they arise at a certain point in time, in a certain place, and with a certain mission which represents, according to Sarason, a protest against the adequacy of existing settings. Thus, the study of the creation of settings begins with an assessment of the ecological context and its implications for how the setting is conceived of and developed. As ecological influences, Sarason nominates the Zeitgeist and its implications for the range of alternative ideas considered by the setting's creators.

A. The Zeitgeist and the Range of Alternatives: The term *Zeitgeist* is invoked to highlight the general importance of the larger social and cultural context in creating and sustaining new settings. *Zeitgeist* evokes an image of those ideas, values, and assumptions that are "in the air" as the new setting begins; the "climate of opinion" surrounding the problem against which the new setting is a complaint. The Zeitgeist may provide the resources and energy which activate the idea of creating a new setting. It provides a framework for defining both the nature of the problem and the domain of possible solutions. A Zeitgeist simultaneously shapes what is unthinkable as well, providing cultural blinders which exclude some possibilities from conscious consideration. The same cultural conditions that give rise to the possibility of a new setting constrain the range of alternative assumptions on which it may be built.

There are, of course, pragmatic reasons why those who create settings operate from a restricted range of alternatives. As Reinharz (1985) reports, alternative settings are seldom the result of long-range planning by community groups or organizations. Rather, they are more likely to emerge from the efforts of dissatisfied citizens or professionals who generally lack the resources for a protracted planning period.

The more important long-term implications of the Zeitgeist, however, are conceptual, and involve the implicit assumptions governing the thinkable. For example, in commenting on various proposals for educational reform in the 1980's, Sarason (1983) points out that they shared the implicit assumption that education should be carried out in buildings called schools. His point was not that education *could* not or *should* not occur in schools. Rather, it was that the range of possible alternative conceptions of educational reform was constrained by this implicit assumption. Because this assumption was implicit, it was not available to scrutiny. This, in turn, meant that reform proposals based on different assumptions were unlikely to be considered. Thus, the Zeitgeist operates not only in the broader climate of opinion but in the sociocultural ideas that individuals take for granted. As the old saying goes, "the fish are the last to see water."

2. Internal Assumptions of those Creating Settings. In addition to these ecological factors, Sarason postulates a number of internal assumptions which characterize setting creators and exert their own influence on the process of creation. These internal assumptions, of course, are influenced by the Zeitgeist. Each of these assumptions implies both costs and benefits to the new setting.

A. The Myth of Unlimited Resources: The myth of unlimited resources is the initial belief that "we can do it all" and "we have all we need" to do it all. The hope and resolution this inspires provides the determination for risk-taking so necessary to the creation of new settings. However, one predictable consequence of this myth is the penchant for creating goals so varied or general that they inevitably exceed the resources of time, people, and energy necessary to implement them. Because of the discrepancy between available resources and scope of perceived mission, a confrontation with this assumption must eventually come about.

Two things happen when such a confrontation occurs, says Sarason. "One confronts the context of one's values (i.e. choices, previously denied, must be made), and the formulation of the problem and its solution take on different forms" (1972, p. 108). How new settings anticipate and cope with this inevitability thus becomes an important aspect of how they evolve.

B. Superiority of Mission: A second assumption is that the creation of settings is accompanied by a sense of superiority of mission; a belief, whether or not openly expressed, that the new setting is not merely an alternative to existing settings but a superior alternative. A correlate of this assumption is that the new setting will somehow transcend the mundane problems confronting other settings.

Such an assumption may, of course, provide benefits and exact costs for the new setting. On the positive side, a belief in creating "the best" can energize creative talents, focus efforts, and allow individuals to endure stresses and strains they otherwise would not. However, this same sense can increase the denial of real problems in the setting and feed a sense of failure when the "bubble bursts" and the "same old problems" arise again.

C. Agreement on fundamental values is necessary and sufficient: A third assumption useful in understanding the early history of a setting is the belief on the part of setting creators that they agree on fundamental values. Sarason asserts that such an agreement may be a necessary condition for getting a new setting off the ground, but, like the myth of unlimited resources, is not sufficient to maintain the setting over the long haul. Shared values, in the early evolution of a setting, provide an energizing sense of solidarity and mission in what is often a risky and vulnerable undertaking. Further, they tend to serve as a buffer against internal conflicts at a time when it is organizationally important to pull together in the act of setting creation.

For varied reasons, however, shared values, while perhaps necessary, are not sufficient over time. First, there is no absolute correspondence between shared values and agreement on how those values should be implemented. Many distinct specific action choices may be made, all of which may be compatible with shared underlying values. In addition, because any basic value exists in a matrix of other values, the salience of any single value may be supplanted by other competing values over time as the context changes. This further diminishes the chance that values over time will be shared. Finally, as the new setting evolves, it must shift from being held together by a dynamic of "being against" the old setting to "being for" its own agenda. As this process occurs, different kinds of values emerge which were not necessarily primary in earlier stages. The sense of solidarity which characterizes the early life of the setting thus gets tested as the setting confronts more complex and differentiated challenges to its initial values and their implementation.

D. Settings are for clients, not service providers: A fourth assumption mentioned by Sarason involves the degree to which new settings emphasize the importance of the needs of clients and minimize the importance of the needs of setting members. Particularly for those settings fueled by a sense of social mission, the commitment to a cause or an oppressed group is absolute and determining. Responsiveness to the perceived needs of disenfranchised clients is likely to be acute.

Over time, however, such an assumption may set the stage for either disillusionment or burnout unless attention shifts somewhat to the working conditions themselves. Goldenberg's *Build Me a Mountain* (1971), the story of the creation of a residential youth center for inner-city school dropouts, demonstrates how awareness of this assumption can mediate its potentially negative impact. From the planning stages on, the residential youth center operated on the self-conscious assumption that it should provide for staff the same conditions for growth that it wished to provide for its clients. According to Sarason, this assumption is not usually made. Consideration of the setting as a workplace is more likely to be preempted by consideration for client needs.

E. Denial of the necessity of leadership: While the preceding four assumptions may have a generic and relatively content-free emphasis across settings and over time, Sarason's fifth assumption is quite linked to the Zeitgeist when *The Creation of Settings and the Future Societies* was written. The denial of the necessity of leadership was based on the assumption that power corrupts and leaders, to the extent that they are necessary, are necessary evils. Consistent with the times, the downplaying of leadership was intended to provide an egalitarian sense of ownership and control on the part of individuals creating social settings. However, "by denying the necessity of a leader it is assumed that a major source of individual and social corruption has been eliminated" (p.237).

The definition and role of leadership in creating new settings are predicted to be complicated by ambivalence over their necessity. On the one hand, leaders are willing to become leaders to have some distinctive influences over how the new setting evolves. On the other hand, settings created at this time were likely to be founded upon egalitarian ideologies and efforts to minimize or deny "the necessity of leadership." Under such conditions, asserted Sarason, leaders are likely to experience an increasing sense of frustration and isolation from their colleagues over time.

The ideological tendency to negate the authority of the leader, plus the fact that many leaders in new settings are themselves new to the role, increases the likelihood that the leader will lack "an organized conception of the nature of the process in which he and others are engaged" (p.245). This further frustrates the leader's ability to be influential. It does, however, suggest the value of focusing on the dynamics of leadership as a central part of the creation of settings story.

F. Relationship of the new setting to existing settings: Implicit in the previous assumptions is the notion that the ways in which new settings are created influence their relationships to existing settings. First, Sarason asserts that new settings arise as a critique of existing settings and are usually in competition with these settings for resources. This situation, augmented by the myth of unlimited resources and the superiority of mission, vastly increases the chance that new settings will, in their early stages, tend to "go it alone." They will not be interested in creating what may ultimately be mutually beneficial relationships with external agents who may have useful resources. Over time, however, the issue of needed resources is likely to push the new setting toward greater interdependence with its external environment. This, in turn, may heighten issues of how to maintain ideological commitments while compromising to gain external resources.

Taken together, these six assumptions form a useful perspective for assessing the creation of settings. They suggest that the nature of early assumptions on the part of setting creators insures later confrontation with their unrealistic hopes and/or unanticipated consequences. They suggest that assumptions adaptive at one stage of a new setting may be maladaptive at other stages. They further suggest that as settings evolve, a variety of differentiations occur; in values and their implications for how the setting should function; in the degree to which working conditions are seen as linked to the quality of staff life and quality of service provided; in what missions the setting can accomplish and what it cannot; and in the relationship of the leader to his/her colleagues.

Within this framework, new settings are *inevitably* created in such a way that longer-range consequences of initial formative decisions and assumptions will not be well anticipated. There are at least two partial antidotes to this situation. One involves an awareness on the part of setting creators of the assumptions they bring to the setting's initial stages. Such awareness could presumably allow for anticipatory activities which could moderate their negative impact (see Cherniss and Deegan, in press). A second involves the development of both attitudes and mechanisms conducive to self-scrutiny and future planning. This formulation suggests, then, that a prognostic sign for the fate of new settings may involve how they deal with early evidence that things are not going as planned.

B. STAGES IN THE EVOLUTION OF SETTINGS

Embedded in the varied assumptions discussed by Sarason is the notion that settings change over time and progress through different stages, such as an initial stage of hope and high energy followed by disillusionment and the potential for burnout. The issue of stages in the development of new settings has been discussed both in business and industry and with respect to alternative settings.

Greiner (1972), for example, asserts that "the future of an organization may be less determined by outside forces than it is by the organization's history" (p.38), and that "as a company progresses through developmental phases, each evolutionary period creates its own revolution" (p.38). He postulates five stages through which organizations pass, with "each phase (being) both an effect of the previous phase and a cause for the next phase" (p.41). The first phase, Creativity, ends with a crisis of leadership. This is followed by the phase of Direction, which ultimately yields a crisis around the lack of autonomy resulting from Direction. The third phase is one of Delegation, resulting in a crisis revolving around control in the organization. Next comes the phase of coordination of activities, which eventuates in a "red tape crisis" caused by the organizational needs related to Coordination. Finally, a Collaboration phase follows, and no predictable crises from this stage of evolution can be currently ascertained with certainty (see also Van der Ven, Hudson, and Schroeder, 1984).

Within the realm of alternative settings, a less differentiated set of stages has been described. Reinharz (1985), for example, suggests two consistent and meaningful stages: creating the setting and maintaining the setting. Here, the important change in the life of the new setting occurs when the emphasis shifts from getting the setting going to keeping the setting functioning. This literature suggests that the transition between stages is often accompanied by a change in leadership; that individuals who start settings are either uninterested in or unable to provide the skills necessary to maintain them. Thus, the two stages of the organization require different types of leadership skills which, in turn, are reflected in the selection of different types of leaders.

While not specifying discrete stages, Cherniss and Deegan (in press) outline a general process through which alternative settings pass. "Over time, alternative settings that survive change in character. They often become more formal, more differentiated, and more bureaucratic. Power comes to be exercised by a small, select group of people. Roles become more clearly defined and rigid... In other words, alternative settings over time come to resemble traditional settings" (pp.12-13).

Not all writers, however, find the stage theory useful in describing the evolution of new settings. Sarason strongly supports the notion that new settings go through phases as they encounter the implications of their initial assumptions. However, he does not articulate a series of stages per se. Indeed, he cautions that "one must be very careful not to overemphasize discontinuities and to underemphasize continuities" when thinking about phases and stages of settings. In this formulation, one must distinguish fundamental changes in the nature of the setting from superficial changes in its ongoing life.

The potential validity of this point is underscored by Hackman's (1984) description of the creation of People Express Airlines. In a paper entitled "The Transition That Hasn't Happened" Hackman describes People Express Airlines as an organization which, while changing strategies to achieve its goals, did not alter its primary tasks or goals over time. During several times of organizational crisis, when new stages might have been expected to develop, "the response (of the airline) has always been the same: a rededication to the *growth* of the airline, greater efforts to sharpen and teach the *precepts* (on which the company was built), and an increased commitment to the *people* of the airline. Those emphases have been present at People Express since it began, and there is no reason to expect they are about to change" (p.28).[1]

STAGE THEORY AND THE PRESENT STUDY

Hackman's paper is a useful example of why it is important to develop case studies of different kinds of organizations with varying goals, structures, and ecologies. As a framework for the present work, it seemed useful to search out both continuities and discontinuities in the evolution of the school. Following Hackman's ideas, the overriding importance of ideology and its reflection in the organizational culture was seen as a critical continuity.

To assess possible discontinuities, the five-stage theory described by Perkins, Nieva, and Lawler (1982) in *Managing Creation: The Challenge of Building a New Organization* was chosen. Their study is relevant in a number of ways. First, they develop their stages in a way which integrates the ideas of such prior theorists as Sarason and Greiner. Second, their account describes the creation of a medical products laboratory built on "two dominant themes: organizational creation and participation management" (p.xi). While their study involved the private rather than public sector, the focus on a participatory and empowering working environment is quite similar to the focus of HSC.

Perkins et al. argue that "social systems progress through a series of five developmental stages" (p.19), that such movement is predictable but not "inevitable," and that a set of developmental issues associated with each phase will become salient during the early life of the setting"(p.19). Their five stages are as follows:

1.The Utopian Fantasy: This first stage corresponds to much that Sarason has described. This stage is described as "one in which communication is frequent and informal, participants work long hours, and financial rewards are modest....the core group is formed and relationships between leaders and their families are negotiated. The stage for later developmental crises is set by the unexamined assumptions of the recruitment process, failure to establish adequate mechanisms for governance, and the 'myth of unlimited resources'"(Perkins et al., p.20). Goldenberg (1971), in describing the creation of the Residential Youth Center, likened the early days to "a love affair; an undertaking which, for all its moments of panic and uncertainty, possessed the binding qualities of revolution" (1971, p.42). Indeed, assert Perkins et al., "without such utopian beliefs few people would have the temerity to create new settings" (p.20).

2. Challenge to Authority: The second stage is "Challenge to Authority." "The failure to accomplish unrealistic goals, coupled with the difficulty in operationalizing the philosophy of the organization, will eventually lead to breakdown in managerial control" (p.24), thus creating a crisis of leadership. This stage of organizational disillusionment is congruent with Sarason's assertion that the failure to confront predictable problems in the utopian period must inevitably result in a "confrontation with reality." During this phase, the familiar group dynamic of "kill the leader" is at its height, and group members in the setting are preoccupied with the issue of power.

3. Resolution: This third stage, if successful, results in a stabilizing of the conflict generated in the preceding stage. Increased attention is paid to articulating the internal workings of the setting and an increase in the degree of formalization and hierarchy in the setting's organizational structure is found. The primary task is recovery from the previous stage, and, in the service of achieving harmony, conflicts, though present, are masked.

4. Intergroup Conflict: The fourth stage is a return to "Intergroup Conflict." The dynamics behind this return to conflict, however, are different from those fueling the conflict in Stage 2. Here, "This new disturbance originates in needs for autonomy. Members of the organization find themselves thwarted by cumbersome procedures and a centralized hierarchy. These constraints lead to dissatisfaction, disenchantment, and, in some cases, departure from the organization" (p.27). These conflicts seem to surface around issues of resource allocation, influence with the leader, and a feeling of equity in terms of how setting members view the costs and benefits of their participation in the setting. Intergroup conflict is further heightened by the ambiguous contract between leaders and other setting members.

5. Quasi-stationary Equilibrium: Implicit in the stage theory approach is the notion that at some point in time an organization "matures"; that "growing up" is in some fashion accomplished. Perkins et al. call this fifth and final stage "quasi-stationary equilibrium." "This phase is intended to convey the sense that the future state of an emergent organizational system is a dynamic one that cannot be precisely determined. Some organizations succeed and others fail. But there is reason to believe that the level of equilibrium realized in maturity — measured in terms of organizational effectiveness — will be directly affected by the skill with which developmental issues are negotiated in the critical first stages of growth" (p. 32).

LIMITING FACTORS

The model described by Perkins et al. provides a useful roadmap for focusing on stages of group life in emerging organizations. Indeed, in the case study presented in their book, the authors find support for their stage theory. Still, the approach does seem to minimize three other factors of additional concern in the present study.

The first, which Perkins et al. acknowledge is underplayed in their work, involves what Sarason has called the "pre-history" phase of the new setting. *Pre-history* includes those events and processes which lead up to the actual opening of the new setting. Because the hopes, assumptions, and ideology underlying the setting are likely to be particularly vivid in its pre-history, this aspect of setting creation is critical to document. Further, it is during this pre-history that the new setting's overriding vision may become articulated. Such a vision can provide a perspective to assess setting continuity over time.

A second limiting factor involves the relative emphasis placed by Perkins et al on "*internal*" vs. "*external*" *influences* on the development of different stages. In their perspective, the tasks facing the setting are defined primarily in terms of group interaction and group development. The tasks faced by the group are defined mainly in terms of the *internal* dynamics activated at previous stages. Thus, the focus centers on the interplay of group dynamics and its implications for organizational structure and process.

An alternative approach to the notion of stages highlights the setting's relationship to its *external environment*. This may be particularly useful when the setting is at the mercy of environmental influences to which it must constantly attend. For example, many alternative settings, including the school described in this book, begin on "soft money" which cannot be counted on over time. An ongoing task in the creation of this type of setting involves the constant search for a secure funding base. Do such environmental constraints override or simply influence the usefulness of stage theories which focus primarily on the internal workings of the setting?

A third factor currently limiting our understanding of the stages new settings go through involves the dimension of time. Most published accounts of the creation of settings describe events occurring over a relatively short period of time, often two years or less. While a great deal certainly occurs in the first few years of a setting's life, a longer time frame allows a more comprehensive tracing not only of possible stages of development, but also of how the initial assumptions underlying the setting endure or are modified in response to internal and external events. The 14-year period covered by the present study allows such an examination.

The intent of this book, then, is to tell a story that adds to our understanding of how settings are created and evolve over time. Using the general themes of ecological context, internal assumptions, and stages of development as organizing principles, the present study builds on the ideas of Sarason, Perkins et al. and others who have contributed to our knowledge in this area.

As is clear from a perusal of the literature, there is no agreed upon overarching framework for the study of the creation of settings and the problems they face. For some new settings, understanding the overall ideology may be a core problem (e.g. Perkins, Nieva, and Lawler, 1982). For others, fending off community pressure to alter the agreed upon ideology assumes dominance (e.g. Gold and Miles, 1980). The leaving of a charismatic leader may be seen as a pivotal event in some settings (e.g. Reinharz, 1983), while the withdrawal of external funding has been the death knell for others.

This is one reason for telling a tale rather than testing a theory. Almost 20 years ago Sarason commented that "one of the thorny obstacles to understanding and formulating the creation of settings is the lack of well-described instances" (p.21). Out of such descriptions may emerge a richer and more ecologically valid set of concepts which, over time, can form the basis for a more inclusive perspective. Setting the stage for the present story requires a description of the larger social movement out of which the alternative school described in this book emerged, for this larger Zeitgeist was decisive in its influence.

THE ZEITGEIST AND THE ALTERNATIVE SCHOOL MOVEMENT

Murray and Adeline Levine, in their insightful book *A Social History of the Helping Professions* (1970), hypothesize a cultural regularity useful in characterizing the Zeitgeist which spawned the alternative school movement. In describing the history of such helping professions as social work, child guidance, and psychology, the Levines were struck by the relationship of broad cultural forces to the ways in which these professions tended to define problems. They observed that during those times when society is peaceful or quiescent, the helping professions tend to attribute the causes of individual difficulty to individual deficits rather than social policies or institutional structures. The attribution of cause funnels downward, and individuals become troubled, truant, or truculent because of family situations, inadequate internal processes, genetic predispositions or lack of moral fiber.

During times of social turmoil, however, the tendency is to attribute responsibility for individual difficulty to flaws in social policies and institutional practices. Here, the spotlight shifts from the micro to the macro. Ryan's (1970) eloquent book *Blaming the Victim* states a basic thesis of this perspective; that individuals are victimized by larger social forces which should themselves be the focus of concern for the helping professions.

These contrasting perspectives on how problems are defined do not represent pure cases. Rather, they represent the waxing and waning of different *emphases* prevalent at different points in time. Attributing responsibility for behavior to individuals *or* social structures and policies does, however, represent an important aspect of the Zeitgeist. As Caplan and Nelson (1973) point out, the way problems are defined tends to shape the kinds of solutions that are developed.

During the late 1960's, when the alternative school movement began, attribution of responsibility for many social problems rested on the shoulders of social policies and social structures. The civil rights and Black Power movements were providing incisive critiques of the more subtle as well as obvious structural supports for racism. The student power movement, the Free Speech movement, the women's movement, and the hippies also forced the ongoing analysis and questioning of the social structure and one's relationship to it.

Dr. Martin Luther King, Jr. beautifully described both the tone and content of the Zeitgeist in an October 1961, speech to the Transport Workers Union:

> There are certain words in every academic discipline which soon become stereotypes and cliches. Every act of democratic discipline has its technical nomenclature. Modern psychology has a word...It is the word "maladjustment."
>
> Certainly, we all want to live the well-adjusted life in order to avoid neurotic and schizophrenic personalities...I say to you today that there are some things in our social order toward which I am glad to be "maladjusted" and I call upon you to be "maladjusted."
>
> I never intend to adjust myself to slavery and segregation. I never intend to adjust myself to religious bigotry. I never intend to become adjusted to economic conditions that will take necessities from the many to give luxuries to the few.
>
> I never intend to become adjusted to the madness of militarism, for in a day when Sputniks and Explorers are dashing through outer space, and guided ballistic missiles are carving highways of death through the stratosphere, no nation can win a war. It is no longer a choice between violence and nonviolence. It is now either nonviolence or nonexistence.
>
> And I never intend to adjust to the madness of militarism and the self-defeating effects of physical violence.
>
> And so I call upon you to be "maladjusted" and continue in the maladjustment that you have already demonstrated, for it may well be that the salvation of our world lies in the hands of the "maladjusted."

Themes of Empowerment: The Specific Context for the Alternative School Movement:

During this time of questioning various aspects of the social structure, several specific themes emerged which became embodied in the alternative school movement. All of these themes stemmed from a commitment to the empowerment of those perceived as being vulnerable and victimized by the larger social order.

1. Participation in Decision-Making: Of the various forms taken by the push for individual and collective power, none occupied a more central role than the quest for participation in decision-making. Through such activities as voter registration drives in the South, advocating affirmative action in the workplace, and promoting participatory democracy on college campuses, participation in decision-making became a primary forum for actualizing power. Empowerment did not simply mean a "sense of control" in a psychological sense. Rather, it meant having a slice of the political action by actively participating in how issues were decided.

(2) Revising the Concept of Authority: In the larger struggle for social justice and empowerment, the concept of authority was a primary target. In the social arena, the authority of law became suspect, and police were symbolically and actually attacked to protest laws seen as repressive and disenfranchising. Institutional authority based on role and expertise was likewise thrown into question as the consequences of institutional structures and policies came under attack. Here, empowerment of the individual was linked to the overthrowing of people and policies exercising "arbitrary" influence that undercut the wishes and needs of those influenced by them.

(3) The Vilification of Bureaucracy and the Search for New Institutional Forms: The vilification of bureaucracy represented the institutional focus of the revision of the concept of authority. Bureaucracy was not only seen as constraining the freedom of individuals; bureaucracy also stood for hierarchical and role-based relationships among people rather than more egalitarian and "humanizing" interactions. Bureaucratic structures stood for "the establishment"; manifestations of where we had gone wrong. They were too big, too impersonal, too immune to self-examination, too resistant to change. The vilification of bureaucracy spawned the search for alternative institutional forms designed to empower individuals.

(4) The Positive Value of Cultural and Lifestyle Diversity: The celebration of diversity of people and cultures constituted another thrust toward empowerment. On the individual level, the development of varied lifestyles, often punctuated by one's personal appearance, served as a critique of societally imposed "shoulds" and as a statement of personal liberation. The affirming value of cultural heritage was concurrently strong, both as a critique of the ways in which the dominant culture had disenfranchised groups and distorted their history, and as a positive statement about the qualities and contributions of varied cultures. Here, the development of pride, self-esteem, and a caring appreciation for one's own culture were emphasized as empowering goals.

(5) The Politicization of Experience: Within the Zeitgeist of the time, the motivational basis for commitment to social change was linked to the politicization of experience—the importance of understanding social structures, policies, and cultural attitudes within a political/ideological framework. This perspective was captured well in Eldridge Cleaver's now famous phrase "if you're not part of the solution you're part of the problem." There was no room for political neutrality. The draft was defined as a policy designed to discriminate against the disenfranchised; admissions policies at universities reflected efforts to maintain the class structure in the broader society; school curricula portrayed the white experience as the only experience worth portraying. The intent was to reframe current social reality in terms of political struggles, thus developing a new consciousness about the ways in which the broader culture discriminated and disenfranchised.

The foregoing is not an exhaustive set of the social agendas which characterized the Zeitgeist during the late 1960's. It is intended to convey the spirit and content of some primary themes of empowerment salient at the time. Most important is the notion that *all* these themes reflected efforts to realign the relationship between the individual and the social structure, with the greatest emphasis placed on examining and altering aspects of the social structure rather than focusing on individual determinants of behavior.

The Alternative School Movement: Manifesto and Themes

The alternative school movement which started during this time was a direct reflection of the larger Zeitgeist. Its manifesto was clearly articulated in testimony by Mario Fantini, Donald Harris, and Samuel Nash given in summer, 1969, before the Senate Select Committee on Educational Opportunity. It links the national Zeitgeist directly to the realm of public education and the rationale for the alternative schools movement. Their prepared remarks were entitled "Public Schools of Choice."

> We have entered an age of education and the American public knows it.... The term "survival" is particularly appropriate for describing the role of education in an advanced technological society which needs and wants universal education. To be denied quality universal education today is to be denied the means for societal survival.
>
> The case for political survival is also clear. The quality of education affects the role of citizen. Political socialization is an educational process. Participation is learned. Unless an individual is fully aware of his rights in our political system, his chances of surviving are seriously jeopardized. Blacks, Chicanos, Indians, and other minorities are especially sensitive to the importance of education to their political survival.
>
> If schools produce illiterates among Blacks, Chicanos, Puerto Ricans, and Indians, as they have, then the quest for group economic and political power is crippled. Without access to this power, these minority groups cannot play in the political arena. Hence, when they claim that schools are engaged in a systematic conspiracy against them, when they use "educational genocide" to describe their frustration, it is all wrapped around the political survival needs of minority groups.
>
> It is clear that public schools as they are presently set up cannot meet the growing demands that are being thrust on them. In a pluralistic society, diversity is an important value that our educational institutions should express... Minority parents are demanding a quality of education that guarantees equality of educational performance. We are asking the schools to deal with such societal problems as poverty, alienation, delinquency, drug addiction, pollution, and racism. The result is that while these demands are legitimate, the schools cannot now satisfy these demands.
>
> We need a process today in which each user of our public schools can make a decision concerning the type of education which makes the most sense for him. This means giving parents, teachers, students, and administrators a direct voice in educational decision-making. Parents, teachers, students, and school administrators—those closest to the learning front—have traditionally been those farthest from participation in educational decision-making.
>
> How can we enter a new state of participation in which the rights of the plurality of school publics are protected? Two

movements which started at the tail end of the sixties offer us some signs for the seventies.

The first of these is the movement of alternative schools outside the bureaucratic public school system. These new schools have increased in number over the past few years as conditions in urban public schools continue to decline.

The second movement is an attempt to reach the educational consumer directly through a tuition voucher which can be used to purchase superior education. This latter form attempts to generate needed change by altering the dominant structure of American education, that is, increasing the purchasing power of the educational consumer to purchase different forms of education in a type of free market enterprise...

What is needed is to bring these two developments and individual decision-making into the context of public schools where the majority of students are enrolled. What we propose is a new system of public schools of choice...

The citizen consumer should be able to decide on the kind of school his child should attend or the kind of educational environment he would like his children to have...

EMPOWERMENT THEMES AND ALTERNATIVE SCHOOLS:

It is beyond the scope of this book to review in detail the nature and scope of the alternative school movement outlined in the previous manifesto. The interested reader is referred to Duke's (1978) *The Retransformation of the School*. That book's very title, however, reinforces the notion that the emphasis underlying the creation of alternative schools was structural and intended to transform the nature of schooling through transforming the ways schools were organized and run. These new settings were based on a variety of ideological assumptions about how students learn, where they can learn, and what kind of organizational structures they can best learn in. All were fueled by the broader Zeitgeist's emphasis on empowerment.

1. Participation in Decision-Making: The broader Zeitgeist emphasis on participation was reflected in various ways in the alternative school movement. Teachers were empowered to shape the curriculum and organizational structure of the newly created schools. Students, at least at the high school level, were provided opportunities to create their own course of study and participate in decisions affecting the school. Active parent involvement in the school was encouraged.

The specific mechanisms to increase participation in decision-making differed from school to school. In the area of governance, for example, some schools attempted a participatory democracy where all students and teachers were given equal voting power on decisions affecting the school. Other schools adopted a form of representative democracy where students and faculty representatives decided on a narrower range of school issues. Still, the value of soliciting input on various matters, the extensive efforts to create schools that were responsive to students and parents, and the many ways in which student and faculty choice was built into the school experience all signalled the belief in participation as an empowering ideology.

2. The Commitment to Nonbureaucratic Organizations: A second response of the alternative school movement to the broader Zeitgeist reflected the vilification of bureaucracy. This was expressed in the creation of a variety of nonbureaucratic organizations for schooling. Hawley (1974) cites five aspects of nonbureaucratic organizations which were reflected in the organizational structure of alternative schools:

> (1). Key decisions would be made collegially instead of by those atop a hierarchy of authority. While hierarchy might exist for administrative purposes, such authority would be delegated by the work group. Thus, the "vertical span" of organizational hierarchy would be zero.

> (2). Specialization of roles would be minimized and those played by specific individuals might vary from time to time; status divisions would not exist.

> (3). While goals may be externally established, the means for achieving them are largely determined by the organization. In this sense, the organization is relatively autonomous and the distinction between policy and administration is blurred.

> (4). Interpersonal relationships are determined by social needs and technical requirements with respect to specific tasks rather than by standard operating procedures and formal positions. Continuity of position or role is not stressed.

> (5). Standardization of organizational activities (the ways problems are dealt with), the extent to which established and uniform procedures and rules govern the execution of function, is low. Formalization is low; procedures, rules, instruction and channels of communication are not codified or otherwise well defined (p.3).

3. Expanding the Explicit Goals of Education: A third alternative school response to the broader Zeitgeist was to expand the goals of education beyond academic skills to include personal development. "Knowing each student as an individual" was important both as an antidote to the fragmentation of experience caused by bureaucracy and as a means of stressing that education was a holistic rather than academic experience. Alternative schools differed in the degree to which this expansion of educational goals implied a diminished concern with academic achievement per se. The broader concern, however, was to redefine the goals of education to include socialization goals as well as academic ones, and to redefine the very notion of achievement in a broader way than could be tapped by standardized tests.

4. The Community as an Educational Resource: A fourth influence of the larger Zeitgeist was the notion that education can occur in a variety of settings outside the school and invlove a variety of persons not formally part of the educational system. This idea represented several Zeitgeist influences. First, it helped "liberate" students from the bureaucratic structures of the public schools and diminished the distinctive professional role of teacher by asserting that "we all have things we can teach each other." In addition, it increased the opportunity for student empowerment through allowing increased choice and options around constructing a more personalized curriculum. Further, it provided a potential vehicle for both the school and community to learn about the strengths and weaknesses of the other, bringing education into contact with the "real world" in a pedagogically useful way. Finally, it provided an opportunity to involve parents as educators of students in the school. For these reasons "the community as educational resource" was congruent with the broader empowerment ideology.

The sum total of these varied emphases — on participation, nonbureaucracy, expanded educational goals, and community as resource — implied a reconstructed educational environment in marked contrast to the public schools of the day. In structure, norms, educational values, and relation to the community, the alternative school movement was intended to create not only a choice, but a distinctively different choice. Relationships among teachers and between teachers and students would be less role-related, decision-making would take on a different form, and parents and the broader community would in some fashion take on more meaningful roles in the educational process. This implied restructuring on a rather major scale.

The following chapters tell the story of the creation and evolution of one such school: New Haven, Connecticut's *High School in the Community*. Its goals, ideology, and structure were explicitly intended to test out the previously described themes of the alternative school movement. The story is told from the perspective of Sarason's framework for

CHAPTER 2

What if There Were a School Where They Tried All the New Ideas?[1]

Such was the title of High School in the Community's first annual external evaluation report. More than merely offering a choice for students, the evaluators claimed that HSC "may be the most ambitious effort at comprehensively restructuring and reorienting secondary education now being supported by any public school system in the United States" (Hawley et.al., 1972).

HSC began in the fall of 1970 as an alternative to one of New Haven's three high schools: Hillhouse High School. Its purpose was articulated in a 1970 grant application for Connecticut State Aid to Disadvantaged Children (SADC) funds:

> The H.S.C. will offer students an alternative school structure, one designed to link school with the outside world and to be highly responsive to individual student needs.
>
> The High School in the Community Program (HSC) is based on the belief that the greatest strength of a democratic society is its ability to absorb a wide range of different opinions, and to make it possible for different groups to have their own social and political institutions. In a democratic society it is imperative that institutions become and remain pluralistic in character. Public schools provide a number of educational options that meet the needs of different groups of students.
>
> Many students, particularly those with disadvantaged backgrounds, do not fully develop — either educationally or psychologically — in the standard high school framework... Their negative feelings are the result of three primary factors:
>
> (1) The students find school divorced from life in general. They feel little connection between the hours they spend in a school building and those spent on the job, in playgrounds, walking in city streets... Such students need immediate perception of the relevance of their school work to life in the city.
>
> (2) The students need more individual attention than a large high school can give. Few students are able to move at their

own educational pace. Some fall behind in their classes and get discouraged; others find the pace of their classes too slow and grow bored. In general, these students feel that no one focuses on them as individuals with concern for their particular needs, talents, and interests.

(3) The students are unhappy with what they see as a rigid, unresponsive school administrative structure. Some are suspicious of authority in general and their suspicious attitudes extend to teachers and school officials.

HSC's organizational structure affirmed its alternative nature. During its first few years, it had no building of its own; its offices and classes were scattered throughout the city. The role of the classroom teacher was enlarged to include guidance and liaison between students and community placements. Community placements were made for credit through a Community Orientation Program (COP) in local businesses and service agencies. It had no principal. A Policy Council, consisting of equal numbers of students, parents, and teachers, held a major decision-making role in school governance. Student evaluation was accomplished through written teacher assessments of student performance rather than through letter grades. And state-mandated course requirements could be filled by any number of appropriate courses rather than a specific course. Through these structures, HSC created a fundamentally different school experience for the high school students of New Haven.

How did such a school come about? What were some of the forces which led to its taking the form it did? These two questions, relating to what Sarason and others have called the *pre-history of a setting*, get to the heart of the "idea" of HSC, and are the focus for this chapter.

First comes a discussion of the development of crisis in New Haven in general and Hillhouse High School in particular. During the 1960's, rapid demographic changes and social instability took place in New Haven. The lack of quick response on the part of city government and the public school system to the changing needs of the community, and the more widespread urban unrest of that time, created both crisis and the opportunity to innovate. Next, the reactions of the school system to this crisis are described. It will be seen that a climate of support for innovation existed among key administrators and teachers who found common cause in the idea of creating an alternative school. The focus here is on how different key actors viewed the idea of an alternative school and why they supported it. Finally, the process of developing funding and school system approval for the project is outlined.

THE DEVELOPMENT OF CRISIS:
NEW HAVEN AND HILLHOUSE HIGH SCHOOL

On December 15, 1967, riots broke out at James Hillhouse High School in New Haven. The incident that sparked the outburst had racial overtones — a white boy had punched a black girl in the back three days earlier. She had declined to stand for the Pledge of Allegiance because she was tired. In the minds of many, the boy was not adequately disciplined for his actions. The black girl noted, "He wasn't punished the way a black would have been punished who had done that" (New Haven Register, December 15, 1967).

The Black Student Union at Hillhouse protested the situation by walking out of the school, en masse, during the lunch hour. They were looking for resistance, but Assistant Principal Eugene Vitelli cautioned the staff to let them go. With no direct provocation, the group re-entered the school and started to break plate glass, tables, and chairs. A few white boys were "selected" for roughing up. Four minor injuries were reported in the press. After an hour the group took to the streets, blocking traffic and throwing bottles at cars.

George Foote, then a teacher at Hillhouse, felt the riot was never out of control in the sense that the kids were "crazy." On three separate occasions Foote easily broke up large groups of blacks who were beating whites. No girls were involved and no teachers were threatened.[2] Foote recalls: "About a half hour after this thing was over, I remember the assistant principal walking down the hall talking to himself. It was funny... It was tragic. He was saying, 'Never thought it could happen here.' It was like a movie scene, but would have been corny in a movie."

John Santini, then Superintendent of Schools, initially reacted to the riots in the following way: "What happened here is part of the illness that besets the whole country. We have people — extremities of the left and right — preaching hate. Some of this preaching hatred has infected our young people" (*New Haven Register*, December 18, 1967). While there was much evidence on the national level that such was the case, in retrospect it seems clear that local conditions in the school also contributed to the rioting.

New Haven as an Urban Setting: Before 1967, New Haven had been considered America's Model City by many: an example of how much a city can do for its people. Mayor Richard Lee perceived a need for the renewal of New Haven when he took office in 1954. One key to renewal was money, and Lee's success can be linked at least in part to his unusual ability to receive outside funding. Over the course of Lee's 16 years in office, $120 million in federal funds — $800 per inhabitant — was funnelled into the city. This was supplemented by $60 million in state and local money. The primary uses of the government funds were road construction and demolition of deteriorating housing. Two hundred and fifty million dollars of private investment was attracted to rebuild the downtown area (Powledge, 1970), an impressive face-lift for the central business district. Lee's success at fund raising and his entrepreneurial spirit not only increased New Haven's resources during this period, but also helped create a "can-do" climate of innovation in the city bureaucracy.

The population of New Haven was rapidly changing, however. According to census data, the city was 5.8 percent black in 1950; 14.5 percent black in 1960; and 26.3 percent black in 1970. Much of this increase was due to blacks emigrating from the South. As the black population increased, middle class whites moved to the suburbs (only 2.3 percent black in 1970). As a result, the city's overall population dropped from 164,443 in 1959 to 137,707 in 1970 in spite of a 13,000 increase in the black population.

Lee was fully aware of the changing populace of New Haven and responded by emphasizing "human renewal." In Lee's eyes, the keys to making human renewal work were community organization and participation — concepts which had earlier been bulldozed over in the drive to achieve physical renewal. In 1962, $2.5 million came from the Ford Foundation to support a poverty program that served as a model for the Johnson administration. Community Progress, Inc., the original poverty agency, became an important and visible symbol. (See Sarason et al, 1966, for an interesting perspective on Community Progress, Inc. and its role in community organization in New Haven).

The schools were also involved in human renewal through the creation of "community schools" — the opening of schools for 16 hours a day to serve as the focal point for community activities. The "community schools" idea signalled a readiness on the part of the school system to transform the school into a community resource.

The changes were slow in coming, however. In August, 1967, New Haven was hit by three days of vandalism, arson and looting. The incident that incited the rioting was the non-fatal shooting of a Puerto Rican by a white restaurant owner who claimed he had been threatened with a knife. The damage, estimated in the millions, was isolated primarily in the poor Hill and Dixwell communities. Participants commented that "the Mayor's building all the houses for white people," and "Yale is taking over New Haven." One black woman said, "Lee was so sure nothing would happen to his pretty city... As far as I am concerned, this (the violence) is a good thing." (*New York Times*, August 21, 1967).

Lee had indeed thought that New Haven was immune to the kind of violence that had struck so many other cities. His initial reaction was: "None of it makes sense." After some reflection, however, he made a comment which was similar to the one School Superintendent John Santini was to make: "I don't know whether any city can avoid major violence, through the dedication of a mayor or through the leadership of the community itself beyond the political power structure. Some of these things are just signs of our times" (Powledge, 1970, p. 111). While both Lee and Santini sought to lay much of the blame on national trends, the inadequate response of the city to its new constituency and new problems was certainly a contributing factor to the violence.

Tensions were slow in easing after the riots, in part because the issues remained and in part because of a series of events that served to further polarize the community.[3] From opening day on, schools were tense from the aftermath of the riots. At Hillhouse, it was particularly noticeable. The Black Panthers were an organized group in New Haven, and one of their favorite meeting places was in the park across from Hillhouse. George Foote recalled that it was not uncommon to be sitting in a class and hear the Black Panther sound truck broadcasting: "If you're truly black, then come out of the building...walk out...walk out." The people across the street often included some Panthers of national reputation. It provided ongoing discussion for Foote's current events class: "And who is making the news today? Well, it is across the street in the park and it is focused at Hillhouse."

HILLHOUSE HIGH SCHOOL

The site of the riot, James Hillhouse High School, had been originally conceived of as a college preparatory school and had a fine reputation during its early years. At the end of the 1940's, the school board decided that it should become a comprehensive high school; it should provide curricula and guidance for non-college bound students as well as for those who were college bound. In the late 50's, the school moved to a new building which was better equipped to meet all students' needs.

But even in 1963, the school had not changed its fundamental approach to education. It retained many of its old teachers — the average years of teaching experience was close to 30. Some teachers did not have a college diploma — they had been given tenure in the system at a time when one was not required. In addition, almost all were white.

The school board and the superintendent decided the time had come to induce changes at Hillhouse. In 1963 concerted efforts were made to force incompetent teachers out of the high school. One of the four new young teachers added at this time was George Foote. In that first year Foote had 34 students in each of five one-hour periods each day with only one free period per week. Classes were tracked, and there was a strong sense among teachers that college-bound courses were given as rewards. Five non-college bound classes was equivalent to saying to a teacher, "hope you don't come back next year." The school was as orderly as it was traditional. In fact, Foote recalled that he was reprimanded by an administrator for walking "up the down staircase" in his first year.

During the few years following Foote's arrival at Hillhouse, critical demographic changes were occurring which drastically altered the racial composition and socioeconomic characteristics of the student body. In 1963 the black/white ratio was 20 percent to 80 percent. By 1967 the school was 60 percent black, rising to 67 percent by 1970 (Abraham, 1971). The immigration of blacks into the previously white community was compounded by the relocation of local blacks forced to move because of redevelopment. Thus the Hillhouse community was highly unstable and the population of the school changed rapidly. The school's response to this change was sluggish.

Even thirty years of teaching in the New Haven system did nothing to prepare a large number of Hillhouse teachers and the administration for the events of 1967. At the first of the school year, the issue was whether or not a teacher was allowed to have a beard. By December, the principal had been confronted by seven Black Panthers in his office with a list of demands. The crucial issue raised by the blacks was racism. As the leader of the Black Student Union at Hillhouse said after the riots: "It's a whole range of things — the attitude against us that white teachers have — that's why we revolted." A white English teacher agreed. "You see it all the time, even though it is subtle. The fact is that, subconsciously or not, we just don't treat the Negroes the same way as whites and they know it" (*New York Times*, December 16, 1967).

The New Haven Commission on Equal Opportunities issued a report on the causes of the Hillhouse problems. The report placed the blame directly on the school for failing to recognize the changing needs of a changing population. The Commission found that (1) prejudice did exist in Hillhouse; (2) students showed an appalling inability to read; Hillhouse was failing in its primary function; (3) the guidance counseling was geared to the middle-class college-bound students; and (4) more community participation was needed in the operation of Hillhouse (New Haven Commission on Equal Opportunities, 1969). In short, the Commission charged that the school had changed little and lost touch.

Gerald Barbaresi, Associate Superintendent of the New Haven Schools in 1967 who became superintendent two years later, placed the blame on "dead wood" in the public schools. They were responsible not only for allowing the Hillhouse situation to develop, but also for the failure of Mayor Lee's broader goal of human renewal. In Barbaresi's view, they could not look beyond the classroom walls to see the potential role the schools could play in organizing and coordinating community services. Barbaresi favored the community school idea as the first step of a master plan to coordinate all human services out of the school at the community level. In this theory, he was supported by Sam Nash, Director of Special Projects and Program Planning.

By December 1987, several trends had combined to create crisis conditions in New Haven and, in particular, Hillhouse High School. Though unusually adept at developing external support for urban renewal, New Haven was still unable to stem the national tide of violent reaction against racism and poverty. The population of both the city and school system was becoming increasingly black and poor, and the public institutions were unprepared for the implication of these changes.

There were, however, several forces for change emerging at this time. Regardless of Mayor Lee's initial response of blaming the riots on the national Zeitgeist, his administration had, over time, created a positive climate for social innovation. New Haven was a place where problems could be acted on and solved. This spirit was found in the administration of the public schools, where Barbaresi and Nash were developing their own ideas about how the crisis might be turned into an opportunity for educational innovation.

Responses of the School System: An Idea Gains Momentum

Superintendent of Schools John A. Santini announced a shortened school schedule for the week following the Hillhouse riot. This was to allow time for students and teachers "to assess current school problems and to work on ways to improve learning and teaching conditions." He said that the school board and staff were willing to be advised by any "person interested in public education." But he emphasized that the final responsibility to take corrective action lay within the system. For the time, "the welfare of our students requires that we maintain order in the schools" (*The New Haven Register*, December 16, 1967).

If Santini did not know he was walking a tightrope on December 15, the day of the Hillhouse riots, he knew by the 18th. Parents kept their children at home. In all, two-thirds of the students stayed away from Hillhouse. The majority absence led to a special student-faculty meeting to discuss school problems. Those who did attend talked mostly about discrimination. When someone asked why only one-third of the teachers were at the meeting, Santini offered the comment that maybe some of them had to see sick aunts; everyone stormed out. On the whole, however, the student-faculty session was calm compared to a parents' meeting which was held earlier. Most parents wanted to know why their children's lives were in danger (*New Haven Register*, December 18, 1967).

There were also parties not directly involved who took an interest in the school proceedings. The Republican Town Committee came out in favor of firing the superintendent and school board for not being able to maintain order (*New Haven Register*, December 27, 1967); and the Black Panthers continued to make appearances in the school.[4] Peace was fragile and tension was high.

Two approaches were taken by the school system to improve the situation. The first was to reduce the student-teacher ratio at Hillhouse by adding 10 teachers after the Christmas recess. Its effect on relieving the tensions was minimal. Secondly, the school system encouraged negotiations among representatives of the discontented black students, teachers, administrators, and parents to discuss demands for change at Hillhouse. Sam Nash was appointed by the superintendent to negotiate on behalf of the school administration.

George Foote, recognized as someone who could communicate well with the students, was elected chair of the Teachers' Liaison Committee. It was this committee's responsibility to represent the views of the faculty in the negotiations. Foote recalls that this was practically impossible as the faculty itself was deeply divided. The primary demographic division was in terms of age and seniority. The majority of teachers had been in the system a long time, tended to be politically conservative, and wanted little change. However, a group of young teachers had been added over the preceding four years who tended to be politically liberal, if not radical, and supported proposals for changes at Hillhouse. The younger faculty members had formed a group immediately after the riot called the Teachers' Collaborative, headed by Torrey Orton. By December 21, they had already published a letter to the editor of the *New Haven Register* espousing support for the black students and their demands for change.

The split in the faculty was exacerbated by the students who referred constantly to the "good, young teachers" versus the "old, bad ones." The generalization was unfair to some teachers but, as Foote noted, many older teachers had not been able to adjust to the changing demands that the 60's had brought. They reacted unsympathetically to the events of 1967, which further alienated them from black students. The younger teachers were perceived by the blacks as being on their side. But of more importance, the older teachers were the symbolic targets of the riots. They embodied the historical discrimination and failure of the system to teach basic skills to blacks[5] and the favoritism shown to middle-class college-bound students.

Thus Foote was faced with the impossible task of representing the faculty which could not iron out its own internal differences. The chances of working out an acceptable solution in the discussions with black students were reduced further by the faculty's failure to include any black teachers in electing their representatives. The election was very democratic, Foote recalled, but insensitive to the demands of the situation. The effect of this election, then, was that an all-white committee was sent to "discuss" (defend itself against) charges of racism made by black students. Though black teachers were added to the group, the tone of the sessions had already been set.

On February 5, 1968 new riots struck Hillhouse. Rumors of a planned riot had surfaced and the authorities were expecting trouble. The newspapers reported that the black students had been split on tactics — some wanted to boycott the school because nothing was resulting from the sessions while others wanted to "bust the place up." Thus, not all the discontented black students participated in the riot, and after it was over the Black Student Union denied having had anything to do with it (*New Haven Register*, February 6, 1968).

The new disturbances brought a strong reaction from the faculty. In a wide-ranging faculty meeting, the majority of conservative teachers instructed Foote to tell the central office that they would not teach if police were not in the halls the next day. Foote conveyed the message over the objection of the Teachers' Collaborative, whose members were adamantly opposed to bringing the police into the school. Superintendent Santini was neutral on the question but the police were not. They said they were ill-prepared to deal with the situation at Hillhouse and that bringing in police would be a big mistake. Foote, not wanting to tell that to the faculty himself, suggested to soon-to-be Police Chief James Ahern that he explain the reasoning behind the refusal. Ahern, after a very emotional session with the teachers, agreed to have the police there the following morning.[6]

Mayor Lee, whose daughter attended Hillhouse, was also moved to action by the second outbreak. He came to the school and personally ordered the arrest of any student breaking school rules. By the end of the week, 27 students had been arrested for violations in the school halls (*New Haven Register*, February 9, 1968).

Hillhouse quieted down for the remainder of the year, but tension was still present between the factions of students and teachers. The principal resigned and was replaced by Robert Pleasure, the black principal of Martin Luther King Elementary School. Pleasure's appointment was accompanied by high expectations. The school board thought it would go a long way in easing tension and solving the fundamental problems of the school. The faculty supported it with similar hopes. The black students, however, were not so convinced. They wanted to know what he was going to do, and whether or not he was going to act like a black.

After assessing the atmosphere at Hillhouse, Pleasure decided on an unusual course of action. He suggested that the riots be recreated under controlled circumstances so that everyone could understand what had happened and relieve themselves of residual tensions. Fifty people — a cross-section of students, parents, teachers, and administration — gathered for 72 hours of group confrontation. The session failed in its goals. George Foote recalled how hostile everyone was: reacting with a lot of yelling and resulting in badly hurt feelings. One teacher with 20 years experience, selected for the session by Foote, quit shortly after. She simply could not face students in the school. It was apparent that frustration and hostility ran deep and was not merely a residual of the riots. This was the beginning of the end for Pleasure, who was deeply disillusioned by the fate of his approach to helping what now seemed to be an impossible situation.

The Solution: An Alternative School

The problems at Hillhouse were concurrently being approached from a different direction by some teachers led by George Foote. After the February riot and the month of frustrating negotiations, Sam Nash suggested the idea of starting an alternative school as a solution. It made sense to Foote: "If you take what the conservative teachers want and you take what the liberal teachers want and have them negotiate, you end up with mush. Nobody's happy. So you give the conservative teachers what they want and so forth...that was the kind of thinking we started to do at the time." Torry Orton of the Teachers' Collaborative also joined in the discussions. There were no specifics worked out, just a process: Involve parents, teachers and students in designing their ideal school. The idea was intriguing to all.

Robert Pleasure's failed 72-hour confrontation did serve one important function — it put Foote and Orton in contact with students and parents interested in creating an alternative school. In late 1968, eight parents, six teachers, and eight students began to meet together regularly at parents' homes to discuss the possibility. The group disbanded after a few months, however. Most did not believe that the system would support them.

By this time, Foote and Orton were committed to the idea. Foote recalled that it was very difficult to teach at Hillhouse after having thought about starting an alternative. With the help of Sam Nash, the two applied for an Office of Economic Opportunity (OEO) planning grant in January, 1969, asking for $80,000 to support a one-year organizing process for an alternative school. The process called for the specifics of a school to emerge from discussions among students, parents, and teachers. The proposal was sent but they heard nothing. Foote felt there was some politicking going on in which he was not included. His suspicions were partly confirmed when he met a person in New Haven who said he had some influence over the Washington proceedings and could possibly get the grant approved *if* Foote were willing to include some of his ideas on "ideal" schools. Foote refused to have the form of the would-be school dictated to him by anyone. That, he felt, should be determined by the participants. No money came.

This perspective was corroborated by Sam Nash. He recalled that the Nixon administration was just taking over when the proposal arrived in Washington, and that the Nixon philosophy on the OEO was different than that of his predecessor. More specifically, Nash recalled that the people reading the proposal had very set ideas about the kind of programs they were willing to fund. OEO requested several changes in the proposal as a condition for funding. In Nash's eyes, these changes watered the idea down. Like Foote, he was ultimately unwilling to compromise. The request for funding was denied.

The turmoil had taken a heavy toll on Superintendent of Schools John A. Santini. He resigned in the spring of 1969, noting that a person can run only so far before passing the baton. The person who received the baton was Gerald Barbaresi, his associate superintendent throughout most of the turmoil.

According to Nash, Santini had supported the concept of creating alternative schools, albeit cautiously. In addition, the school board was hesitant in pushing the idea. However, before his departure, Santini and Nash had initiated discussions about restructuring secondary education, with the concept of alternative schools playing a central role. These discussions gained momentum under Barbaresi. He was not only supportive of restructuring secondary education; he had been helpful to Orton and Foote in their efforts to secure federal funding for the creation of an alternative school. With Barbaresi as Superintendent, "downtown" became more active in the process of educational reform.

Having exhausted possibilities for OEO funding, Nash, with the help of Barbaresi, turned to the State Title III. The proposal, entitled "Restructuring Secondary Education," was submitted on May 1, 1970. It was rejected by the Title III Agency which noted "The underlying thinking reflected (in the proposal) is fuzzy and various aspects of the proposal require clearer definition." However, because of the high priority of the problem, the agency agreed to consider a revised application.

The revised application had three primary objectives: 1) The development of a planning process involving community members in active decision-making and problem-solving roles; 2) The development of initial projects, like an alternative school; and 3) The development of plans for system-wide restructuring of education. This approach was acceptable to the Title III Agency, but it was not funded for lack of money.

Thus, the school system initiated several types of responses to the 1967-68 Hillhouse riots. First, attempts were made to improve Hillhouse. Teachers were added and discussions were held to deal with the problems underlying the riots. Over time additional staff changes were made: seven of nine department chairmen were replaced, new guidance counselors were brought in, and some clerks were removed. Two new positions — an assistant principal and a community coordinator — were added. Both jobs were held by blacks.

In addition, a core group of persons in the school system began to discuss the idea of creating an alternative high school. George Foote and other teachers initiated discussions with interested parents and students. This effort was supported by Sam Nash, who was working within the administration of the school system to push the idea of schools of choice. And Superintendent Barbaresi, along with Nash, began a search for funds which would allow New Haven to plan for a "reconstructing of secondary education." The idea was gaining momentum.

A CLOSE ENCOUNTER BETWEEN THE IDEOLOGICAL AND THE PRAGMATIC: SYSTEM SUPPORT FOR AN ALTERNATIVE SCHOOL

In reconstructing the creation of settings, it is useful to ferret out the varied agendas of key players. It is clear from previously published accounts that individuals involved in the creation of settings are motivated by quite different reasons (e.g. Gold and Miles, 1981; Smith and Keith, 1971). In some instances, motivations may be role-related: The Superintendent of Schools lives in a very different world of pressures and influences than do teachers and parents. These pressures and influences constrain what is seen as feasible for the school system to undertake. Differences may also be due to personal philosophy or political persuasion. Implicit in these varying agendas are differing images about what the potential setting will look like and differing assumptions about what problems it is intended to solve.

The idea of creating an alternative high school in this case surfaced as a partial solution to the problems at Hillhouse. Most importantly, it represented an opportunity for all parties directly involved to further their own agendas. For George Foote and some of the teachers, it would provide a chance to escape the hostile atmosphere at Hillhouse and search for "new ways to work with Hillhouse kids." Starting a school meant being empowered to implement their own educational agenda within an organizational context of their own. Teachers who sought to be more egalitarian with students could be. Teachers with creative ideas about how to structure learning experiences for students would have the freedom to test their ideas. As has been aptly characterized by Sarason (1972), creating a new school would serve both as a critique of policies and practices at Hillhouse and as a promise of creating a more vital antidote.

For Sam Nash, Director of Special Projects and Program Planning, creating an alternative school represented an important step in his agenda to create a system of public schools of choice. Nash viewed the alternative school as another force pressing for his vision of a responsive and varied public school system. For Nash, a local alternative school might serve as a model for how public school systems might be structured.

In 1969, more than a year before the opening of HSC, Nash had addressed the American Orthopsychiatric Association (Nash, 1970). Public schools, he stated, are fueled by the value of the "will to produce" — a production ethic with homogenizing consequences for the structures and goals of a public school system. Nash advocated an alternative metaphor — "the will to govern" as a superordinate goal. To quote Nash: "The will to govern is an individual's insistence and sense of obligation that everyone, in community, have clear and increasing access to the society's decision-making apparatus. Thus activated, the community can frustrate and replace coercive and manipulative topside decision-making. The form that school assumes must be shaped by the nature of its task, its task of arousing in the young the will to govern, to develop the skills to manage the affairs of society" (1970, p. 609).

"Our institutions have the power to deal with the symptoms but lack the capacity to deal the causes... In the name of equality sameness is imposed; diversity is suppressed in favor of uniformity; passivity is rewarded over involvement and dogmatism over problem-solving. ...The task is to manipulate and bend the social environment to enhance personality rather than, as we do now, manipulating and bending personality to fit an increasingly malign environment...Institutional restructuring is obviously needed" (p. 609).

Thus, by 1969, Nash had taken the position that the time was right for educational alternatives. His language blends nicely the ideological and the pragmatic: "Massive and swift transformation of schooling requires an idea. The idea must rally national energies... It must be one which can be stated clearly; which does not threaten to dismantle institutions more quickly than they can be replaced; which does not require human financial resources beyond our means; which conforms to the best aspects of our democratic traditions. In short, it must be an idea whose time has come. The idea I wish to propose is that within the next decade public school systems be transformed into confederations of schools of choice" (p. 610). The starting of a public alternative high school represented the start of such a system.

Nash's support for an alternative high school was both pragmatic and ideological. Pragmatically, the system was under stress and consequently more open to consider significant structural and conceptual changes. The Superintendent was seen as an ally towards these goals. Ideologically, Nash believed that it was important to create schools which were planned and organized by people who would participate in them. The process of creating the alternative school should, in Nash's view, mirror the underlying rationale for schools of choice. It is possible that had Foote not shown interest or the energy to organize the program, this particular alternative might not have existed, as Nash was ethically opposed to forcing one on the system.

Superintendent Barbaresi also supported the creation of an alternative school but for different ideological and pragmatic reasons. Barbaresi viewed the current school system as unduly restrictive: Students were forced to fit into the structured school day without regard for individual needs. He envisioned a public school system where some students would be in a traditional school full time, some part time in school and part time out, and some whose education would occur entirely outside of the traditional school setting. Barbaresi also believed in supporting creative teaching; he felt that the energies of the more creative teachers could be better expressed in nontraditional school structures. Such structures would also serve to attract creative teachers to the school system.

There were also two practical consequences of which Barbaresi was fully aware. First, the creation of an alternative school would help resolve the Hillhouse stalemate by allowing some teachers and students to leave. Second, if New Haven had a viable alternative program in operation, it would greatly increase the chance of getting outside money to plan for a total restructuring of secondary education. As one former state funding official noted, Barbaresi simply realized that the New Haven schools could not go it alone.

The idea of creating an alternative school, then, appealed to people in key roles for a variety of pragmatic and ideological reasons. The idea was relatively free of controversy since each of the key figures saw it as being in their interest. In Nash's words, it did not "unduly perturb" the system; it promised answers without asking too much of the system's energies or resources.

At this point, however, it was an idea based solely on process rather than substance. There was no articulated image of what the school might be like. The very notion of an alternative school developed by those who would participate in it *precluded* specification about its particulars. Still, there was basic agreement on the value of pursuing the idea. It was decided to actively search for the necessary external funding sources; too great an initial reliance on school system resources would have "unduly perturbed" the system.

High School in the Community is Created: Funding and Approval

In late 1969, Sam Nash approached Gerald Barbaresi with the suggestion that 10 teachers take sixty to eighty students out of Hillhouse and start an alternative school. Barbaresi had been thinking along similar lines. The outside funding they had requested from OEO was apparently not forthcoming, but it was agreed they needed to start such a program. With Barbaresi's support, Nash approached George Foote with the proposal. At that time Foote was working on a project for Earth Day with some other teachers. Nash suggested that two of these teachers — Nancy Shestack and Rich Solacka — Foote, and himself meet to discuss a possible program for the following fall, 1970. Foote and the others were still interested.

Now that a core group of teachers had been assembled, three broad hurdles needed to be crossed — funding, obtaining the approval of the school board, and planning the structure of the program. In January 1970 an event occurred to help all three areas. Dr. Richard Mastain, Director of the New Haven Educational Improvement Center (EIC)[8], had taken an interest in a high school in Philadelphia called the Parkway Program. The Parkway Program was hailed as the prototype of the school without walls — an innovative educational alternative congruent with the general ideas of Foote and Nash (see Bremer, 1973, for a detailed description of the school).

Mastain, wanting to promote a similar effort, brought the head of the Parkway Program, John Bremer, to New Haven. While in New Haven, Bremer talked to Yale about a job, to Barbaresi about the Parkway concept, and to Foote and the other teachers about how Parkway worked. All parties were favorably impressed with the model, which was committed to individualizing and personalizing the educational process, utilizing community resources, and keeping per pupil costs of education below those of traditional high schools.

In retrospect, Nash saw the visit as a kind of crystallizing event which provided a feasible and exciting example of what was possible. It boosted both the credibility of the idea and the energies of the teachers working on it. It would be a school of 10 teachers and 150 students — similar in size and teacher-student ratio to the Parkway Program — and would open in September 1970.

FUNDING

State Contributions: The task of funding the program fell into the laps of Barbaresi and Nash in the central office. They reasoned that if 150 kids would be leaving Hillhouse, the city would be justified in taking some of the Hillhouse budget and transferring it to the alternative. They needed other money, however, and turned to the State Bureau for Compensatory and Community Education Services, headed by Dr. Sandy Plante. Barbaresi justified the request for funds under the State Act for Disadvantaged Children — classifying roughly 40 percent of the students in the alternative school as disadvantaged.

The State Act for Disadvantaged Children allocated some $27 million a year — primarily in urban areas. To obtain it, a proposal had to be made specifying the need and the uses to which the funds would be put. The State Bureau, under the direction and influence of Dr. Plante, decided upon the appropriateness of the request. Dr. Plante, described by Barbaresi, Nash, and Foote as a long-time friend of New Haven, assured the school system that funds would be available for the alternative school. In all, the State Act provided $43,200, broken down as follows:

Personnel:

4 teachers	32,000
part-time staff	2,800
summer planning	5,750
fringes	2,600

Non-Personnel:

supplies	1,050
Total	$43,200

It is interesting to note that the final description of High School in the Community sent to the State Bureau did not even mention the percent of disadvantaged students who would be served. Plante was willing to accept the proposal on the basis that it was strengthening the school system and would therefore benefit disadvantaged children. The proposal's description included the following justification:

> Public school systems should provide a number of educational
> options that meet the needs of different groups of students. In
> particular, educational alternatives must be tailored to the
> needs of the so-called disadvantaged students — those whose
> economic and cultural backgrounds are not conducive to suc-
> cess in the standard high school structure. The High School in
> the Community is such an alternative.

Yale University Contributions: Shortly after Barbaresi took over as
Superintendent, he was contacted by Jonathan Fanton, Yale University's
Coordinator of Special Education Programs. Fanton was an advisor to
Yale's President Kingman Brewster on finding ways to relate Yale to the
city. Because New Haven had lost about $17 million annually due to
Yale's tax-exempt status, Yale had been under pressure to find alterna-
tive ways of contributing to the city. In addition, black organizations
within and outside of the University had criticized its leaders for not
living up to their responsibility to the community. Fanton was attempt-
ing to open channels of communication between Yale and the New
Haven Schools. The initial idea to create the Educational Improvement
Center as a clearing house for school assistance emerged from early
Fanton-Barbaresi discussions.

Fanton recalled that Richard Mastain, the Director of EIC, was interested in developing a Parkway-type alternative program in order to
strengthen EIC. It was thus understandable that Barbaresi approached
Mastain and the EIC for financial support. The close relationship that
Fanton had developed with Barbaresi played an important role, as
Fanton personally presented the proposal to Brewster. Seeing it as a way
to improve relations with the city leadership and the community as well
as a means to strengthen EIC, Brewster approved the giving of $40,000
to the alternative school through EIC. In giving the money, it was made
clear that the money would be available only for one year. After that, the
program would have to find support elsewhere.

Local Contributions: The EIC share of the budget paid for three teachers
and various other expenses. It was no problem for the city to find the
remaining money, approximately $31,500 for two teachers, books,
supplies, and operating expenses. Thus, the total budget for the school
was about $111,000, of which $85,000 was for salary to 10 full-time
teachers and the remainder for supportive services and operating costs.

Several budget items clarify assumptions behind the school. For
example, the total operating expenses for the school were $2,400 to be
spent on utilities. At this time the school did not have a particular

location, but from the level of funding it clearly would not be in its own building — it would be "in the community" somewhere. Thus, finding a home would be an early task for the school. The $4,000 in the budget for "Renovations" suggested that it could make a small contribution to its host environment.

The structure of the budget, put together with state, Yale, and local funds, suggested in addition that the school was on flimsy financial footing. Yale's contribution would run out after the first year, and state SADC funding was not secure. There was no commitment on the part of the New Haven school system to fully fund the venture. This meant that one of the ongoing tasks would be the development of funding after its first year. The power of this reality in shaping the activities and dynamics of the school will be clarified in succeeding chapters. At this point, however, funding for the first year of HSC had been found.

THE BOARD APPROVES

The last obstacle was approval from the Board of Education. As Nash noted, the school board was hesitant about alternative schools when Barbaresi took over the Superintendency. The event most responsible for turning them into supporters was John Bremer's visit. The Parkway experience showed the board that an alternative school could work, both in terms of educating students and in terms of saving money on a per-pupil basis. After funding was found through the State Act for Disadvantaged Children and EIC, the last major barrier to approval was removed.

Foote recalls that the first time the proposal went before the board it was rejected. Foote maintained that Barbaresi failed to deliver the votes as promised. Foote personally explained the proposal to board members to gain approval. Barbaresi, however, recalled the disagreements as minor. Some board members were apparently unclear about the cost of certain aspects of the program and just where the $30,000 would come out of the system's budget.

Barbaresi felt at the time that the biggest problem was gaining approval of the administration at Hillhouse. He correctly anticipated the possibility that bad-mouthing of HSC at Hillhouse would reduce the quality of students going to HSC. The justification he gave to Hillhouse administrators was that they would have fewer students to worry about and that if the program did not work well, the students could always be funneled back to Hillhouse. Hillhouse promised its support. With all of the minor details ironed out, the board approved the proposal for High School in the Community in June of 1970, to begin operation the following September with 10 teachers and 150 students.

The Pre-history of the School: Processes, Themes, and Structures in the Planning Process

The notion of "pre-history" refers to those events, decisions, and assumptions that guide how a new setting is conceived of before it opens its doors. Pre-history yields a set of constraints and opportunities operative in the new setting. It forms the basis of the hopes and anticipations for the setting while simultaneously defining what is ignored. The purpose of this chapter is to outline the part of HSC's pre-history that dealt with planning. Fortunately, a significant amount of archival material was available to supplement interviews with participants in the pre-history process.

Evolution of the Idea

Discussion about the school had been ongoing for some time before the Board of Education approved the proposal to create HSC. Teachers had met on and off for two years with students and parents to discuss the possibility of an alternative school. George Foote and Sam Nash had been talking informally for some time. Beginning in late 1969, Foote organized a small group of teachers to discuss the possibility again, this time with the explicit support of the Superintendent. The January 1970 visit of John Bremer, who met with both the Superintendent and this group of teachers, also proved vital in shaping what an alternative school might look like. Indeed, many of the basic structures of HSC would be similar to Bremer's Parkway program.

The first documented evidence about the image of the proposed alternative school can be found in the funding proposal sent to the State of Connecticut for Title III funds. The proposal, entitled *"Hillhouse Alternative Program,"* was submitted on January 19, 1970, about the same time as Bremer's visit to New Haven. The document included ideas about the role of teacher, the structure of the curriculum, and the emphasis on active student involvement in shaping their educational experience.

The proposal outlined the threefold role of the teacher as follows:

> (1) to help the student identify the different alternative plans of
> action which would lead to the goals the student has set for
> himself; (2) to teach classes in which the students have indi-
> cated interest; (3) to act as a liaison between community re-
> sources and the students. This, in essence, means that teachers
> are truly public servants, in the sense that they serve, explore,
> and learn with their students — instead of simply managing
> them.[1]

The role of students is defined as identifying their own needs,

> a task which requires introspection and independence, being
> responsible for planning and executing the daily program of
> study, mastering subject areas relevant to the student's goals,
> helping to evaluate the overall program, helping other stu-
> dents solve their problems, and learning to be a functional
> member of the school community.

The proposed structure of the academic program included a seminar,
staff-taught courses, and institutional offerings. The seminar was intended to be a daily meeting "with 15 to 17 fellow students and at least
one faculty member." It was designed to serve varied functions:

> to provide an opportunity for individual and group discussion
> of a guidance nature...to serve as a forum for student-teacher
> dialogue about the nature and operation of the Program...to
> provide an opportunity for the development of special group
> projects such as plays, workshops, field trips, etc. In summary,
> the Seminar will offer the individual a chance to be heard, and
> at the same time, will encourage (the student's) successful
> participation in group activities.

Staff-taught courses would include both basic subject area courses and
electives, and would mirror the teaching role requirements of the more
traditional schools. The ideology behind the teaching, however, was
distinctive.

> The subjects offered, as well as the content of courses, will
> reflect the talents and interests of the teachers and students in-
> volved. As a result, credit requirements will be distributional
> rather than specific. For example, a student needing an English
> credit will not have to take a prescribed 'English III' course.
> Rather (the student) will be able to choose among a variety of

courses ranging from a grammar and usage workshop to a seminar in modern poetry.

The "institutional offerings" concept was elaborated in terms of the community as a learning environment.

> Where a student studies will depend on the student's needs and interests. A student may study marketing in a department store, lab technology in a hospital, auto mechanics in a repair shop, art in a museum, practical sociology in a social agency, law in a courthouse, money and finance in a bank, computer science in a data processing concern. Clearly, the variety of organizations is as unlimited as the variety of organizations in the city itself.

Program staff would be responsible for locating such institutional offerings and for collaborating with them in designing courses of study, maintaining attendance records, and reporting on student progress.

The document also outlined the anticipated size of the program and some staffing requirements.

> The program will consist of one unit head, eight to nine Hillhouse teachers, ten teaching interns, one hundred and fifty students, and those parents and members of the community who have some contact with various areas of the program.

The school would include grades 10-12 with approximately equal members of males and females and have a racial proportion similar to that of the ongoing student body at Hillhouse. A lottery would be used to achieve the desired gender and racial balance.

The similarities to Bremer's Parkway program are clear in both tone and structure. Both schools were *in the community* and had classes that were designed to be held in various donated spaces throughout their respective cities. The total number of students (150) and the proposed student-teacher ratio (15 to 1) were similar. Both schools were organized into administrative entities called "units" led by a "unit head." Students in both programs were encouraged to develop courses appropriate to their needs if they were not available in the school.

Two other aspects of the proposed structure reflected the general thinking behind the Parkway model. The concept of *institutional course offerings* to be provided in the community reflected one of the most innovative and challenging features of the Parkway Program: the use of the community resources on the Benjamin Franklin Parkway for educational purposes, including museums, businesses, the Academy of Natural Sciences, and even city hall.

Secondly, the idea of an ongoing *seminar* serving a variety of administrative and cohesive group functions was similar to the Parkway *tutorial*. At Parkway, the tutorial consisted of 16 students selected at random, one teacher, and one intern. It met daily to deal with administrative matters and any personal issues students might have. It was further responsible for monitoring whether students were learning necessary basic skills.

Teachers Plan Their School: The Spring Meetings

As the winter of 1970 progressed, so did the possibility of creating an alternative school for the fall. Both Nash and Foote believed the next step was to recruit a core group of teachers to plan the school. Though the general contours had been developed by the school system, they felt specific planning should be left to those responsible for the school's operation.

Most, if not all, of the recruiting was done by Foote and Nancy Shestack from among their like-minded peers at Hillhouse. Predictably, the ten teachers who assembled in the spring to work on the school were younger, more politically liberal, more dissatisfied with Hillhouse, and more likely to value personal relationships with students than the average teacher at Hillhouse. Of the original group, five were male and five female, two were black, and all saw themselves as sharing a concern for educational reform.[2]

From early April to late May 1970, this group met 11 times to plan the school. Tom Nelson, a Yale Divinity School student, was hired by Nash to keep a written record of the meetings. "I tried to write everything down," recalled Nelson. From these notes, plus the recollections of several teachers who participated in these meetings, a rich picture emerges of the planning process and its dominant themes.

The Overarching Ideology: Empowerment

From the very first meeting of April 9, 1970, empowerment represented the school's basic ideological premise. To quote Nelson's notes from that meeting:

> A main problem is that the teacher is prejudiced against (by the bureaucratic system) and made into an object . . . . The first thing of the new school will probably be culture shock. The shock of choices newly made available; the student (teacher, too) chooses rather than someone else asking the 'whys' . . . . Students do not

learn when they feel they are a victim, therefore give the students the sense that there is nobody more important than they are (although there are persons as important); make this school *a community at fingertip response* — to get out of education a sense of worth — to give a sense of control."

Flowing from this premise of empowerment would be a redefinition of how the school would be governed; a redefinition of the roles played by teachers and students; the quest for a sense of community as an institutional value; and, most globally, the creation of an institutional culture vastly different in purpose and structure from that of Hillhouse. The evolution of this fundamental idea would not unfold clearly and coherently in the early planning of the school. Yet, the concept of empowerment — emphasizing control of decisions about how the school would develop — formed the framework. The specific manifestations of the idea are found in the themes reflected in the teacher meetings.

EMPOWERMENT AND CONSENSUS DECISION-MAKING: THE EGALITARIAN COMMITMENT

Perhaps the most basic expression of the empowerment ideology was the governance process adopted during the planning meetings. Reflecting the Zeitgeist of the times, the teachers agreed that if the school was to be a setting where individuals were to control their institutional lives, then everyone had both the right and the responsibility to participate in decisions affecting those lives. They agreed to make all decisions by consensus rather than by some form of majority vote. This decision was not only ideologically congruent with the teachers' notion of empowerment; in all likelihood it reflected the idea that, as Sarason has commented, the teachers deeply believed they shared values and a sense of solidarity which would allow this process to succeed.

It is in the elaboration of these values, however, that their limitations, contradictions, and unintended consequences become manifest. For example, teachers recalled that what initially held them together was a shared reaction <u>against</u> a previous school rather than a shared commitment <u>to</u> a specific alternative. "Fifty to sixty percent of what we were about was reacting to Hillhouse," recalled one teacher. Said another, "the group came together because of what we didn't like. Everyone had a general agreement about liking kids but, beyond that, there were many individualists and strong personalities who had little in common about what they *did* like."

It is not surprising that early in the teachers' meetings tensions arose around the issue of decision-making by consensus. The egalitarian commitment meant that each person's ideas were not only sought out, but were actively valued and considered. If decisions were to be made by consensus, each member's contribution needed to be heard and discussed in the context of other members' contributions. As has been reported elsewhere (e.g. Riger, 1984 ; Freeman, 1973), such ideologies tend to extend discussions of process at the expense of accomplishing specific goals. This was particularly true when the group was comprised of "many individualists and strong personalities" who were more clearly united *against* than *for* something.

By the third teacher meeting in April, the tension between group process and task accomplishment surfaced. Meeting notes record for the first time a discussion of group process.

> We need to get practical and in some ways discipline and formalize the meetings. We need to have an aim for each meeting (e.g., site, selection, philosophy, etc.)...to discipline the group into a *result orientation* [underline in the notes]...Set up an agenda and spend the week aiming at an angle of our plans and problems... (notes from third meeting, 4/14).

One pervasive implication of the egalitarian commitment was the value of questioning any aspect of school structure or policy without any preconceived boundaries or givens. It was not only legitimate to start over, it was necessary as an affirmation that all could question, and hence influence, any aspect of the school. For example, Nelson's notes of 5/15 record a discussion on critical issues of structure and policy which consist entirely of questions.

> "Can a student get out of school early? Can he graduate with a diploma for proficiency rather than time spent? Should we admit students from Hillhouse according to class distinctions and then immediately remove them upon entrance to our school? Can a student drop a class after he has begun? Can a student enter a class after it has begun? Can we set some sort of control so that a volunteer teacher will be assured of having students? If you drop a course, you don't get credit, that's all ? Can we set a time after which you cannot begin a new course for credit? Is there punishment for cutting class? Is this the sort of problem you try to work out in the morning session?" (notes of 5/15).

A second implication of this ideology was that it complicated the task of group agreement on priorities, even in terms of what questions were most important to deal with. One teacher proposed the following plan for the ideal school day:

8:00-10:00   half group stuff, half individual stuff; flexible individual stuff; flexible enough to be made into an all-school meeting — Two hours when something can happen, rigidly scheduled so that it's there to be flexible! Time blocked in enough to make it flexible.

10:00-5:00   kids on their separate schedules (get the computer!); time in the community will most likely be quite *rigid*.

Evening   take kids to lectures, symphony, etc."(notes of 4/17).

This proposal was met by questions, including the following: "Does this vision make some hours more primary than others? All hours are primary" (underline the author's). Such an assertion may be fully consistent with the myth of unlimited resources. However, since resources are inevitably limited, some hours inevitably become more primary than others. At this point in the school's planning process, however, the egalitarian commitment worked against the teachers' willingness to assign group priorities to tasks or issues.

The Egalitarian Commitment and Leadership

The empowerment ideology and the egalitarian commitment also influenced the dynamics of leadership. While many settings begin with an acknowledged leader who sets the agenda and tone for the setting, such was not the case here. Indeed, there was no discussion of leadership until the fourth meeting. It arose in response to a perceived external threat rather than as a way to structure internal issues. The concern was that Yale University, as a condition for providing funding, would attempt to influence the school's direction. The need to create a buffer, a negotiating agent, or a structure to fend off this potential threat caused the discussion.

George Foote, because of his central role, had been authorized to serve as "coordinator" of the group. As the meeting notes of 4/21 indicate, however, he held no formal status as leader. "Shall there be someone within this group as administrative head? Should such an administrator have a teaching role as well? Should the coordinator have any more say than anyone else?" The questions continue: "Should we have a three-person revolving triumvirate? Why should the coordinator be one person? Do we want someone to be vulnerable for getting the blame? Accessible for getting the credit?"

Following these questions came a proposed solution:

> This situation is not a typical hierarchical structure and there's no reason for us governing it as such—so let's rotate—a managerial group of three people always rotating with George (Foote) as a permanent member...We don't want a director and George doesn't want to be it! George has to be able to say 'sorry, I teach today!'...No matter what we do George will be called if there's a gripe. But we want a structure to rely on, for George, as well as each of us, to maintain our *identity as teacher*. Therefore, a triumvirate — structurally, a triumvirate rotating with George as permanent — equal members with George 'more equal' — a built-in structure to be protected from an outside threat (notes of 4/21).

Foote's recollections confirmed that the teachers viewed a formal leader as necessary for responding to external issues, but as having no differential power internally. To do so would have violated the egalitarian commitment. Indeed, the belief in collective responsibility was strong enough to prevent the issue of leadership from arising during any other of the eleven planning meetings held that spring. While this issue would become more acute during the following months, the early meetings showed a determination that everyone would be equally empowered in running the school.

Controlling the School: Outsiders and the Threat to Autonomy

A third empowerment theme was raised with the question of leadership: the importance of being vigilant around threats to the autonomy of the school. Because empowerment rested on the teachers' ability to shape the school, they were sensitive to possible encroachment from external sources. However, they also needed external support and resources. Thus, the planning meetings reflected the tension between the wish to control their own destiny and their need for external support to survive. The two external agents that crystallized this theme were John Bremer's Parkway Program and Yale University.

Parkway as Threat and Promise: It has already been stated that John Bremer's visit to New Haven several months before had been critical in galvanizing support for an alternative high school, and that the New

Haven Public Schools had submitted a funding proposal which drew heavily on the Parkway Program philosophy. In mid-April, Nash suggested a site visit to Parkway so that teachers could talk with Bremer and gather information relevant to their own planning. He outlined several reasons why the school should adopt the basic Parkway model:

> (a) We find ourselves short on time; if we start on a new or different model we should aim at a year from September, rather than September; (b) There is a short period of time to convince people of what you want to do—here's a model that *has* worked, and worked *well*; (c) We have Parkway people we can lean on if we need help.
>
> Teachers responded primarily in terms of issues of autonomy. What we need is two or three days to forget about the Parkway Program and do our own thing. Then, if what we do goes along with Parkway, okay—but we do not so much want to do it because it has worked, nor do we want to rely so much on a program that has worked. Although much of our program planning is in general agreement with Parkway, we have a career at stake and need to talk about our most basic and fundamental needs, and not look to Parkway as a guide (notes of 4/17).

> If we can look at Parkway as a general guide and at the same time be sensitive to the needs of our kids and ourselves we should be able to adopt the program as a generality into which goes our specific time and place (notes of 4/21).

Yale as Threat and Promise: Like Parkway, Yale offered the promise of important resources, but was also seen as a potential threat to the new school's autonomy. One specific concern was that Yale would, as a condition for funding, impose Bremer on them as a director or consultant. The meeting notes show that the teachers discussed strategies for dealing with the possibility of that situation. Initially, the scenario would be to opt for an "advisory committee" if Yale wanted to foist a "big name director" on the school. Concern about becoming too dependent on Yale was voiced, and the threat to autonomy was clear.

> If Yale has something more to offer than advice *it is our fault alone*...If the program changes against our wishes then we should be able to resign and still have a job. . . Advice that we do not have to take is important to the way we operate.

> What is our bottom line of tolerance? At what point do we say 'we cannot tolerate this.' If the integrity and identity of the

group is the bottom line then the worries about the director, etc., may not be all that important—the integrity of the group is the real power and the real control in any relationship with a consultant/director. Therefore, we can or will negotiate the point of director but *not* the point of the integrity of our group. We must not let our group break down into factions, and we must not allow one another to become expendable (notes of 4/ 28).

On May 15, the meeting notes state that Yale had committed $40,000 and that there would be no director as part of the agreement. Indeed, as far as can be ascertained from persons at Yale and in the New Haven Public Schools, there was never any consideration of linking Yale's support to having Bremer in some official capacity. The notes suggest, by their brevity, that this announcement did not occasion much discussion, but by then many things had changed. The trip to Philadelphia had reduced Parkway from a specter to a live, complicated, and useful piece of data. The Superintendent was also sending strong signals that the school would have sufficient funding to open in the fall. Still, the discussions about Yale underscore the degree to which the teachers saw themselves as a band of rebels in potentially hostile territory.

Empowerment of Teachers in The Teaching Role

In addition to empowerment themes of governance, leadership, and autonomy, the planning meetings included many discussions about how to create empowering roles for teachers. "We want to create a situation where persons could be individually assisted in their desires by opening up resources and situations different from those previously experienced" (notes of 4/9). Thus, school would be a place where teachers could experiment and develop. They did not subscribe to the myth, identified by Sarason (1972), that those who create new settings concern themselves with how the setting can serve the clients over how it can enrich the "helpers." Rather, the teachers asserted that students would be better served if the school was a place for teacher growth.

The myth of unlimited resources, however, did seem to characterize the hopefulness of teachers as they discussed their role. "We must be able to administer, teach, negotiate, and do tutorial," state the 5/15 notes. While the empowerment ideology would diminish role distinctions among and between teachers and students, role responsibilities of teachers would be multiplied. In essence, removal of role distinctions meant each teacher would participate in governance, guidance, leading a tutorial, and developing other unspecified educational options in addition to classroom teaching. The 4/21 meeting notes summarize the spirit of the role in a series of agreements: "We should meet individually with the kids. We should as well meet in groups. We have to maintain and instill a sense of responsibility for time. We have to offer course options. We have to offer options for enjoyment and discovery."

There is little indication of discussion about the feasibility of such role expansions. The hopefulness of the empowerment ideology held the day. In sum, the notes show that the teachers self-consciously discussed the school as a place for their development as well as that of students. They envisioned functioning in such a way that their influence would pervade all aspects of the school. The pre-history of the school shows clearly that it was intended, from its origins, to be a teacher-run school.

Empowerment of Students and the Student Role

The sense of superiority of mission is well reflected in the many discussions about how the new school could empower students, helping them succeed where other schools had failed. The role of the school as a setting for student development would greatly expand. Its goals for students would be both broader and more individualized than in other public schools. They would encompass aspects of personal and interpersonal development in addition to the learning of basic skills; they would be individualized so that students could create their own learning agenda and develop, in conjunction with school and community resources, an appropriate curriculum.

The roles envisioned for students would not only place new demands on them, but would also require certain abilities and coping styles. This issue had not been fully discussed. The assumption seemed to be that students, like the teachers themselves, had been victimized by the authoritarian and bureaucratic structures of Hillhouse. Freed from these structural constraints, they would be able to flourish in a school which empowered them, providing avenues for their personal development. The belief in the overriding ideology thus prevented certain kinds of questions from being asked which would have important implications for the school's development.

Discussions of attendance provide a useful example. According to the meeting notes, this discussion focused on such issues as "should we take attendance, and, if so, how?" and "attendance, if we take it, should be taken so that nobody's lost or anonymous, not that somebody *takes* attendance" (notes of 4/17). Questions were not raised about whether or not the ideology and structure of the school might impact negatively on student attendance. This issue surfaced only once, and was introduced by Sâm Nash rather than the teachers: "Problem: are we assuming that the kids are already ready to function like we want them to function?" The notes record no discussion of this question.

There was, however, discussion of what kinds of students might do well in such a school and what kind of racial and ability mix would be optimal. With respect to the former, the idea that students should be risk takers surfaced early, particularly in the context of education taking place in the community.

> Our school (says that) education for some kids is not a room/ teacher thing but out in the community — some kids are not ready for this and should not try to get into the program; if he says 'I don't want the community,' we say 'don't come here.' If he says 'I don't know if I want the community thing,' we say 'Let's find out!' (notes of 4/21)

There is no mention in the notes about how race, gender, or social class may affect *any* issues of student adaptation to the school. There was agreement, however, that the student body should reflect the racial composition of Hillhouse and that a variety of levels of student achievement would be desirable.

The Politics of Survival: Relationships with Relevant External Settings

A final theme emerging from the spring planning meetings was that the teachers were, from the outset, concerned with the politics of survival. Sarason (1972) suggests that the sense of superiority of mission which characterizes the creation of new settings results in a "crusading" attitude that discourages contact and cooperation with existing, "competing" settings. The meeting notes, while affirming the sense of superiority of mission, show an ongoing concern with how the new school should deal with relevant external settings in the service of its survival.

Discussions about the relationship between the new school and the school system serve as an example. On several occasions, teachers voiced concern about how the broader school system might react to their efforts.

> It's safer for us not to get too many people in (this group) that the school system thinks badly of . . . We must individually mind our p's and q's so as not to arouse negative reaction to individual members of our group from persons in the 'system.'

Concern about parental reaction was also expressed.

> Parents will probably like the program idea until they find out that the kids do the choosing rather than the teachers (notes of 5/8).

Special concern was given to their colleagues at Hillhouse who had not been asked to join the planning group. The secrecy of the initial meetings pained some of the teachers who had to hide what they were doing from their Hillhouse friends. Predictably, it also served to alienate these potential allies when they discovered what had been going on. During the spring, however, many conversations did occur between members of the planning group and their peers at Hillhouse. On a personal level, ties with Hillhouse were maintained and the wish for more complete communication intensified. Any sense of superiority of mission was directed at the institutional structure of Hillhouse, not at fellow teachers.

While caution and vigilance were the primary concerns about external settings, the "crusading" attitude also activated a search for external relationships which could aid in the creation of the school. Foote, for example, played a role in courting Yale funds during the spring, and meeting notes suggest extensive discussion about other Yale resources the school might find useful.

From the very beginning, then, the superiority of mission was tempered by an appreciation of the politics of survival. The group understood both the potential long-range importance of relationships with the school system more generally and Hillhouse in particular. Further, they were on the lookout for appropriate external resources.

FROM FANTASY TO REALITY: THE SCHOOL BECOMES "OFFICIAL"

By early May signs were very favorable for the possibility of a new school opening in the fall. The meeting notes of 5/5 start with a message from Superintendent Barbaresi conveyed through Foote— "Barbaresi says we do it and we do it in September." City funding was secured, EIC funds from Yale would soon be officially assured, and Nash was looking for money for teachers' summer planning. Who would work on salary over the summer and what tasks had to be done dominated the teacher discussions. The name of the new school had yet to be decided, and various suggestions — some printable, some not — are recorded in the notes.

While increased certainty about the school provided an impetus for more concrete planning, many issues remained unresolved. Indeed, the meeting of 5/18 closed with a list of 23 unanswered questions, many of which were quite basic.

> Selection? Randomness? What if a student is not selected? What options then? What if a kid doesn't like it or doesn't participate? Credit? Grades? Program or pattern for both college and non-college-bound kids? Evaluation? How many years? <u>Can</u> you return to Hillhouse? Would I get a choice to do my own interest? Transportation? Eating? How will I be guidanced? Sports? Insurance?

Though enormous tasks lay ahead, the teachers were pleased with the process which had characterized the meetings thus far.

> We must remember that the summer is for organizing details. We don't need to worry about being able to get too detailed now. In fact, it may take up valuable time...A function of the school is the process of its definition, this process is an ongoing one — we need not bog down in non-professional details" (notes of 5/15).

Yet there were increasing pressures to begin formulating answers. One of the immediate costs of prolonging the ambiguity about the school was raised by Dr. Richard Mastain, Director of EIC, which had funneled money from Yale to support the new school. Dr. Mastain attended the 5/20 teacher meeting to discuss ways in which EIC could help generate resources from colleges, universities, and the community. He needed answers to several questions about the structure of HSC before the EIC could approach other groups on its behalf. Included among the questions were the following:

> Should it be of Hillhouse alone? Should the staff be from Hillhouse alone? Is the population selection satisfactorily random? Shall there be a coordinator, and, if so, who would he be responsible to? What is the mechanism for the handling of funds? Where is the fiscal responsibility *and* control of the project? Where does EIC fit in? What is the involvement of the community and the parents? (notes of 5/20).

Mastain's questions served as metaphor for the state of the planning process as the teachers ended their meetings in May. On the one hand, teacher energy and group commitment were high, buoyed by the increasing possibility that the school would become a reality. On the other hand, essentially none of the structural decisions about the school had been made. Further, it was becoming increasingly clear that the school needed to make such decisions to become a coherent setting internally, and to publicize its existence externally. Much remained as the planning group suspended the meetings until the end of the public school year.

Summer Planning: Activities and Empowerment Themes

In June, the Board of Education officially sanctioned the fall opening of the school. When the teachers reconvened in late June, they knew that both funding and approval had been secured. The following account comes from documents and recollections of five of the ten teachers involved with the school at that time.

Early Summer Activities: The summer was a time of constant activity. Funding had been found to pay for teachers' time, though the amount in no way covered the time commitments. Students had to be recruited, a building found, and places for classes to meet in the community located. Most importantly, many fundamental decisions about how the school would be structured still had to be confronted.

Finding a building for the school turned out to be relatively easy. Nash called the local Redevelopment Agency to find out what city-owned buildings were empty, and he and Foote toured the city. They found a warehouse-type building which previously housed an automobile dealership. In order to fulfill fire safety regulations, a door had to be constructed which exited into the parking lot of the business next door. "They wanted a high school next door like they wanted cancer," Foote recalled, "but I was from New Haven, grew up in a working class neighborhood, and understood the concerns the company had. We were able to work it out."

Recruitment of 150 students was also less problematic than might be expected, as the teachers brought many of the acquaintances they had formed at Hillhouse. Among these were several black and white students who were formal or informal leaders at Hillhouse. These students served as an important resource for the school. And, after a series of debates, the school named itself High School in the Community (HSC), reflecting its Parkway connection.

Empowerment Themes Continue: The early summer also reflected some of the themes which had characterized the spring planning meetings. One recurrent theme involved the issue of consensual decision-making.

During the first part of the summer there was no clear agreement on what had to be accomplished. "I'd never started a school before," recalled Foote, "and I don't think I knew what we had to accomplish before we opened." As the summer progressed, it became clearer that what the teachers stood *for* was more varied and diverse than what they stood against. One staff member recalled debates not about *what* goals the school should have, but *whether or not* it should have *any* shared goals. "Some teachers thought they should be free to determine for themselves what goals to pursue," he said. These differences dimmed the chances of reaching consensual decisions.

Even in the face of these frustrations, the concept of a common external enemy continued to be a binding force. On the local level, "downtown" and the Board of Education were still viewed as threats to the new school. In addition, in 1970 the politically liberal teachers found common cause against the military-industrial complex and such businesses as Dow Chemical. Their identity as a political as well as an educational group was strong. "As I look back on it," said one teacher in 1983, "I think I'd call us paranoid about authority. Then, however, it seemed much more like reasonable mistrust of the oppressor."

This existence of a common enemy, however, could not suppress the fundamental tension between the empowering value of individual autonomy and the need to agree about how the school would be structured. Inevitably, reaching a shared decision meant yielding individual autonomy. At this point in the school's evolution, this was considered disempowering by some teachers, and was resisted. Because decisions could only be made by consensus, any serious individual disagreement thus paralyzed the process of accomplishing specific tasks.

The seminar was the structural symbol for much of this early summer tension. As originally articulated in the January 1970 school system grant, the seminar was intended to be a hub around which many school values revolved. It was intended to be a personal teacher-student connection, a vehicle for guidance, and, most basically, a forum for student empowerment. Through its small size, personal flavor, and open agenda it stood as microcosm of teacher hopes for the larger school experience of creating a responsive, personal, caring environment for learning. Yet the seminar format, and the specific functions it might serve, were unclear as the summer began.

"Everyone agreed on the seminar," stated one teacher, "but no one agreed on its structure." Meeting notes reflect this sentiment:

> Should students be allowed to self-select into their seminar of choice or should they be randomly assigned? Should it be a

place for 'whatever comes up, comes up,' or should more general topics be agreed on by the staff? Do we (the teachers) know enough about leading groups to be successful in this structure? Are there shared goals or should we (teachers) determine our own practices and goals? (notes of 7/15)

These questions depict the ideological rift between individual freedom and group accountability which remained unresolved as the summer continued.

A second summer theme related to the empowerment ideology involved issues of leadership. The spring meeting notes show that while the teachers were unwilling to grant Foote any internal power, they had given him the responsibility of representing the school to the outside world. Foote recalled vividly his frustrations with this set of circumstances. In early summer, for example, he prepared a list of tasks which he felt needed to be accomplished before school opened. Apparently, presenting this list to the other teachers stimulated a great deal of discussion about whether or not certain tasks should be done at all. Some tasks were rejected as not important. The net result of the discussion was, according to Foote, one of "talking it all away," not agreeing on a plan of action, and blaming the leader for trying to lead.

Other happenings at that time suggest that teachers were equally aware of Foote's ambition to lead and their ambition to prevent it. In an effort to "collect the symbols of leadership," Foote tried to appropriate for his office the sole surviving chair in the newly acquired building. Another teacher, recognizing Foote's attempt to differentiate himself from the other teachers, would remove the chair from Foote's office after work and place it in her own work area, where Foote would find it the following morning and re-appropriate it. This interchange serves well as metaphor for the tension between empowerment and leadership.

Late Summer Activities and Empowerment Themes: As the summer progressed, teachers grew increasingly concerned with the amount that remained to be done and with the slow pace of decision-making. Students had now been recruited for the school, selected by lottery. Each teacher, in the spirit of creating a more collegial home-school relationship, had agreed to contact approximately 15 incoming students and visit their homes. By late July, work on the specifics of the curriculum was dragging and the overall school structure was still quite vague.

Foote recruited two advanced graduate students,one a psychologist, the other a social worker,to act as process consultants. These students, an interracial married couple, would have two mandates: (a) consulting with the teachers about their own decision-making proc-

esses, and (b) helping train teachers in the group dynamic skills necessary to conduct their seminars in the fall. Issues of leadership and
followership became central themes in both these areas. Indeed, the
consultants repeatedly stressed that the issue of leadership was the
primary block to successfully moving ahead.

After a series of meetings between the consultants and the teachers,
a two-day experiential learning workshop was scheduled for mid-
August. Based on a Tavistock model of group dynamics, the workshop
included a number of group exercises which minimized the amount of
structure provided by the leader. This format promoted conditions for
maximizing issues of authority and leadership.

Teachers recalled the workshop as a very difficult experience. While
some remembered it positively, the dominant recollection was that it
was more than they could handle at that point. Several recalled feeling
exposed and saying things about one another that could not be adequately dealt with before the workshop ended. Thus, the processes
activated by the workshop augmented rather than resolved frustrations
about authority issues and leadership in the group.

By now the idea of consensual decision-making had been abandoned in favor of a two-thirds majority vote. Believing that the group
process intervention had been almost more than the school could stand,
Foote decided to try to terminate the consultants' relationship with the
school. A meeting was called with the teachers and the consultants
present. Issues and accusations were aired, interpretations and efforts to
understand what had happened were offered, and, at the end, a vote was
taken. While a majority of the teachers were in favor of retaining the
consultants, they did not achieve the necessary two-thirds, and the
consultants were dismissed.

This event was a powerful one. Almost 15 years later teachers had
vivid recollections of both its process and outcome. They considered the
relative openness of the meeting as a positive, though sometimes tense,
situation. They recalled how unusually firm and determined Foote was
to force the consultants out. This determination, combined with his
success, increased their suspicion that Foote wanted power to lead the
school.

This event happened in the context of many other activities during
the last part of the summer. Teachers were meeting students and
parents, planning courses, and meeting almost daily about the school. In
mid-August they discovered that the teacher's union had called a strike
to begin the day school was to open. Though most teachers were not in
the union at this point in the school's history,[3] they supported the
reasons behind the strike. This issue raised pointed questions about how
the teachers would behave. How would going on strike or not affect the

opening of school? On the one hand, there was support for the union and the strike. On the other hand, there was concern that if the new school was not able to open for an indefinite period, momentum would be lost and, possibly, the school would not survive. The teachers decided to attend school on opening day with the provision that if any teachers disagreed, they could protest, picket, or support the strike by staying away. One of the ten teachers decided to picket; the others opened the school.

Finally, efforts were made to recruit volunteers and interns from local colleges before school began. Such individuals were needed to teach courses which teachers felt should be offered but were not because of limited staff resources. In addition, HSC sought to sponsor courses that individuals in the community wished to offer. During August, several teachers recruited volunteers, Foote solicited interns from a local college, and a local foundation sponsored a large mailing which generated the names of over 300 potential volunteer teachers. How to use these resources, when to use them, and who should supervise them was added to the agenda.

SCHOOL GOALS AND STRUCTURE: THE PRE-SCHOOL PLANNING ENDS

In addition to these previously described tasks and struggles, work needed to be done on overall school goals and structures. The focus here is on how the teachers were operationally translating their empowerment ideology into goals and educational structures for the school.

Intended Goals for HSC

In the late summer, plans were being made for a school evaluation by a Dr. Willis Hawley, a Yale political scientist who had been consulting with Superintendent Barbaresi over the previous year. The evaluation was designed to provide the school with information it might find useful, and would be done gratis. It was intended to serve the role of external critic (see Sarason, Zitnay, and Grossman (1970); a source of immediate feedback on how the newly developing setting's programs and processes were working.

Meetings were held during the summer to discuss school goals with the teachers. Hawley's obvious support for the concept behind the school, plus some existing affiliations of HSC faculty to Yale, minimized suspicion of the evaluation as an outside intrusion. Hawley was a "good-natured spy," as one teacher labelled it.

Issues of evaluation were discussed within the more pervasive philosophy underlying the school. The social science emphasis on standardized instruments and quantifiable data often clashed with HSC's ideology, lending a sometimes heated quality to the discussions. Similarly, concerns were voiced about the potential cultural bias of achievement tests and the difficulty in using any standardized measures when goals were to be individualized for each student.

These discussions also indicated the teachers' high hopes and sense of mission. As Foote recalled it, "we generally would start from the position that 100% of our kids will be Rhodes Scholars and be able to walk to England to do the work." The evaluators served a moderating influence by stressing the potential difficulty in reaching such goals and reminding the teachers that it was politically useful to achieve the goals they set.

While all the difficulties involved with designing the school itself pervaded the evaluation meetings, eventually more than 30 specifiable objectives were agreed upon. A listing of these goals (as reported in Hawley et al., 1971) shows the scope of the hopes and intentions of the teachers.

Product Objectives
1. Student tolerance of others will increase.
2. Recurrent incidents of student disorder will cease.
3. Student rates of academic progress will increase.
4. Student absenteeism will be reduced.
5. The number of informal and formal dropouts will be minimized.
6. Students wishing to go to college will have that opportunity.

Process Objectives
7. Students will manifest an increase in their interest in school.
8. There will be an effective parents' organization at HSC.
9. Students will feel they can influence school policy.
10. Students will participate in the governance of the school.
11. Students' self-discipline will grow and capacity for independent study will increase.
12. Students and faculty will develop a sense of responsibility to the program.
13. Students will feel teachers are interested in them.
14. A variety of teaching methods will be used.
15. Student response to particular courses will be sought.
16. Students will receive effective counseling.
17. Teachers will develop college preparatory courses.
18. Teachers will develop methods of effectively teaching basic skills.

19. A unique, diverse, and flexible curriculum will be developed.
20. The staff will derive satisfaction from teaching.
21. Interns will participate in various aspects of the school.
22. Teachers will exercise collegial authority on major issues.
23. Teachers will develop vocationally oriented programs.
24. Teachers and students will utilize informal contact outside of class.
25. Students will have the option of participating in a "community orientation program."
26. Students will receive formal evaluations in their courses.
27. Administrative procedures will support effective teaching.
28. All students will participate in a seminar.
29. Teachers will visit homes of their seminar students.
30. Teachers will regularly consult with each other about students.
31. Teachers will determine the resources needed to improve teaching within their subject area.
32. Students of different backgrounds will apply to HSC.

Several conclusions may be drawn from this list. First, HSC was attempting to achieve a wide variety of goals, greatly broadening the very definition of what a school should accomplish. Not only were more traditional goals involving achievement, attendance, and student retention emphasized, but various socialization goals for students were included, such as a commitment to school and improved interpersonal relationships with peers and teachers. Further, many goals for teachers were articulated, not only in terms of classroom-related activities, but in terms of collegial relationships and more personal relationships with students.

Embedded in the first conclusion is a second; teachers had assigned themselves an unusually multifaceted role which made them fundamental to the operation of all aspects of the school. The goals were thoroughly consistent with a teacher-run school fueled by an empowerment ideology; they also implied an eventual confrontation with the myth of unlimited resources.

The Status of Key Empowerment Structures: The Seminar, the Guidance Process, and the Community Orientation Program

Certain empowerment structures were also evolving as the summer neared an end. Three of these — the seminar, the guidance process, and the Community Orientation Program (COP)—would serve as distinctive contributions to a restructuring of the school experience. Each required an expanded role for the teacher, for at HSC every teacher had responsibility for participating in each of these structures.

THE SEMINAR

The seminar floundered all summer on the issue of whether it should serve a shared group function or be a place where teachers and students could "do their own thing." While teachers agreed it should be "the one absolute of the school," there was no agreement on what that absolute should be. One teacher wanted to be able to choose students for her seminar and did not want to force them to meet as a group. Another wanted students to be randomly assigned to the seminar to enforce the value of learning to interact with people different from oneself — the worry being that self-selection or teacher-selection would homogenize groups.

As the summer drew to a close, a compromise was reached on selection issues. Students would be randomly assigned to seminars and a certain percentage, if they wished, could shift. What was avoided, however, was the fundamental issue of defining the seminar. Consultants were brought in to aid in developing teacher skills in group leadership, but no consensus was reached regarding specifics—whether the groups had to meet as groups and whether attendance would be required remained unsettled issues. How the groups would accomplish the goals of facilitating communication, developing a sense of community, and helping students deal with school concerns also remained undetermined. For some teachers, this ambiguity was congruent with their belief in HSC as a place to "do your own thing." Yet, at the time school opened, the idea of the seminar was not well developed.

THE GUIDANCE PROCESS

Planning for the guidance aspect of the teacher role was minimal, according to notes and recollections of teachers. The basic intent was for each teacher to assume the guidance responsibilities for 15 students whom they could get to know well. This more personal relationship would allow the guidance process to be more informed and satisfying than was possible at Hillhouse. While none of the teachers had prior experience in guidance per se, many had been effective in working informally with individual students at Hillhouse. Still, *how* , *when*, and *where* guidance might occur was not discussed. Further, guidance included not only personal interactions, but a variety of administrative tasks, including record-keeping, checking on grades and attendance, and aiding in the development of post high-school plans. While the intent of the guidance role was clear, how these values would be translated into particulars was not.

THE COMMUNITY ORIENTATION PROGRAM (COP)

The COP was HSC's effort to extend education to include local community resources. Its development occurred on two levels during the summer. Foote and Superintendent Barbaresi, representing the school and school system respectively, went on the "rubber chicken" circuit, meeting with various agencies and business organizations to discuss the new school and the role that community institutions could play in the COP. Particular efforts were made to develop resources through the Chamber of Commerce. The Chamber's Task Force on Urban Solutions issued a supportive report in August 1970 about HSC, the Community Orientation Program, and various ways in which the business community could help the school.

Foote recalled two aspects of his relationship with the Chamber of Commerce. One was the "culture clash" between his ideas and attire and the business people involved with the Chamber. The other was the difficulty he had presenting the COP in a concrete way. The specifics had not been worked out, and Foote could not clearly respond to their questions. "If *you* don't know what you want, *they* won't know to respond," cautioned a friend on the Chamber of Commerce. Still, the group was very interested in linking the business community to the public schools, and a mechanism to direct interested parties toward HSC was developed.

While Foote was responsible for generating COP resources, the teachers were responsible for helping their 15 guidance students find appropriate community placements. Their efforts were limited by a lack of knowledge of the educational needs of their students, however, and the search assumed a low priority. Those teachers who were actively seeking community placements sought out ideologically congruent ones. "It was fine for a teacher to work out a community placement with a civil rights lawyer," said one teacher, "but no one was going to see a sergeant at the recruiting station."

As school opened, the COP was still a relatively undeveloped idea. There was no articulated structure for the program beyond the agreement that students would receive credit for work done in the community and that this work should be encouraged and arranged by teachers. Like the seminar and the guidance program, the COP would have to be developed as the school itself evolved.

Policy considerations: In addition to goals and structures, certain policy decisions were also made before school began. These decisions, whose consequences would only emerge over time, further underscore HSC's commitment to an egalitarian ideology. For example, teachers agreed that students would not be suspended from school; it would be the school's responsibility to work out ways of helping every student find some niche to allow the student to remain in school. It was further agreed that students would not be grouped by ability on the basis of standardized test scores; individual attention and heterogeneous grouping would be the rule. Finally, evaluation of student performance was to take the form of written evaluations of their progress. This would be relative to where they started and their own goals rather than based on comparison to other students. Teachers and students would then meet to discuss the evaluations and the course.

A CONCLUDING COMMENT

By the end of the summer, the contours of the school were beginning to take shape in the form of policies, structures, and the roles of the teachers. The planning process had surfaced a tremendous commitment of the teachers in terms of time, energy, and caring about creating a school responsive to the individual needs of students *and* teachers. It was to be a place where teachers could experiment and learn about *teaching* while students were experimenting with differing modes of learning. Emerging as important themes were: the tensions around the concept of leadership in an egalitarian setting, the integrating of the need for autonomy and the need for giving up some autonomy in the service of group goals, and the unknown implications of a greatly expanded teacher role. Yet, on September 8, 1970, when school opened, it was all theirs.

CHAPTER 4

The Shakedown Cruise

HSC began its formal operation on September 8, 1970 with a student body of 142, 88 black and 56 white students from Hillhouse. It began in a turbulent environment, with New Haven teachers on strike. The scene on opening day was vividly recalled by Ed Linehan, then a new student intern at the school and later its second head: "I grew up here in town, just a little Irish kid. And I come to school, the first day, and walk right into it. Alice [a teacher who later became the third head of the school] picketing, playing her guitar, people stepping over her body to get into the school, Nancy [who later became a lawyer in town] saying 'I'm here and I'll teach but I won't accept my paycheck; I'm not willing to be paid.' And I stand there and say to myself: 'How am I going to understand this? What's going on here?' I said."

"What's going on here" was the beginning of HSC's first year: its shakedown cruise. This chapter follows four salient aspects of the voyage: the organizational life of the school; the evolution of three empowering structures (the seminar, the guidance process, and the Community Orientation Program) and the beginning of role differentiation; mobilizing resources for survival; and the student experience. Together, these provide an overview of the school's first year.

THE ORGANIZATIONAL LIFE OF THE SCHOOL

The early months of the school's organizational life were characterized by teachers as involving intense excitement, long hours, "endless" meetings, and an often overwhelming sense of how much remained to be done. "I recall," said the one and only language teacher, "that at one time that first year I was supervising something like 14 volunteers — an *incredible* amount of supervision. But you know at that point in our history we had to offer *everything*, and I was the only language teacher we had." "It was 18 hours a day," recalled another, "but the excitement, the sense of being able to create our own school, the freedom to teach as we wanted, those made it all worthwhile."

Perhaps the most apt image, however, was supplied by Tom Nelson who, after taking notes at the planning meetings the previous spring, had been added to the staff as a student teacher. "I see George [Foote] as the captain of an airplane who comes into the passenger cabin and says 'Ladies and Gentlemen, I have some good news and some bad news. The good news is that we are flying at a record-setting pace, going much faster than anyone thought humanly possible. The bad news is that we have absolutely no idea what direction we're headed!'"

During December of the first year, the evaluation team interviewed teachers about their reaction to the first few months of school. Without exception, the teachers contrasted the positive and humanizing HSC climate with their experiences at Hillhouse. They collectively affirmed that at HSC the teacher role was to facilitate student intellectual and personal development. They cited the freedom to teach as they wished, to use whatever materials they deemed appropriate, the small class size, and the range of alternatives available for students as ways in which HSC was providing a positive alternative.

Yet the fall also marked one of the periods of gravest doubt about the future of the school. Around November, Foote recalls, there was general concern that "the school isn't working." The teacher interviews highlighted a number of issues causing concern at that time. They reflected the unanticipated consequences of the school's empowerment ideology for the life of its teachers and students.

Participatory Governance and Leadership in an Egalitarian Setting: The Difficulties Continue

As the school year progressed, difficulties in reaching decisions through group discussion continued. Because many aspects of the school were vague when school opened, teachers needed to meet continuously to discuss how the school should function — what its structure and rules should be. The existence of an actual as opposed to hypothetical school exacerbated the problems described during the summer, because real decisions with immediate consequences would be made by default if active teacher decision-making broke down.

Many teachers commented on this concern: "The core group of teachers fails to function as a group;" "lack of trust among faculty affects group decision-making;" "Unanimous decision-making means we do not confront problems in the group in order to avoid the pain of disagreement." These comments represent the range of concerns voiced by teachers. "We had an incredible tolerance for debate," recalled one teacher, "and sometimes someone would just go on and on until people got tired and the issue was dropped. It was like voting with your lips!" "It was bullshit," said another.

A related issue involved the difficulty in enforcing group decisions that were made. Often decisions reached in the group were ignored by some of the teachers outside the group. This unwillingness to abide by group decisions seemed particularly intense around policies in areas such as attendance which highlighted the power and role differences between teacher and student. In addition, there was no sanction against teachers who did not behave in accordance with group decisions. While providing a sense of ownership and energy, the empowerment ideology was also complicating the task of making decisions which would be carried out and enforced.

These frustrations around governance heightened the issue of leadership. When school opened, George Foote was informally acknowledged as a driving force behind the creation of the school, instrumental in securing funding, and the conduit for information and support from downtown. However, he was granted no legitimacy to lead internally around such tasks as agenda-setting for the group and allocating tasks to others. He had no formal title which differentiated him from the other teachers, even though he had unique responsibilities and accountabilities.

This situation remained during the fall, and contributed to the decision-making problems which increasingly concerned teachers. On the one hand, the need for leadership in structuring meetings was becoming increasingly apparent. On the other hand, efforts by *anyone* to lead were fought by faculty. This led to a kind of group stalemate which increased the teacher focus on Foote as leader. Several faulted his leadership style as too laissez-faire. "He's not a big enough boss," said one. Yet from Foote's perspective, leadership involved a delicate and often untenable balance. He recalled that his efforts at leadership were greeted with caution and suspicion, even when the difficulties in the meetings suggested its need. He cited the familiar group dynamic of "kill the leader" as a metaphor for his experience.[1]

Foote recalled one other aspect of this role which contributed to teacher suspicion of his leadership. During HSC's first year, he was primarily responsible for developing support for its continued survival. This required time away from the school dealing with the Superintendent and central school system administration. Foote's absence from the school and his powerful position as conduit for important external information made him increasingly suspect as an overly influential person in the school.

Boundaries in an Egalitarian Setting

Related to the two previous manifestations of the empowerment ideology and egalitarian commitment was a third: the blurring of various boundaries among teachers and between teachers and students. Boundaries refer to those organizational norms and practices which define the appropriate and inappropriate, the acceptable and the unacceptable, the included and the excluded (see Alderfer, 1981; Smith and Corse, 1986). At HSC, the empowerment ideology supported individual preferences over group norms. This resulted in the blurring of boundaries about who was authorized to do what.

Three brief examples highlight the kinds of issues which resulted from this blurring of boundaries. They show simultaneously the "good instincts" of the empowerment ideology as well as its costs. The first example involved the interaction of a black male student and a white male faculty member. In an effort to be accessible for students, HSC decided to remain open after school into the evening, with one staff member locking up at the end of the day. One day a white teacher negotiated with a group of students to stay until 7 p.m. As this time approached, one student said he did not want to leave. The teacher tried to argue him out of it. "You can go if you want," said the student, "I'll lock up. You just don't trust me because I'm black." "I just didn't know what to do," said the teacher, "he strung me out till about 8 p.m."

Here, the teacher was caught in the ambiguous authority boundary which the empowerment ideology fostered. In the spirit of this ideology, he wanted to be responsive to the student, and did not want to appear racist. However, with boundaries around authority blurred, the teacher was unclear about *who* was authorized to make the decision to close the building. Without institutional legitimacy for his authority, his only justification was seen as personal, i.e. selfish or racist. "It wasn't until people could say 'I don't want to be all things to a kid' that we got beyond that kind of thing," he commented later, "but at that moment it was just me and the kid." "But you know," he added "the same qualities that got people like me in trouble around these kinds of issues were the ones which attracted me to the school in the first place and allowed me to make such a commitment to it."

The second example was more systemic in impact. Early in the fall, representatives of the Black Panthers were invited to discuss their views in an assembly. It was a preplanned event, and classes were cancelled so that students could attend the assembly. A few weeks later a student, without prior warning, showed up at school accompanied by two Mormon missionaries. She thought the Mormons would provide an interesting contrast to the Black Panthers. In an effort to be student-oriented, flexible, and responsive, classes were interrupted for an assembly with the Mormons. While the assembly did indeed provide a contrast, teachers were concerned about the disruption of their classes. They did not know what control they had over participation in the assembly. The blurring of boundaries made them unclear about whether or not they could protect their classes from external and unpredictable intrusion.

The third example involved the unintended consequences of teacher autonomy around discipline. By agreement, teachers were free to set their own classroom standards for appropriate behavior. Vastly different expectations about student behavior resulted from this stance. The same student would thus be treated very differently in different classes. In the absence of shared expectations around discipline, teachers who were seen as more strict were labeled "unfair" or "uncaring." This, in turn, pressured teachers to be more accommodating to student influence than they wanted to be. Like the teacher in the first example, they did not want to be seen as authoritarian or, where discipline involved cross-race interactions, racist.

These three examples highlight the difficulties resulting from the uncertainty about the boundaries governing organizational life. In expressing concern about these issues, teachers signalled an acknowledgement that they may have to relinquish individual autonomy in favor of developing more clear and shared boundaries. At this point in HSC's history they did not state the issue this way; rather, they were more frustrated about finding themselves in such situations. However, they were inching toward a confrontation with this aspect of their empowerment ideology.

School Structure and the Student Experience

A fourth theme involved teachers' assessment of the impact of the school on students. When HSC opened, its predominant belief was that its empowering nature and humanized atmosphere would enrich all. The December interviews, however, suggested that different groups of students were responding to HSC in different ways.

Two kinds of student distinctions emerged. The first was between students who were self-directed and self-starters and those who needed structure to anchor their school existence. "The program is designed to help the bright, self-motivated kid — it's not taking care of kids who need special attention" said one teacher. "Some kids simply aren't good at taking responsibility for their own education," said another. HSC's loose structure and lack of norms about attendance and discipline were allowing some students to flounder.

The second distinction involved race. Black teachers in particular were concerned about the impact of the school on black students. "There's not enough structure, too much freedom, teachers' fear of imposing their own views. Black kids are 'let go' too much. Teachers need to understand cultural diversity, but they're too afraid to be the 'bad guy,'" said one black teacher. And from a second black teacher:

"Teachers are not assuming proper roles as authority figures. Kids, especially black kids, want people to care about what they are doing — a sure way of showing that one doesn't care is to ignore disciplinary problems; kids want to be told when there are limits. Teachers try to ignore 'racial matters' by not provoking (or trying extremely hard to avoid) confrontations; this is unnatural; teachers should learn to deal positively with such situations."

Racism

Because of the school's origins in racial unrest, its commitment to egalitarianism, and the faculty's belief in racial integration, racism was often discussed during the fall. When asked about it by the evaluators, teachers gave several responses. First was general agreement that whatever the racial issues at HSC, they were more manageable, less severe, and more readily confronted than they had been at Hillhouse. No specific "incidents" were cited which could be clearly labelled as racist. Indeed, several white faculty recalled a frustration in discussing racism with black teachers because "there was nothing specific to point to."

Still, the year was 1970 and there was the strong belief that the society was racist. It seemed implausible that *no* racist attitudes or structures could be found in the school. Black and white teachers brought differing perspectives to the issue. "We talked about it all the time," recalled one white teacher. "I remember several of us not really knowing how to understand the ins and outs of racism. I remember one teacher saying, 'I know I'm white but I'm not a racist' when he was given the message that to be white was to be racist. He kept protesting." At least one white teacher dismissed the issue out of hand. "This racism is silly," he stated, "we wouldn't be in this school if we were racist." In another context, however, this same teacher asserted that, "Italian parents back up teachers, black parents back up students."

The recollection of that time by a black teacher put another perspective on interracial dynamics. "You know," she said, "when I got involved with the school, and I walked in the door and saw Alice, a young, fair-skinned, long-haired, blue-eyed blonde with a Southern accent, I said to myself 'she's *got* to be a racist, and she isn't.' None of us black teachers had ever worked closely with whites before, and it took some getting used to."

In sum, the teacher interviews supported the belief that HSC was concerned about racism in the school. Black teachers in particular felt that the issue needed more discussion. In December, they asked Foote to arrange a group process workshop on race relations among staff.

Teachers differed in their recollection of the value of the workshop, but all stated that the short-term impact surpassed the long-term benefits. "It was just a very hard issue to deal with," said one white teacher. "Sometimes you're not sure whether or not it's there and you're afraid to get into it in case it is." "I'm not sure why the workshop didn't work," said another. "Either the technique was wrong or there wasn't enough racism." "Sometimes the reason you don't know something is that you don't *want* to know it," countered a black teacher.

Such was the organizational life of the school during the fall. The central themes involved decision-making, leadership, boundaries, the student experience, and racism. Tensions between the autonomy of the individual and the needs of the collective were experienced, and the differential impact of HSC on black and white students raised concern. However, many of the anticipated positive outcomes of HSC's structure and ideology were being realized.

Let us turn to a second aspect of the school — the evolution of its innovative structures and the development of clearer role differentiations among faculty. Here HSC quickly was forced to confront the unanticipated consequences of its initial grand assumptions. As one teacher stated that fall, "HSC is failing only if its definition of success is to succeed at *everything*." One aspect of the shakedown cruise was the realization that "everything" was too much, forcing a confrontation about priorities.

The Evolution of Structures and the Differentiation of Roles

HSC had designed several structures for students to individualize their education and teachers to humanize its process. At the time school opened, these structures included the seminar, the guidance process, the use of outside volunteers, and the Community Orientation Program. In the spirit of the egalitarian commitment, teachers were responsible for participating in each: leading a seminar, being guidance counselor for students in the seminar, coordinating volunteers in their area of expertise, and serving as liaison with community placements for a small group of students. Any discussion of specific structures cannot be understood without remembering that teachers were involved in *all* of them.

The seminar: As originally conceived, the seminar was intended to be a setting where students could bring up issues, voice problems, and develop a sense of community at the school. While the idea of the seminar had been much discussed during the summer, no shared agreement was reached about how it might be implemented. Shortly after the beginning of school it became clear that the seminar concept was not accomplishing its mission. The format of the seminar varied widely from teacher to teacher. Some resembled organized classes, while others drifted into free-floating discussions. Student attendance quickly became a problem.

Teachers differed in their response to the seminar. Those teachers with particular competence in leading such groups continued throughout the fall. Several teachers, however, found the seminar concept to be unworkable within the first month of school and ended it. As a school-wide structure, the seminar did not survive the first half of the school year.

In May of the first year, teachers were interviewed about the seminar and its future. Teachers expressed strong support for the idea behind the seminar, and hoped it would be reinstituted in a different form the following year. The most frequent explanation for its lack of success was the belief that teachers did not have the necessary skills to run such groups. Other reasons surfaced as well, however. "The seminars failed because they were imposed on students, not developed with students. They should be reinstituted if there is agreement with students that they want it," stated one teacher. "Seminars failed because we didn't want them," said another. "We avoided real talk about what they could do — a totally unstructured situation, with no one wanting it enough to think about it."

On the positive side, several teachers saw the process surrounding the seminar as one of strength. "We didn't simply go on pretending that it was working when it wasn't," stated one. "I think it's a sign of our organizational flexibility that we decided to drop the seminar and think about planning it more carefully — like you plan a course." "We were very honest in dealing with the issue of the seminar," said another, "even though we were unhappy that it wasn't working better."

The seminar, then, provided one of the earliest sources of feedback that the teacher role was being stretched in ways which some could deal with effectively and others could not. Further, it underscored how lack of clear and shared goals interfered with the success of one particular school structure. The continued interest in pursuing the seminar, however, suggests that it represented an important idea.

The guidance function: Early discussions about the role of teacher as guidance counselor focused on personalizing the teacher-student relationship. Through being responsible for 15 students each, teachers could better appreciate students' life circumstances and educational/personal needs. This aspect of the teacher role was both successful and a source of teacher satisfaction during the first year. Teachers reported spending a great deal of time with students talking about personal and career-related matters. As student data will later show, students also felt supported by and cared about by teachers.

Over the course of the year, however, two forces combined to push HSC toward centralizing some of the guidance functions. The first involved the need to coordinate the flow of information around course planning and students' cumulative records. To plan courses, for example, it was necessary to compile a complete list of available offerings and distribute that list to students and teachers. In addition, students' progress in other courses needed monitoring to insure that requirements for graduation were being met. Doing this required access to each student's cumulative record as each semester progressed. In the service of efficiency, it became clear that centralizing such tasks would be necessary.

The second force toward centralization involved planning for post-high school education. The complexities of this aspect of guidance only became clear as those seniors in the class began to face the issue of what they wanted to do after graduation. While HSC eventually did a good job at placing its graduating seniors (see Chapter 7), a more centralized process was needed to deal with this aspect of guidance as well. The institutional mandate for a guidance counselor had emerged.

The Community Orientation Program

The Community Orientation Program (COP) was designed to be a vehicle for students' use of community resources as learning experiences. During its first year, the evaluation team interviewed teachers, students in the COP, and field supervisors about their reaction to the program.[2] In framing their report, the evaluators noted the central role of the COP in HSC's structure and the importance of the teacher role in carrying out the COP. They further noted that "vocational education exists entirely within the scope of the educational offerings of the COP," thus emphasizing its distinctive importance for noncollege-bound students.

The evaluators reviewed the history of contact between HSC and the Chamber of Commerce, emphasizing how HSC's lack of a clear understanding about the goals of the program impeded the efforts of the business community to be useful. Lack of clarity about goals plus a more general sense of ambivalence about the business community contributed to the relative exclusion of business-related COP offerings during the fall.

The overall conclusion of the report was that the COP quickly lapsed into a secondary priority as the fall progressed. While several teachers and students took the initiative to develop community placements, the extensive role demands on teachers prevented the necessary follow through. A few weeks after school opened, the liaison activities of the COP were delegated to student interns. The lack of any codified procedures for running the COP and the interns' uneven knowledge of city resources combined to reduce its coherence.

Though the COP became increasingly peripheral to the teacher role, HSC remained committed to keeping it in the educational program. In January 1970, the evaluation team provided the teachers with extensive feedback on the initial months of the COP. They pointed out the structural problems with the program and made recommendations for its improvement. This document was discussed by the teachers and led to several changes in how the COP was structured. One immediate consequence was to have a single person—Tom Nelson—begin to coordinate the administrative tasks. In addition, HSC decided to create a formal role of COP coordinator beginning the following year.

The Creation of Formal Roles and Structures — Secretary, Coordinator, and the Policy Council: As the first year progressed, three additional organizational changes occurred. First was the addition of a part-time secretary in November. When school opened, HSC had no secretary — a decision which faculty recalled as primarily ideological; the idea of a secretary invoked status and role differentials which could not be reconciled with the egalitarian commitment.

The organizational need for such a position, however, quickly became evident. Within two months, a part-time secretary had been found. Her position was funded by external resources secured by Ernie Osborne, head of Yale's Council of Community Affairs. Teachers described her as a competent, unflappable woman whose ability to be both calm and organized contributed significantly to the school. In addition to her secretarial duties, she voluntarily assumed other responsibilities, such as developing a listing of COP placements.

A second change was the decision to provide George Foote with a title: Coordinator. While acknowledged as informal leader of the school and its primary liaison to the external world, Foote was not initially accorded any title which would differentiate him from the other teachers. The motivations behind the decision to give Foote the title of 'coordinator' are not clear. Some teachers recall that it was primarily a move to clarify for persons outside the school that there was actually someone in charge. They also recalled that it held little meaning *inside* the school. Still, it did convey some internal meaning. "Just *when* I went from 'Hey you' to 'Coordinator' I don't remember," said Foote, "but it *was* a sign of legitimacy for the role I was playing anyway."

The final change during the first year involved the decision to create a Policy Council, consisting of equal numbers of teachers, students, and parents. This decision, made around Thanksgiving, was designed to serve a number of goals. First, there was concern about how the school was working. The Policy Council was seen as one possible mechanism for re-energizing the school and bringing new resources to bear on its functioning and development. Such a vehicle for students could also provide a possible antidote for the problems around group cohesion caused by the demise of the seminar. In addition, it would further the school's commitment to parent involvement. Finally, during this time plans were being made to secure federal funding for the school. Federal guidelines around parent involvement may have helped stimulate the creation of this specific mechanism.

A more complete story of the first several years of the Policy Council is found in a later chapter. However, it is useful here to state that by February, a Council consisting of five teachers, five students, and five parents had its first meeting. Its mandate was both broad and vague, and its domain of responsibility still needed clarification. But the intent was to give the Policy Council considerable policy-making authority.

Thus, during the first year of the school, a variety of new structures were created and teacher roles began a process of differentiation. These modifications in part represented reactions to the unanticipated consequences of HSC's initial assumptions. However, they also represented adaptive efforts to survive without diluting the basic empowerment ideology of the school. While stress was high, so too was energy, commitment, and hope. Nowhere was this combination more evident than in HSC's efforts to develop funding for the following year.

MOBILIZING RESOURCES FOR SURVIVAL: INSTITUTIONALIZING HIGH SCHOOL IN THE COMMUNITY

Though HSC had become established as an experimental alternative high school, its funding base was only sufficient for its first year. A significant portion of its budget came from state and local funds which could presumably be tapped after the first year. However, Yale's $40,000 contribution was a "one-time only" commitment. For the school to continue, it needed future funding. Sam Nash had previously been told that funds for special projects such as HSC might be available under Title III, Section 306 of the 1965 Elementary and Secondary Education Act. Nash and Superintendent Barbaresi believed that a successful application could both expand the size of HSC and signal the beginning of the school system's comprehensive restructuring.

Nash and Barbaresi's interest in expanding HSC caused internal debate. Some teachers felt that HSC had not yet adequately demonstrated that it could succeed. "If we're having such trouble getting our own act together, how can we advocate expanding and potentially magnifying the problems" was their position. Others believed that new opportunities should be available for people like themselves to test their mettle. "Why deny others the same opportunity we have had?" captured this position. Foote, supporting the latter argument, joined in the grant-writing process with Nash and Barbaresi.

On February 9, 1971 a preliminary grant application, "Organization of Community and School Staff for Restructuring the School System," was submitted to the Office of Education, Department of Health, Education, and Welfare. The proposal was for three years of funding to support an expansion of HSC based on two approaches: first, organizing the community — students, parents, businesses, colleges, agencies, and concerned citizens — to participate in the planning process for the restructuring of the schools; and second, developing additional alternatives into a system of "public schools of choice," essentially as Nash had envisioned. "The same education isn't the best education for everyone, and we believe that it's necessary to provide educational alternatives" (comment from Gerald Barbaresi in the Superintendent's Bulletin, January 25, 1971, and cited on page 4 of the grant proposal). On the basis of this preliminary proposal, the Office of Education requested a formal grant application.

Notification of acceptance of the preliminary proposal was received on April 9, 1971; the deadline for the formal proposal was in late May. This allowed six weeks to clarify with the federal government what the proposal needed to contain *and* write a final grant proposal. This time proved pivotal to the development of HSC for a variety of reasons. First, it showed how many diverse resources could be mobilized on behalf of the idea of HSC and educational alternatives. By late April, nine task forces and an oversight community council had been formed. Teachers, members of the New Haven community, students, and parents were involved in each group. The final week's schedule of events captures well the intensity of the effort: May 13 — final task force reports submitted and budget task force begins cost analysis; May 15 — budget task force report due; May 17 — distribution of working drafts for criticism; May 19 — final proposal writing begins; May 21 — final proposal (180 pages) sent to the Office of Education.

Second, the federal guidelines for developing the proposal helped shape aspects of the school. For example, the guidelines stressing community involvement helped consolidate the idea of a Policy Council as an important vehicle for parent and student involvement. The need to specify a project director was a force toward making the title of Coordinator a formal school role. The mandate to specify roles and job functions provided an opportunity to request funds for a guidance counselor, full-time secretary, and coordinator of the Community Orientation Program. Finally, the mandated external evaluation of the project set the stage for an ongoing relationship with an evaluation team.

The ability to mobilize the community, the existence of HSC as an indication of school system commitment to educational alternatives, and the narrative of the proposal itself were convincing. The proposal was funded for three years at a level which would allow HSC to expand to two units in the following fall. Foote would become coordinator for those units, and in addition to new teachers, a guidance counselor, secretary, two administrative assistants, and a COP coordinator would be hired.

Foote, Linehan, and Nelson, the three HSC staff primarily responsible for coordinating the task forces and writing the final proposal, recalled both the excitement and exhaustion of that month. "It was a heady feeling," recalled Linehan, "working on your own school like that, being part of that dynamic. It was exhausting, but it made a lot of things worthwhile."

The Student Experience: Results from the Evaluation

In addition to data on HSC's development as a new setting, the evaluation team also gathered information on the student experience. These data add greatly to our understanding of HSC's first year of operation. Three general areas bear specific mention: (1) grades, attendance, and dropping out; (2) the "affective dimension" of the school experience — student attitudes about themselves, teachers, and the process of learning; and (3) post-high school plans.

Grades, attendance, and dropping out: At HSC, students were given written evaluations of their classroom performance rather than grades, and the evaluators had to devise a means of translating these evaluations into grade equivalents. This was done using a five-point scale, with the following criteria for translation: 1 = failure; 2 = incomplete; 3 = credit given with improvement needed; 4 = credit given for satisfactory work; and 5 = credit given for excellent work. Using these admittedly rough criteria, over half of the HSC students stayed in the same quartile of grades at HSC that they had the previous year at Hillhouse, about a quarter of the students improved, and a fifth obtained worse grades.

Just as assessment of grades was made more difficult because of HSC's policy of providing written evaluations, so the issue of attendance was complicated by policy ambiguities about what was recorded as attendance. Margaret Miller, a teacher at HSC, captured one dimension of this issue: "We have a number of 'phantom students' at HSC who are enrolled on our books but they have received no credit all year. In a sense, they come to school: they show up every morning at a fashionably late hour to play cards in our front window..." (City Notes Bulletin of the Center for the Study of the City, 1971).

The evaluation report (Hawley et. al, 1973) states its findings as follows, beginning with the goal that HSC set for itself.

> *The attendance of individual students will improve compared to their attendance at Hillhouse High School:* This objective is modestly stated: many teachers and parents hoped that HSC would inspire almost full attendance by most students. Our analysis suggests that poor attendance is as serious a problem this year at HSC as it was last year at Hillhouse, perhaps more so. Over the entire year students attended school at HSC about 74 percent of the time while they had attended school — or at least appeared in homeroom (where daily attendance at Hillhouse was taken) — about 82 percent of the time in the previous year. This judgment must be considered tentative, however, since neither Hillhouse nor HSC keeps attendance records in a way which allows one to reliably know whether students actually attend classes. At HSC a student is recorded being present if he or she attends one or more classes in a given day. At Hillhouse students are counted present if they attend the short meeting of their homeroom. . .(pp. 13-14).

In addition to goals for attendance, HSC also aspired to minimize the proportion of students who "formally or informally" drop out of school. To quote again the Hawley et al. evaluation:

> If one defines a formal school dropout as a person who no longer attends classes and evidences no intent to preserve the continuity of his or her education, it appears that only 6 of the 40 seniors at HSC dropped out. It is difficult to determine whether sophomores and juniors have discontinued their formal education but 13 percent of these (approximately 110) students did not receive credit for a single class during the final

quarter and did not attend classes during most of this period (p. 14).

By these criteria, then, approximately 13 percent of HSC students had functionally dropped out during the year.

Additional data suggest that this percentage would have been greater had the HSC students stayed at Hillhouse. In January, students at HSC were asked whether or not they had considered dropping out of school. Nineteen percent reported that they had considered dropping out of HSC while 77 percent of these same students reported that they had thought about dropping out of Hillhouse the previous year. On the level of self-report, students viewed HSC as having more potential "holding power" for them.

Additional data were gathered on "informal dropouts." These were students who, by the end of the third quarter of school, had not received credit in 60 percent or more of their classes because of poor attendance. Twenty-one percent of HSC students fell into this category.[3] Interviews with a random sample of this group revealed several themes. First, there was general agreement that students should assume significant responsibility for their own education. Still, they were also ambivalent about the lack of structure. Further, they felt that HSC did not hold them accountable for their absences. Their most common explanation was "that they 'messed up' by not going to class or by not doing their work because they were 'messing around' with their friends or with activities which they momentarily found more interesting than class" (Schultz, 1971, p. 9).

Many students had very positive things to say, however. Racism was seen as greatly reduced from their previous school experience, and many commented favorably on the concern and helpfulness of teachers. Several stated that their parents were happier with HSC than they had been with Hillhouse. In addition, they appreciated HSC's commitment to students. "Here," said one student, "if a girl gets pregnant they don't make her feel bad or kick her out; they let her stay in school and help her as best they can." It's a real friendly atmosphere," said another. "I get a lot of individual attention."

In general, however, student reactions reflected an issue of compatibility between the demand characteristics of the school and the abilities and coping styles of students. Those students who were identified as informal dropouts included many students who were unable to take advantage of the freedom HSC offered. "Messing around with friends" and "hanging out" took precedence over school, particularly when *not* attending school held no clear consequences for students. "There is just too much freedom here," said one sophomore, "I'm going back to Hillhouse."

The Affective Aspects of the School Experience: During the spring of HSC's first year, random samples of students completed surveys at both HSC and Hillhouse.[4,5] Results from these surveys led the evaluators to the following conclusion:

> The most dramatic achievement of HSC centers on what educators like to call 'the affective dimension' of the school experience — the students' attitudes about themselves, others (especially teachers), and about the process of learning itself. HSC students appear to manifest little of the alien feelings toward teachers and school, little of the intergroup hostility, and little of the sense of futility that characterized students in so many other schools. HSC has been virtually free of student disorder, physical or psychological intimidation, vandalism, or other types of antisocial behavior (Hawley, et al., 1973, p. 3).

More specific data from these surveys clarify the reasons for that conclusion. For example, 87 percent of the HSC students reported less interracial tension at HSC than had been present at Hillhouse, and 55 percent stated that there was more interracial contact at HSC. To the statement, "Most of the time I'm proud to go to this school," 93 percent of HSC students answered affirmatively compared to 49 percent of Hillhouse students. In like manner, only 7 percent of HSC students seemed to feel "less interested" in school this year than last, while 43 percent of the Hillhouse sample reported less interest.

In addition, HSC students reported an increase over time in their belief that they could make a difference in how the school was run. To quote the evaluation:

> When we conducted our first student survey in December and January, a majority expressed a certain amount of cynicism as to whether the faculty really intended to grant them a substantial role in the governance of the school. However, by late April, after the Policy Council had been established and was working, better than three-fourths of those students we interviewed indicated that they felt that, in one way or another, students had a meaningful role in making school decisions (p. 22).

Student satisfaction extended to other aspects of the school as well. With respect to the curriculum, 81 percent of HSC students who participated in the spring survey answered "yes" to the question, "Did you get what you wanted from most of your courses?" Teacher treatment of students was also an important contributor. All but one of the 58 HSC students surveyed in May agreed with the statement, "Most teachers at my school have respect for their students as people."

While quantitative data anchor the conclusion that HSC was seen positively by students, the spirit of the school shines brightest in one anecdote reported by Tom Nelson.

> Ten students were suspended from Hillhouse and decided to come down to HSC to raise hell and make their presence known. They did, and they were doing it quite successfully. The staff had pretty much forgotten what it was like to teach at Hillhouse and stood awed, remembering how bad it had been and not being able to remember what they did when it was so bad... It was educating to the staff to see the incredible contrast between our students and the ones 'left behind,' but in the meantime things were being broken and stolen by the 'rowdies.' The staff was let off the hook by our students, who grew so angry at their friends of former days disrupting their school that a group of them got together and literally kicked them out. The staff spent the remaining days of the week basking in the difference of their students and the rowdies, and remembering that last year the kids that disrupted and the kids who kicked them out were the same kids.

Post High School Plans: While it is not uncommon for high schools to be judged by their success in placing students in college, such was not the intent of HSC. Rather, their goal focused on helping students fulfill their own aspirations, regardless of whether or not those aspirations involved college, vocational training, or the world of work. Still, it was important to assure prospective college-bound students that coming to HSC would not interfere with, and indeed might enhance, this option.

Teachers understood the importance of this issue for the school as well as for students. They also knew that aspects of HSC's innovative structure, such as use of evaluations rather than grades, might work against college admission. To deal with this, many teachers and, particularly, George Foote, spent considerable time developing contacts with colleges in the region. They attempted to provide more information about prospective students and the school than colleges would normally receive. The results of these efforts yielded a quite favorable outcome for HSC students. Of the graduating seniors, 76% were accepted by and planned to attend a four-year college the following year. Of those students not planning on attending college, all had specific plans for employment or duty in the armed services.

SUMMARIZING THE FIRST YEAR: SPRING TEACHER INTERVIEWS

As can be seen, HSC experienced many changes during its initial year. These changes were necessitated in part by unanticipated consequences of the ways in which the school implemented its empowerment ideology. Of central importance was the degree to which the multifaceted teacher role placed excessive demands on their time and resources. This pressure pushed the school toward more differentiated roles, thus shrinking the role demands on teachers (e.g., dissolving the seminar and placing COP in the hands of the student interns). Further, HSC created new roles to carry out the school's many tasks.

There is no compelling evidence that, at this point in the school's evolution, any serious thought was given to redefining the school's goals or abandoning the structures related to those goals. The COP, for example, was not discarded as being impractical or educationally unsound; rather, funding for a COP coordinator became one component of the federal grant written by the school. Though the seminars were temporarily dropped, teacher consensus was that they should be revised and reinstated the following year. Throughout the year, the empowerment ideology made each decision to formalize, create boundaries, and become more bureaucratic a painful one, filled with debate about whether or not the decision was consistent with the school's fundamental values.

In spring 1971, all HSC teachers were interviewed about HSC's first year. Their comments highlight certain more specific themes. First, teachers showed great caring for and thought about the school. Many discussed why the seminar had failed and how it could be improved. They argued that both the guidance process and the COP needed additional thought, structure, and resources to succeed. They remained positive about the autonomy that HSC afforded. And they were clearer than in the fall that some students needed far more structure than others; that more attention should be devoted to reading and math; and that vocationally oriented students were not being served as well as the college bound. Like the organizational structure of the school itself, teachers were becoming more differentiated in their assessment of the school and its students.

Teachers also reemphasized the ongoing problem of governance and leadership in the school's organizational life. Not only were the frequent faculty meetings still a source of frustration, the creation of the Policy Council as another decision-making group added further ambiguity around how policy would be made. The need to deal with such issues was repeatedly stressed. Related to that were an increasing number of concerns about Foote's leadership. Foote himself reported feeling more and more isolated as the year progressed.

The first year of HSC, its shakedown cruise, ended with a number of processes related to organizational evolution. Tenaciously holding to the original spirit of the school, its ten founders were attempting to adapt their original conceptions to the context of their first year experiences. A second unit of the school would become operational in the fall, and summer planning would be necessary, as would such pragmatics as finding a site for the new unit. New positions, such as guidance counselor and COP coordinator, needed to be filled, and the first year's experience needed processing. Though many issues remained, much had been accomplished, including the basic task of survival for the next few years.

In June 1971, HSC graduated its first class. Fittingly, each senior walked individually to receive his/her diploma to music each had personally selected. Music from classics to soul was heard. Each student was marching metaphorically to the beat of his/her own drummer.

CHAPTER 5

Evolution of the School, 1971-74: Organizational Themes and Leadership Issues

HSC began its second year with new hopes, new plans, and an enlarged organizational structure. The three-year Office of Education grant allowed the opening of a second unit of the school called Unit II, thus essentially doubling its size. In addition, it provided resources to hire specialized personnel, including a guidance counselor, two administrative assistants, and a coordinator for the COP program. This expansion would not only provide a broader base to test the potentials and problems of the empowerment ideology; it would also raise issues of collaboration and coordination between HSC's two administrative units.

This chapter follows HSC as an organization over the next three years. How did teachers cope with their extensive roles over time? How did the empowerment ideology affect leadership issues? And how did HSC's empowerment structures fare after the first year of the school? Though not definitive, three years represents a reasonable time frame to document whether the organizational themes and issues outlined in the previous chapter reflected transitory processes or more enduring ones crucial to HSC's evolution. In the following sections, we follow the evolution of the themes, processes, and structures introduced in the previous chapter.

Summer Activities

For the entire original staff (hereafter called Unit I), summer was a time of reflection on the past year, planning for the fall, pre-school meetings with the parents of incoming students, and developing placements for students in the upcoming Community Orientation Program. While partial summer funding was available for staff, it was not equal to the amount of staff effort.

For George Foote, the Coordinator, the summer not only included participation in these tasks but finding a new home for Unit I and another site for the new unit: Unit II. The original site for Unit I had been deemed structurally unsound by the city. Foote recalled vividly the time and energy it took. "Often Sam Nash and I would track down buildings owned by the city. Then we'd pound the pavements seeing what was available and what could be negotiated. It wasn't exactly what I thought I'd be doing as an educator, but you do what you have to." By mid-summer, two sites had been secured. Unit I was down the street from its previous home, and Unit II about a mile away.

The biggest set of planning issues for the fall were necessitated by the creation of a second unit of the school. Faculty hiring and student selection had to occur. New faculty had to meet both among themselves and with Unit I faculty to decide how the new unit would be structured. Students would come from the other New Haven high schools, thus making HSC a city-wide alternative. Unit II would be 60% white, reflecting the racial composition of these other high schools.

By the fall, the requisite steps had been taken. Students had been selected by lottery from among those who had applied. A full staff had been hired. Like the original staff at Unit I, Unit II teachers were young, ideological, predominately white, and committed to making inner-city public education "work." Unlike Unit I teachers, several had worked together before on political causes and had experience in organizing which, in retrospect, they felt came in handy in beginning a school on such short notice. They also had the advantage of Unit I's first year experience and had Ed Linehan, who had previously been at Unit I, as their Unit Head.

Structurally, Unit II closely mirrored Unit I. Teaching would be individualized, volunteers would be used, governance would occur through a Policy Council of parents, students, and teachers, the idea of a seminar would be maintained, and teachers would serve a guidance function. While Foote would serve as coordinator of both units, Unit II would be functionally autonomous. There were no plans for coordinating the curriculum or sharing of resources. Each unit would have its own Policy Council. Further, each unit would have its own Unit Head, with Foote Coordinator of both units.

1971-72: FORCES TOWARD ROLE DIFFERENTIATION AND BUREAUCRACY INCREASE

The 1971-72 school year began with a renewed sense of excitement and mission. Not only had Unit I survived its first year, but the school had secured three years of funding and added a second unit. As the year progressed, however, the primary organizational issues of the previous year became increasingly salient. They are captured well in a March 1971 memo from Ed Linehan, Unit Head of Unit II, to his teachers. In both substance and tone, Linehan's memo reflects the ongoing paradoxes of HSC's empowerment ideology: how to balance individual autonomy with group commitments, avoid bureaucracy and still accomplish tasks, and encourage broad participation without becoming swamped. It also, however, reflects a new level of concern about the need for a more planned and differentiated approach to making HSC work.

> Greetings one and all! Throughout the year at different times I've played at being Unit Head. Sometimes only to the extent of recording staff attendance every two weeks and at other times by really trying to coordinate activities. I don't think it's vain to say that I've grown in my position to the point where I keep very good attendance records. All of the above is by way of introduction to request for you to seriously consider what is or isn't going to happen over the next six months.
>
> All of us have been working together and facing problems together for three-quarters of the school year. Each of us started with an ambitious work load either just at HSC or here and at college, and/or at some other place we're committed to. As the year has gone on we've picked up additional things that needed to be done, usually when it was critical for us to do so. One of the strange experiences for me about working here this year has been never really feeling good about what I was doing... Sometimes I would focus in on myself and feel guilty, other times I'd get angry at one or all of you for being 'irresponsible' about doing something. For the last two months I've been really hassling through this problem of what I'm supposed to do and what I can expect from others. The more time I've spent thinking about it the more convinced I am that feeling guilty about what I'm doing and occasionally angry about what others are doing are different perspectives of the same issue and very much share the same causes.
>
> It was either Tom or Ed Lichtenstein over at Unit I that described the school, as it has been operating, as a laissez-faire system. Each of us making decisions independently about what we are going to do, and not being answerable to anyone else. Even when there has been a group decision, we actively support it to the extent that we favored it or have time to fit it in. Our decisions have for the most part met particular realities at school — each of us responding to the one that we feel most interested in or the one that demands, as in a crisis, that we not ignore it. The fault I find with the laissez-faire system is that it makes us compete. The valued commodity is simply time...
>
> The most common frustrations that the evaluation team found when they interviewed us was 'time vs. task.' Clearly there are more things which could be done that can be done,

primarily because of lack of time. We first realized this last summer, when as best we could we tried to talk about our priorities and how we would achieve them. The pressure we are presently working under is in part the difference between what we anticipated last summer and what we've learned since then. Today we are in a much better position to know what amount of time and effort is demanded by something like seminar, COP, counseling, Policy Council, basic skill development, and so on. We also know considerably more about the various administrative functions which need to be done, and what it means not to have an administration separate from the teaching staff. If we are going to improve the operation and productivity of our school, however we define it, then now is the time to begin for next year. We have to determine our new priorities based on a better understanding of our capacities.

My personal goal is for us to eventually have a general plan for next year and a specific list of responsibilities for each of us. A list to include at least all the responsibilities assumed this year and an agreeable distribution of them among us. The one fear I have in pursuing this goal is that others might feel that their own freedom, academic or otherwise, might be in jeopardy — sort of an Organization vs. Freedom dichotomy. Assuming that these two things are polar, I hope we can reach a workable balance between them, the main criteria being the best structure which will allow us to reach our priority objectives without overcompromising the rest. In a sense there is freedom in organization. Freedom from loneliness of direction and helplessness of action. We can't achieve this absolutely through any kind of organization, but I do think we can to a degree greater than this year.

I really hope that I don't sound (or read) like I think I have all the answers or even know all the problems. I just wanted to let you know how I felt about the school this year and to suggest a way of thinking about change for next year.

-the little Irish kid

The Linehan memo reflects the realization that the unanticipated consequences of HSC's structure were becoming increasingly intolerable. This did not imply a revision of HSC's basic commitment to empowerment. For example, teachers the previous year had expressed frustration with various aspects of the school. They did not, however, want to change any of the basic tasks their roles involved. Rather, they had committed themselves to doing all of them better.[1] Nor were they looking to the Coordinator for organizational accountability. Indeed, in the egalitarian spirit, none of the 1971-72 evaluation's 61 goals mentioned the role of Coordinator. The final chapter of the evaluation, entitled "Report on the Evaluation of Management-Centered Objectives," begins: "This chapter will be brief since there is not much 'management' at HSC; a basic assumption of HSC is that schools need not be bureaucratized and that administration is a responsibility to be shared to some extent by all who participate in the program" (p. 137).

Yet by spring 1972, both Units of HCS felt compelled to examine their processes. Foote and the Unit Heads initiated meetings at both units in March. The flavor of staff concerns was voiced in a meeting nine days after Linehan's memo:

> We at HSC have to be able to agree on certain things in order for HSC to have an identity and sense of direction. For example, we should be able to agree that fundamental/significant/meaningful educational freedom or creativity should not be impinged on.

> HSC is not everything to everyone—it is not a place for everyone to do exactly what they want to do, but a place where everyone is responsible for getting the idea of HSC off the ground and on the move.

> We should be able to say to students, parents, and ourselves, in general, this is what we're trying to do, and this is how we're trying to do it.

> Can our vigor maintain itself much longer only on the fact that we are a little different?

After sharing these general issues, the staff meeting turned to a discussion of values, the top four of which further clarify the teacher perceptions of the school.

(1) we respect individuals (perhaps too much);
(2) we respect each other (perhaps too much);
(3) we respect students' expressed needs (again perhaps too much), feeling if they are expressed they are at   least important if not 'good';
(4) maybe we have respect for students but don't care enough to demand or challenge.

The meeting ended with a vigorous call for a systematic look at the school and a need to clarify its structure. "If we do not begin to look at HSC PROGRAMMATICALLY [capitals in original notes], then we'll get into the mud of ineffectiveness and isolation next year—we have to be able to tell each other to leave if they are not 'about' HSC and we have to be able to tell each other to stay."

The Push for Organizational Coherence: An Example of a Systemic Event

In community psychology, the term "systemic event" has been used to describe those key events in social systems which "speak volumes" about core issues and processes in the system (see Kelly,1986; Trickett, Kelly, and Vincent, 1985). Such an event occurred at HSC during March 1972, closely following the memos and meetings described above. Because it crystallized so much about the school culture it deserves the label of "systemic event."

The event itself was the production of a student play, Euripides' *Lysistrada*, in which the women of Athens, tiring of war and bloodshed, enforced their point of view through sexual abstinence. The vivid portrayal of sexual content was quite apparent to the head of the Board of Education, who attended the play's premier performance. Subsequent phone calls to members of the Board from a small number of concerned parents added fuel to the fire. Foote, whose title was now Facilitator, was called downtown to explain, and several emergency staff meetings were held to discuss how HSC put itself in this situation and what they should do about it. For a few weeks, considerable concern was expressed about whether or not the Board would permit HSC to survive.

While, in retrospect, one may view the decision to produce such a play as provocative, the teacher involved did not view it in those terms. "There was some giggling at first around its sexual aspects," she said, "but the kids quickly got over that." Most important, however, were the processes that allowed the play to reach final production without any clear accountability to the rest of the school staff or Policy Council. While the teacher had discussed the play informally with some of the staff members, she did not have to have anyone else "sign off" on her decision to produce it. The unusual degree of autonomy granted her by the school made this kind of accountability to the broader community unnecessary. "We respect each other (perhaps too much)" said the meeting notes only days before.

Yet the circumstances surrounding the play accentuated the importance of examining HSC's structures and policies. Teachers in general did not oppose the production of the play or the right of the teacher to produce it. Indeed, they were very supportive of the teacher and quite cognizant of their own collusion in the process. "Staff didn't take any responsibility for the play — none of us made it an issue. She [the teacher who produced it] was left to defend the situation without any support from staff. This is our failure." They did realize, however, that the larger issue was how to balance the empowerment of individual teachers with accountability to the other teachers and the school. This systemic event also forced the realization that, while functioning autonomously, the two Units of the school were themselves interdependent. "How can they put on this play and jeopardize the school without our Unit even knowing about it?" asked one teacher.

Through various school meetings and, for Foote, meetings with the School Board and downtown administration, HSC survived the scare. The incident, however, sharpened the importance of attending to HSC's internal structure and lent an urgency to dealing with the organizational themes of the Linehan memo.

The Spring Debate Over Leadership: Defining the role of Facilitator

During the spring, the most sustained discussion of organizational structure revolved around leadership. Teachers did not, as a group, show any inclination to grant any special power to the Facilitator. Yet, their history around decision-making and the vulnerability which the play had revealed pushed the issue of leadership to the fore. It was not surprising that discussions of how to structure the school more coherently started with the question, "what should the role of the Facilitator be?"

The vehicle for these discussions was the continuation grant requesting federal funding for the following year. It was prepared by Foote, Sam Nash, Director of Special Projects, and the Unit Heads during the spring of 1972 when the general momentum for self-examination was strong. The document outlined the responsibilities associated with all the major administrative roles in the school — Facilitator, Unit Head, and COP Coordinator. Written under severe time constraints, the continuation grant had not been circulated to all the teachers for input before its submission.

Several teachers expressed concern over what HSC had "agreed to" without the teachers having approved the continuation grant beforehand. Given the context at that time, it seems unlikely that teachers had the time and energy necessary for such discussions. However, their exclusion from the process fed into their more general leadership concerns. Thus, they decided to develop their own ideas about what they wanted the Facilitator to do so that the school, as a school, could sanction the role in a mutually understood way.

As a prelude to this process, Foote drafted a memo recounting the grant-writing process and clarifying what he had written. The following excerpts from this May 11, 1972 memo outline his thinking:

H.S.C. Facilitator:
In June 1971 each staff member received a copy of our initial Title III proposal. Included in this document was a description of the responsibilities of each H.S.C. staff member. The Title III proposal still is the only complete and current description of the program. Unfortunately, Title III is only reflective of the thinking of a minority — those who prepared the document. Yet, it still should be most useful as a place to start reacting to the program as a whole. If you are serious about changing the program you need to read this document.

Facilitator Responsibilities:
"Will supervise the entire H.S.C. staff and twice each year submit to the Director of Personnel an evaluation on their performance." Time alone prevents the Facilitator from fulfilling this requirement in other than a cursory manner. Assuming that we cluster teachers around themes, which won't include teachers from both units, the job of supervising and assisting clusters should logically be the Facilitator.

"Will maintain an overview of the entire H.S.C. project. In this capacity he will coordinate joint unit activities, insuring sharing of resources when needed and the prevention of unnecessary duplication." For at least six months of this year there was little desire to share either people or facilities at the two units. Undoubtedly, this was viewed as necessary to insure the individual identity of each unit. There is a growing desire, at least at Unit I, to increase the amount of sharing toward a theme-orientated curriculum and therefore, the amount of work in this area for the Facilitator should increase.

"Will identify possible funding sources and negotiate for physical resources." (Note: We have been operating under the assumption that 111 Goffe would continue to be available for the next few years. As of Mon. May 8 our future use of the building has come into question. The Supt., Sam Nash and I will be talking with Bill Donohue (Redevelopment) during the next few days about sites for both units. At least a portion of my time will be needed for proposal preparation (State & local funding sources)).

"Will work together with individual units in maintaining the core teaching staff." Most applicants have initially come to me for information about H.S.C. I have been able to screen out some candidates who undoubtedly would not be hired. This procedure should continue.

"Will work as a change agent within the H.S.C. program in conjunction with other members of the staff." The Facilitator is in the best position to act as a change agent. During the greater portion of this year it has been unclear to me (and most people) what direction the program should take. Along with many, it now seems clear that we must move away from a supermarket curriculum toward a 'themes' orientated curriculum.

"Will be responsible for the smooth flow of information between the two H.S.C. units."

"Will disseminate information about H.S.C. outside its local community." One of the Title III requirements is dissemination of info about H.S.C. Our efforts have helped Watertown, Hartford, and Bridgeport (next yr.) establish H.S.C. types of schools. While this effort must continue (throughout grant period) I would like to see more staff involvement.

"Will act as a clerk to insure the integrity of the H.S.C. model. He will work to include students, parents, and teachers in decision making." The individual units have more than accomplished the first objective. As to the second point, does anyone have any ideas?

"Will act as a liaison between the H.S.C. program and local educ. agencies, (i.e. Bd. of Ed., 200 Orange St. Admin.), as well as colleges and universities." Next year, Sam Nash will be on sabbatical. Many meetings and routine jobs which his office has been handling will now be picked up by the Facilitator. In addition, much more time must be spent by me in the coming year working on individual Bd. of Ed. members. We must get the city to absorb more of the H.S.C. costs, let alone vote for continuing the program.

"Will prepare regular reports on the progress of H.S.C." This is basically for Title III and has been done. Increased sharing of staff and a move toward a theme-orientated curriculum would suggest that similar reports will be necessary for internal H.S.C. use. Critical questions which must be answered: (a) Will we be moving toward a 'theme or topic' centered curriculum? My opinion: we must. (b) Teacher accountability even if we begin clustering the staff, which will improve communication, we will still need to deal with the question of staff accountability. Given the model that we use it isn't an easy question.

What I'm suggesting is that the Facilitator be responsible for most of the above areas.

— George

Foote's memo elicited a range of reactions from the teachers. While most faculty agreed that the Facilitator should serve as a mediator between HSC and its external environment (particularly "downtown"), they differed over many specific aspects of the role. Some felt the Facilitator should teach at least one class at each Unit, while others responded that the Unit Heads, not the Facilitator, should be responsible for evaluating teachers. What was clear from the teachers' responses was that there was no consensus on what the Facilitator's role should be.

There was also some anger in the teacher responses about Foote's leadership in general. One faculty member went through the memo, commenting in detail on Foote's ideas. He disagreed with Foote's statement that "there was little desire to share either people or facilities at the two units." "Even if this was the case," he wrote, "it should not be allowed. I see the Facilitator as being too passive in this . . . waiting for people to bring up cooperation when it should have been demanded/suggested/explained/implemented." In response to Foote's comment that he had screened out non-hireable teacher applicants, he wrote "Facilitator does not have the authority 'to screen out some candidates who undoubtedly would not be hired' and that procedure should not be continued." Finally, in response to the notion of the Facilitator as change agent came the comment "it's extremely unclear to me what the change is that the Facilitator should agent."

The Foote memo served the useful function of providing substantive ideas for discussion. From the response to the memo, however, it seems clear that teachers had differing opinions about what the Facilitator role should include, and differing implicit understandings of what kind of leadership they expected. The fundamental nature of this uncertainty about the role is found in one of the spring staff meetings on role definition. "Is the Facilitator on the bottom or at the top of our administrative pattern?" In May 1972, the answer seemed to be a confusing "yes."

TEACHER MEETINGS ON THE DEFINITION OF THE FACILITATOR ROLE

During the following month, teachers met to draft guidelines for the role of Facilitator. These guidelines covered a wide range of areas, including coordination of internal communication ("Facilitator should report weekly"), external communication with "downtown" and the media ("next year he has to enjoy the sanctity of a telephone"), supervising the procedures for getting appropriate interns and volunteers, and responsibility for keeping HSC informed about the necessary maintenance tasks (e.g. number of staff to be hired, etc.).

While these meetings were important steps in structuring HSC more coherently, the job description failed to grant the Facilitator any distinctive power to lead. It thus perpetuated the leadership issues facing persons in that role and failed to solve the issue of how policy would be made. This dilemma was articulated in notes of a staff discussion on June 20, 1972 about the Facilitator role. "The job we have just described is not a policy-making job, not a decision-making, not a 'being responsible for HSC job," said one. "Externally the Facilitator is looked upon as a policy maker; internally the Facilitator is not looked on like this. There is as yet no one or nothing to look forward to for policy. We need more effective policy making whoever or whatever does it. The Policy Council reviews decisions that are made but does not design useful, on-the-scene, operating policy."

Overall Organization: A summary comment

The overall state of organizational affairs at this stage in the school's history is captured in that year's final evaluation report (Hawley et al., 1973):

> HSC could not be described as a 'tight ship'. Leadership and administrative responsibility are widely shared. There are costs to organizations thus arranged in terms of lowered efficiency, frustration, and time sometimes lost in making decisions. There are also some real benefits to nonbureaucratic organizations, not the least of which are the commitment to group goals and adaptiveness to new demands which HSC demonstrates. Schools are not factories, commitment and adaptiveness are more important than the chains of command, specialization, and economic efficiency.
>
> Nevertheless, as HSC evolves, there is a growing awareness on the part of faculty that (1) the capacity to obtain and retrieve information related to program effectiveness is important; (2) roles can be set out more clearly without overspecializing; (3) delegation of administrative authority and tolerance for administrative discretion need not mean a loss of ultimate power (and may be essential to exercise of power); and (4) special skills are required to work with a collection of one's peers, and these skills can be learned (pp. 142-143).

1972-74:
PLANNING, STRUCTURING, DIFFERENTIATING

The momentum for increasing clarity of roles, accountability of teachers to each other, and decreasing of teacher autonomy to "do their own thing" continued during the 1972-74 years. The empowerment ideology remained a constant standard against which all decisions were made and all proposals for change evaluated. Still, internal forces at HSC required a rethinking of how the school was operating. Over time, the interdependence between the two units became clearer; survival needs became more prominent as the end of external funding got closer; and the importance of improving the decision-making process was heightened as HSC struggled to accomplish its self-examination. The recurrent struggle was how to adjust the structures and processes of the school without simultaneously sacrificing its empowerment ideology and becoming the kind of school to which it began as an alternative.

1972-73: A Year of Internal Assessment

The move toward internal coherence carried over from the previous spring into the 1972-73 school year. In contrast to the 1971-72 evaluation design where no managerial goals were mentioned, the 1972-73 evaluation design specified several managerial objectives for both Facilitator and Unit Heads. In addition, HSC set as a goal the creation and approval of revised job descriptions for Facilitator, Unit Head, Outreach Worker, Unit Aide, Guidance Counselor, and Teacher. The plan was to devise such job descriptions during the fall and implement them during the spring.

During the 1972-73 year, the leadership structure of the school changed. A group consisting of the Facilitator and the two Unit Heads began meeting regularly. They were later joined by the head of the COP to form what would be called the following year the Facilitating Unit (FU). The purpose of this group was twofold: (1) to conduct coordinated planning for HSC as a whole, and (2) to provide a broader leadership structure, taking some of the burden off the Facilitator "to do it all."

These pushes toward managerial accountability, clarification of roles, and organized planning spread throughout all aspects of the school. During the winter, a decision was made to conduct a thorough review of the school in June 1973. The meetings would involve the teachers and staff of both units. The themes for these meetings were outlined by Tom Nelson in a May 2, 1972 memo. His 20-item agenda covered a variety of "traditional" areas of organizational concern at HSC.

> *The review of job descriptions and responsibilities:* We've got a lot of different jobs in the school, some that seem institutionally well defined and some that are individually defined. In order for the school to get its work done, and in order for us as

individuals to feel that we've accomplished our function, a clear discussion and sense of agreement should be made as to what our responsibilities are, both interdependent and independent. . .

Writing evaluations: Evaluations are a major task — four times during the year. Most often (always) the task is not done on school time but on personal time — this can lead to resentment because of the school's intrusion on personal time or to poor evaluations because of not having or using that private time. ..

Curriculum: We've got a lot of work to do with our curriculum. . . what we have to do is get some continuity into our curriculum — work cooperatively with Unit II on the courses we offer — clarify the patterns of basic skills and college skills — and be able to offer educational justification for what we offer. There should also be some systematic involvement of students and parents in the curriculum so that they do not become, or see themselves, as victims of the catalog. . .

Student membership: We've. . . done some good work on procedures for students who never show up, do not register, etc. while staying on the school rolls. Perhaps we can 'tighten up' (without getting anal retentive) . . . What does a student have to do in order to continue as a member of HSC?

Policy Council: We've let the Policy Council drift away from the intimate involvement with the school. . . . In a lot of ways the PC is seen as a pain in the neck — meeting often and not clearly accomplishing much — but it started out as one of the central components of our HSC experiment. Finally, it is the only channel for student or parent involvement in effective decision-making, and we can't afford to let that involvement just float away — at least as long as we're serious about teacher, parent, and student participation in governance.

Parent and student organizations: We've not been very helpful to parents and students who have tried to organize themselves. . . I don't think we can say 'well, if they can't get organized then they must not want to badly enough.' This stuff could get to be very important if HSC ever hopes to establish effective political means of support — it can also be important in that parents are coming out with a lot of bitches that 'go nowhere' — they don't have any channels of power to help the school handle the complaints and then resentment builds up. Examples of the complaints are: too much free time, teachers coming late to class, or not coming to class at all and failing to call, no homework, no skills are being acquired, etc. These are important.

Relationship of I and II: HSC is one school in funding, in the eyes of the Board of Education, in the eyes of colleges, in concept, in general design, and intention. But we have acted as if we were foreign to Unit II. . . . Courses are duplicated — people teaching the same subjects never talk or compare notes of their work. . . . We simply are not working with, or learning from, each other as we ought to . . .

The June Meetings:

The plan for the meetings was to break down the agenda into different key issues and spend time on each issue separately, finishing with a summary meeting reviewing agreements which had been made. It covered a two-week period and included a full review of the curriculum, content area by content area, with separate meetings on Guidance, the Policy Council, the Community Orientation Program, the role of the Teacher, Outreach Worker, and Facilitator.

Both in structure and tone the June meetings show how the school had been evolving over its short history. For example, in the discussion of the curriculum, each substantive area (e.g. Math, Languages) was charged to develop a concrete proposal which was then discussed by the teachers as a group. Previously, these matters had been left to the individual teacher and/or group of teachers in the specific content areas.

The tone of many of these discussions reflected the need to "tighten up" on a number of levels. For example, in presenting the curriculum for English, the English teachers stated, "we want to respond to individual students according to their needs, and we recognize the variety of those needs. . . . However, reality should be a compromise between standards and free choice. Students must realize they will have to deal with standards which exist in society as a whole, which may not be similar to their own standards. In developing student skills, we do not wish to disregard the value of ethnic language skills such as Black English, street slang, and other language used for communication. We want to emphasize the need for students to develop 'bilingual skills' which we believe should be an asset to students in dealing with the world. . . . We need to be able to negotiate an 'expectations' contract with students."

Differentiation among students, something the school was ideologically opposed to three years before, was also discussed in the context of curriculum planning. Three groupings, "the graduating, the disenchanted, and the underclassmen," were defined as needing different resources and structures. It was a clear step toward increasing teacher authority vis-à-vis students by defining some of the boundaries which differentiated the teacher role from the student role.

THEMES IN THE DISCUSSION OF JOB DESCRIPTIONS

As previously mentioned, one goal for the 1972-73 year was to create job descriptions and assess how well those descriptions fit the work that was done. The Facilitator, in conjunction with appropriate school personnel, did develop the requisite job descriptions. However, according to the evaluation report, "after the job descriptions... there were no meetings to discuss implementation, revision, or progress toward bringing the long-standing descriptions into line with actual work time until June" (pp. 81-82). The June meetings represented the first opportunity for thorough discussions. While many different roles were considered, the Facilitator and teacher roles provide the most general examples of ongoing organizational forces.

Foote's frustration with the Facilitator role is contained in his comments during one of the meetings. "It's hard to tell which specifics the Facilitator is responsible for. Being responsible for everything sometimes feels like being responsible for nothing. The meetings with Karen, Ed, and Tom (the Unit heads and COP Coordinator who formed the Facilitating Unit) are really helpful in getting a focus on what needs to be done and talking about how to do it. It's helpful to split things up. It's hard to work between two (geographically separated) units. It leads to 'Where is George?'"

Foote's comments precipitated a discussion which resulted in the development of a 22-point job description. The Facilitator should exercise more leadership, be available at agreed upon hours, have a centralized administrative place, and serve as the primary mediator between the school and the outside world. "The role is to create an atmosphere and boundaries which the Unit Head further creates and defines to execute the rules of the game by being on top of it." "The credibility of HSC rests upon the credibility of the Facilitator; therefore, we feel the position should be formalized." There was no discussion of how such formalization might occur, or of specific steps toward concretizing the role. Teachers did, however, acknowledge, that "HSC owes an historical debt to George (Foote)."

Discussions of the teacher role were pervaded by issues of accountability, beginning with the agreement "that any decision to move away from these guidelines (for the teacher role) not be an individual decision but a department or staff decision." In addition to class time, teachers' responsibilities were defined to include two staff meetings a week ("the time boundaries of the meeting should be clearly defined"),"four committed, expectable, agreed-to office hours" a week, guidance responsibilities, active support of the Policy Council, involvement in one ongoing or several short-term extracurricular activities, supervision of student teachers and volunteers (at the discretion of individual teachers), and supervision of tutorials and independent studies ("should not be taken on at the cost of the other duties we've assigned ourselves"). Accountability of teachers to students and students to teachers was also discussed.

In assessing the scope of these duties, it is useful to recall that many teachers were required to teach each day in more than one location. This broke up the day into several small chunks of time between classes. Indeed, one proposal made during the curriculum discussion was to schedule "a 15-minute break between classes to allow for transit time..."

OVERVIEW OF THE JUNE MEETINGS:

The June meetings provided evidence that HSC was moving toward increasing the clarity of shared understandings, developing boundaries around roles, and lessening the individual autonomy of teachers and students to use the school as they pleased. There was increasing collective agreement that teachers could not act on their own, and that individual initiatives (such as *Lysistrada*) needed some mechanism for accountability to the collective. This theme is further reflected in a discussion of a proposal about the COP brought by then COP Coordinator Ed Linehan to the teachers. The meeting notes state: "This COP pattern is the only one that has been presented to us by an individual rather than a group. In effect, Ed thought about this, designed it, proposed it, and defended it without institutional or group support mechanisms. We should think about whether or not this is a satisfactory pattern of working in the school, and could we consider the existence of a COP committee?"

ORGANIZATIONAL THEMES FROM TEACHER INTERVIEWS:

During May and June of 1972, each of HSC's 25 teachers and staff were interviewed about their perspective on the school. In general, teachers remained very committed to the ideology on which the school was founded. They cited their autonomy and positive collegial relationships as major strengths. The development of supportive and friendly relationships with students was still a priority, as was the creation of classrooms that were comfortable, noncompetitive, and participative.

Some changes and concerns were mentioned. More emphasis was placed on teaching basic skills than had been the case in previous years. "I once felt a teacher could be an aide, counsel, learner, and guidance person," said one teacher. "Now it seems that more folks need guidance; directness with a pinch of beating them over the heads before they graduate." Teachers were also critical of themselves, citing as a major frustration the difficulties they were having trying to implement the HSC ideology. Among the impediments were lack of prior experience with innovation, trouble tolerating diversity, and an unwillingness to confront each other.

Most clear from these interviews, however, was the growing consensus about leadership issues and the wish to centralize the school. A majority of teachers were not satisfied with Foote's performance as Facilitator, suggesting that he was not an active enough leader. A sizeable minority of teachers said that it was hard to say whether or not they were satisfied with the Facilitator because they weren't certain what he did. On the other hand, one teacher provided a more sympathetic perspective: "He's not the problem but he's getting blamed for the failures. Group interaction makes him the scapegoat. There is a tendency to see problems and seek quick solutions . . . This has not been an understanding and gentle staff to work with, no praise or interstaff recognition [for the difficulty of the Facilitator's job]. I've been part of it — it's very difficult to break old patterns."

In spite of these concerns, when asked about how teachers wanted to see the organizational structure changed, only a few suggested changing the Facilitator. A majority stated that centralizing the school would represent the most significant positive change.

1973-74: Administrative Consolidation and Survival

During the following year consolidation continued and efforts to insure the school's survival increased. The internal consolidation took two forms. First, the Policy Councils of the two units became combined into one. Second, the Facilitating Unit (Facilitator, Unit Heads, and COP Coordinator) became formalized as part of the HSC structure. One of their primary tasks involved the survival of the school after the federal grant ended.

THE FACILITATING UNIT AND SURVIVAL

The formal integration of the Facilitating Unit into the school represented the culmination of two years of informal interaction. It started unofficially during the second year of the school when two Unit Heads were appointed. It added the COP Coordinator during the third year, and became an "official" planning and coordinating group in the fourth year of school. "It was a wonderful, cohesive, hard-working group," said one member, "and it really thrived on differences. One of us was 'the intellectual, a little commie kid,' another 'just knew all the right answers,' one was a structure freak, and one a very savvy local politician. Some of us were real 'straight arrows,' some of us weren't. You could not have imagined a more unlikely crew, but we did a tremendous volume of work and had a real caring for each other. To give you an example or our differences, one year one of us spent his first paycheck on silverware and another put it in the bank for a trip to Europe." Foote recalled how important it was to finally have a constituency. "We'd argue over a position, and then take a position. There was honesty, support, and solidarity."

The issue of survival had always been a "bottom line" issue for HSC, and during these years the Facilitating Unit assumed increasing responsibility for this task. As they viewed it, survival depended on the accomplishment of several goals, including maintaining good public relations with the community and upper-level school system administrators, developing support among parents, *and* insuring that students in New Haven were interested in sufficient numbers to keep enrollment up. The evaluation report of the 1973-74 year, for example, stated that unlike previous years all students wanting admission to HSC were admitted. This signalled the importance of recruiting students for the coming year.

Complicating the survival situation was a change of superintendents. No longer was Barbaresi, the superintendent who had initially supported the creation of HSC, in office. His replacement was not seen as a strong supporter of the school. Debate about the future of the school was ongoing in the downtown administration. An April 1972 memo from two Assistant Superintendents to the Superintendent included the following:

> During the almost three-year history of the (HSC) project, as with you, we have heard critical remarks leveled at the project, its administration, staff, students and methods. Some of the criticism is justified, some not. We hear of staff and student laxity, a great measure of nonconformance, extra low teacher-pupil ratio, and too much emphasis on 'exotic' curriculum offerings. On the other hand, we hear very little, in spite of these comments, that more graduates of this program enter college than graduates of the traditional high school. We believe the philosophy of an educational alternative of a school without walls is sound, positive, necessary, can be productive, and

displays evidence of a truly progressive urban school system. We firmly believe that negative attitudes toward the program can be reversed to such a degree that both parents, students, and nonparticipants will literally 'tear the doors' down in order to become part of this innovative educational alternative. Therefore, we recommend that the project be allowed to continue on a probationary basis for at least an additional year, possibly two, based on the following plan of operation.

The proposed plan would reduce the size of the school and the number of courses while increasing the accountability of staff. "Continuation of the program beyond the one- or two-year probationary period would be contingent on many factors, including, at minimum, evidence of serious progress in individual study courses, exceptional attendance, absence of disciplinary problems, and seriousness of purpose."

From April 1973 through the following school year the Facilitating Unit met regularly to discuss the school's survival. They decided to initiate ongoing meetings with the Superintendent to promote HSC and gain a better understanding of his concerns. At an April 1973 meeting, the Superintendent articulated the issues outlined in the preceding memo and suggested that increased efficiency and accountability would be necessary. He also, however, supported the general idea behind the school and assured them that funding would continue through the following year.

On May 1, 1973, the Facilitating Unit, representing HSC, responded to the Superintendent's concerns in a lengthy memo. "Tightening up" was seen as a key to survival. The overall document represented an affirmation of the critical components of the HSC experiment (e.g. COP, teachers providing guidance, Policy Council as governance structure) and an accommodation to the organizational concerns expressed by the Superintendent.

> We have taken your suggestions seriously. . . and hope to respond to them here as the continuation of a supportive conversation between our school and the Superintendent's office. . . . It is important to us that our conversation here handle both the educational and administrative angles of HSC. Educationally, HSC is an alternative and thus is committed to encouragement of individuality over conformity. . . . Administratively, HSC chose to flee from one structure into a poorly defined structure. During the past three years we've learned the value of structure and organization, and now feel confident in the establishment of our own structure model for productivity and efficiency. Our experience has brought insights and

skills in organization, which has resulted in this year's operation being a vast improvement over last year's.

They then presented a series of recommendations designed to tighten up administrative processes while maintaining HSC's basic structure.

During the 1973-74 year, meetings with the Superintendent continued. In April 1974, they submitted a formal report to the Superintendent, "done with a look to the future when the school system will face the issue of High School in the Community's no longer being able to acquire federal funding." It began by outlining the 4-year accomplishments of the school as reflected in the evaluations (presented in detail in Chapter 7). Most important in terms of the organizational evolution of the school were two concerns: (1) "the need for a single HSC facility," and (2) "the need for a more collaborative relationship within the school system."

With respect to the first issue, the report stated that "HSC clearly sees the need for a building which it can use as its own center. The administrative and guidance offices would be located there, as well as the majority of the classes. In the past, due to various limits set by the fire department and landlords, the school has been found to spread itself over too wide an area. This was an exciting novelty for awhile (to students as well as staff), but the novelty has worn off." With respect to the second concern, the document asked that HSC be seen as part of the system and have access to the kinds of resources and legitimacy other schools had. Its isolation from the rest of the system had finally become a liability.

The memo ended with hopes for the future. "Paramount in the minds of most of the HSC community is the desire to feel a sense of permanence about the school. . . . We need to see the school ultimately being absorbed into the school system with a clear legitimacy which is not contingent on 'next year's funding.' It seems that incorporation involves at least the following: (1) Inclusion of HSC in the 'regular' city budget; (2) an HSC facility which would house most of the school programs; (3) the formalized acceptance of the HSC administration structure by the Board of Education." (In the past, for example, the Facilitator was not treated like the principals of the other high schools in terms of access to information about resources, meetings with the Superintendent, etc.)

TEACHERS REVIEW RECENT DEVELOPMENTS AND HOW THE SCHOOL HAD CHANGED

The teacher interviews conducted during the 1973-74 year were wide ranging and included their observations on both the current organizational state of the school and how it had changed over time. There was by now near unanimous agreement that the school needed to consolidate. "We all suffer from being nomads," said one teacher. Great ambivalence was expressed about the Facilitating Unit. On the one hand, there was begrudging respect and appreciation for the amount of work the FU had done on behalf of the school. In addition, they had successfully imposed some structure on HSC's ongoing life. "The FU was very powerful and organized this year," said an FU member. "To get things done you need an organized group in an unorganized environment. It helped George because the FU, not George, took responsibility for a lot of decisions. Next year the FU should become a planning group; This year we cleaned up the shit work."

On the other hand, both FU members and other teachers saw its formation as creating what one described as an "in group/out group" phenomenon. Comments ranged from guarded support to bitterness. "The FU functioned well but was somewhat exclusive," said one. "The FU makes teacher influence harder but it's still significant," said another. "The FU should be more open and honest; it's effective but closed," added a third. A minority of teachers felt more negative, however. "FU is a privileged class who introduce policy and pass the privileges of membership among themselves," was one such response. The overall response of the teachers, however, was one of understanding the need for the kind of direction and structure provided by the FU, even if "in their ideological bones" they could not fully trust it.

Teachers were also asked to reflect on how the school had changed since its inception. There was remarkable agreement among teachers about the nature of the changes, though some teachers felt more positively about them than others.

> HSC is now much more organized, it has been establishing boundaries, staff are now demanding accountability from each other, we are able to make decisions. We have lost some of the excitement of being a new program, lost a sense of community though not a sense of allegiance.

> HSC has changed from being a pretty novel place with a lot of spark to being a place that wants to get down to business. Some of that involves being tired, some involves deciding to really teach people things in a really organized way — people getting serious about teaching . . . . This year was deliberate hard work on a different level than last year's frenzy on smaller administrative issues.

> HSC has gotten old and not adapted to its age, not trying experiments, innovations. But it's more organized, easier to get things done.

> There are enormous changes at HSC — more stable, more organized, more focus on classes, less dynamic but still exciting... still easy going and student-oriented, this year was one of strengthening the structure and organization of the school.

> The membership-leadership relationship within the staff has changed. It is no longer seen that unanimous decisions are necessary — consensus is still sought but it's not seen as a no-no if people are pairing up. The school has moved to having real leadership — not a figurehead — leadership for different functions from different people. There is a better defined structure — much less a nebulous romantic liberal view — more of a clear idea of what we're doing.

Many teachers also commented on how the school was being affected by changes in the student body.

> Students now are more passive, harder to engage in school politics. There's less book interest, more kids with attendance problems.

> This year the kids are angrier, more sullen, harder to work with; we're getting more kids other schools didn't want — it puts me more often in a disciplinarian role.

> In the beginning students had incredible enthusiasm for the school which came out of a reaction to where they were. They were following teachers from Hillhouse they liked. Over the past year, a much higher percent are coming in who aren't making it in school — kids suspended from other schools, etc. We've made no structural changes in response to this yet, although our curriculum is reflecting more basics in general.

Finally, it was clear from the teacher interviews that in coping with survival and its internal struggles, the school had experienced a great deal of stress. Some teachers felt that "we've hit bottom and are on our way up." Others suggested that "if we don't get our act together the school doesn't deserve to survive." When asked whether or not the school would survive, a significant majority of teachers who expressed an opinion said no. Still, they had a one- or two-year commitment from the Superintendent and a successful recruitment of student applicants for the following fall. "We would have had it if the recruitment hadn't worked — it was a consensus teacher decision to put effort there," said Foote.

Postscript:

In mid-year, January 1975, HSC moved into its own building, an unused elementary school, where it has remained to this day. It was the eighth move since the school started five years previously.

CHAPTER 6

Empowerment Themes and Structures, 1971-74: Race Relations, The Community Orientation Program, and The Policy Council

HSC was built on the foundation of an empowerment ideology and a commitment to egalitarian norms and structures. The preceding chapter outlined how empowerment was implicated in the school's recurrent organizational struggles. HSC approached empowerment in various other ways, however, which clarify the concept's complexities and provide a more complete portrait of the school. This chapter examines three areas where the empowerment ideology was active. The first, race relations, involves broad organizational themes that cut across attitudes, interpersonal relationships, and school structures. The second and third focus more narrowly on two different structures which represent the most innovative structural approaches to empowerment in the school: The Community Orientation Program and The Policy Council. The COP was intended to allow the school to profit from the resources in the broader community, while the Policy Council was designed to increase parent and student influence in governance.

Race Relations: A Complex Interplay of Culture, Relationships, and Organizational Structure

From its origins, HSC's commitment to empowerment was intimately connected to the goal of creating a nonracist school. Achieving such a goal would empower blacks, promote a more integrated society, and stand as an example of what public education in the inner city could accomplish. However, when HSC began, it had no shared understandings about what racism was and how it might manifest itself in the school environment. Was it primarily a matter of fostering positive attitudes about individuals of varying races and cultural backgrounds? Did it imply the active social integration of different races, or was increased tolerance without significant contact enough? Would structures of empowerment such as the COP and Policy Council serve all students equally well, or would they inadvertently affect blacks and whites differently? These kinds of questions had not been specifically discussed as HSC began.

Data on HSC's efforts in this area come from several sources, including yearly evaluation reports, interviews with black and white teachers, and the report of a black psychologist who spent a year at HSC as a psychological consultant. These data show that HSC made consistent efforts to understand and confront issues of race relations and racism. Many teachers, for example, commented on how much the issue of race was "in the air" during these years. "We'd talk in the halls, in the staff meetings, on the weekends," said one. "We really put a lot of energy into trying to understand racism and how it was reflected in the school."

How it was reflected in the school was itself a very complex phenomenon. In terms of teacher attitudes, for example, the group dynamics workshops, which occurred before and during the school's first year, were continued episodically in later years. Reactions to these experiences were mixed, with some teachers gaining insight about their own reactions to race differences and some simply ending up angered by what they called "wasted time." In general, both black and white teachers did not perceive the group dynamics training to be sufficient, though many felt it necessary.

The issue of recruiting black teachers represented another area where HSC expended considerable energy. Foote, as Facilitator, recalled the extensive efforts — the letters, phone calls, etc. — as important and frustrating. "At that time," he recalled, "competent black professionals were very much sought after, and we had a hard time competing, particularly economically." Over these years, several black faculty were hired, as well as a black outreach worker, to work with "difficult" students, both black and white. Turnover among black teachers, however, was higher than that for white teachers — particularly so for black males. One year a predominant concern of the teachers was the absence of any black male teachers in one of the Units. Those black teachers interviewed cited various reasons for their decisions to leave HSC. These reasons included dissatisfaction with leadership and a wish to attend graduate school. Still, there were suggestions that being a black teacher at HSC posed special responsibilities and stresses.

Each year the teacher interviews included questions about race relations, both among students and among teachers. The consistency of responses from year to year suggested several themes. The two most consistent findings with respect to students are summarized in the winter 1972 interim evaluation report to the school:

Interracial Relationships: One of the objectives which almost all of those involved in HSC have valued has been the improvement of relationships between persons of different races. It would appear that on one dimension HSC has succeeded in that there have been no incidents of overt conflict between persons of different races and we have discovered no evidence of either physical or psychological abuse. And student opinion is generally antagonistic to expressions of racial intolerance. On the other hand, we have systematically observed informal interaction among students and found that only a fraction of such contacts are interracial and that the proportion of such contacts has not seemed to change from the beginning of the year (p. 12).

Across the years, the teacher interviews continued to validate that student-student relationships were much less tense and more positive than they had been in the previous high school, and that blacks tended to stick together, and whites tended to stick together.

Additional issues were evident in the teacher interviews. One recurring theme for white teachers involved understanding their own motivations when dealing with black students and black colleagues. In a setting sensitized to race issues, white teachers felt it very important to avoid acting in ways which might be perceived as racist. "It was very difficult being a white leader of a predominantly black student body," recalled one member of the Facilitating Unit. "There were always issues of whether or not my attributions about blacks when I was critical involved racism or issues of competence." In a similar vein, another member said, "we have a problem with [a black staff member]. It's seen by some as a personality or work ethic problem, that he's not doing enough work. The individual involved sees it as a racial problem."

Black teachers concurred that, while racism was not the issue it had been in other schools, HSC still had issues to deal with. Indeed, the 1973 teacher interviews indicated that all the black teachers except one said white teachers had different goals, expectations, and standards of discipline toward white and black students which, in subtle ways, put down blacks.

White teachers, by and large, did not disagree that there were important race issues at HSC. In response to the question, "Are there any problems at HSC that are associated with racial differences among students or staff?" the modal answer was "sure, how could it be otherwise?" Yet white teachers seemed more likely to see issues of race as less central in the life of the school than did black teachers. Further, for some white faculty, the issues were difficult to pinpoint, though they involved mistrust, suspicion, and the avoidance of controversy in formal meetings.

BLACK TEACHERS IN A PREDOMINANTLY WHITE SETTING: EDUCATIONAL MISSION AND ROLE BEHAVIOR

Interviews with black teachers suggest that they approached their job from a different perspective than their white counterparts. This perspective influenced their mission as teachers and their subsequent role performance. The perspective is linked to the differing sociocultural histories brought by black and white teachers to the school. In discussing select aspects of the experience of black teachers at HSC, the intent is not to suggest that all black teachers experienced HSC in the same way. Neither is it to suggest that white teachers shared a monolithic contrasting perspective on their mission and the school. Rather, it is to highlight the importance of the broad sociocultural contexts which impacted on the teaching experience and the implications of these cultural differences for what was seen as empowering and what was not.

The Black Teacher and Educational Mission. A primary theme of the 1971-74 interviews with black teachers focused on their distinctive commitment to black students, a commitment based on historical mission. To quote Gooden (1978), a black psychologist who consulted to HSC for a year:

> "The sense of responsibility for the black student's education is rooted in the common membership in the black community where these teachers have a status among the local black community that implies an historical mission; i.e. to educate black children so that they can escape the effects of poverty and racism. The historical dimension of this problem is important. Education has been recommended as a remedy for the low economic and social status of black people by such black leaders at Marcus Garvey and W.E.B. DuBois. Self-help and personal improvement have been linked to education and the availability of educational opportunity. Academic achievement has been a value with the more educated segments of the black community throughout its history. This legacy — i.e. to enhance the chances of black students for a better life through education — belongs to the black teacher (p. 34).

This particular sense of historical mission carried implications for how black teachers assessed the efforts of their white counterparts in dealing with black students. Quoting Gooden once more:

> Black teachers complained that white teachers did not know how to deal with black students. The white teachers were too concerned with being liked by the black students. As a result, the teachers did not demand enough from these students. Black students in turn accused the black teachers of being too strict and demanding. Some of the courses taught by black teachers were poorly attended or overlooked by many black students. Black teachers felt further that black students 'conned' white teachers into letting them off easy where the work was concerned. This placed the black teachers in a tighter bind because they were often confronted by students who wanted to know why the black teachers were not as easy or considerate as the white teachers were (p. 33).

Part of the anger against white teachers stemmed from the belief that black students were being cheated if they were not challenged and forced to deal with their academic problems. Academic success was seen as critical for their lives as black men and women of the future. The black teachers believed that, by and large, white teachers did not appreciate these political implications or their own historical mission.

Gooden attributed these different stances toward black students to differing perceptions of the demands of the situation.

> For white teachers, facing potentially hostile black kids with a minimum of understanding, one major demand of the situation was to build understanding and trust so that a viable working — i.e., teaching/learning — relationship could develop. For black teachers, on the other hand, the issue of hostility might not have been as threatening as the issue of the potential charge of blacks being academically inferior. The major demand here would be the implementation of academic standards (p. 35).

These differing perspectives stemmed from different cultural experiences which black and white teachers brought to the school. These experiences in turn affected both how they perceived the school and how they carried out their educational role.

Educational Mission and Role Behavior: The special sense of educational mission influenced black teachers' adaptation to HSC in a way different from whites. One aspect of this was expressed in terms of teacher time spent with black students over and above their already demanding teaching role. The 1973 evaluation, for example, reported that all three black teachers — two of whom had just completed their first year in the school — were unusually overextended. "One person was teaching far too many classes because of student needs. Another had taken over additional classes and counselees after the departure of another teacher . . . . In the first case, she was the only black teacher in her field and was under considerable pressure from black students to teach courses that they needed. In the second situation, she was the only black teacher on the faculty (at the other Unit) and was under heavy counseling pressure from black students . . . (The third black teacher) spent a good deal of her time in extracurricular activities with largely black students. . ." (pp. 80-81).

The unusually strong demands on black teachers, stemming from their special commitments, plus their relative powerlessness in the school, affected their active involvement with white teachers. "Friendships were made," said one black teacher, "and some very good ones too. But mostly, like the students, there wasn't a whole lot of involvement." Additionally, instances were reported where philosophical differences between black and white teachers led to discussions which reinforced their social distance. During a spring 1972 faculty meeting, for example, the following was recorded: "There needs to be some discussion of being white and middle class and working with poor blacks," said a black teacher. "There's so much talk about middle class concepts like 'choosing options!' We have a very unbalanced view of blacks and whites." "I don't like to be told I have no understanding of black kids," responded a white teacher.

Thus, the overall empowerment ideology of the school held implications for black teachers' sense of educational mission which differed not in intent, but in enactment, from their white colleagues. Both their specific commitment to black students and their perception of what black students needed was shaped by a sociocultural perspective which contrasted with that brought by the white teachers to HSC. Because these world views differed, empowerment was seen as involving contrasting concerns.

EMPOWERMENT AND BLACK STUDENTS: CONTRASTING ADAPTATIONS AND UNINTENDED CONSEQUENCES

For students, empowerment at HSC involved the ability to use the school's processes and structures to further personal and educational goals. As early as December of HSC's first year, teachers were concerned that some students were floundering in the lack of structure and the laissez-faire atmosphere of the school. While concern was expressed about both black and white students, black teachers in particular focused on the "white concepts" underlying the school and their unintended consequences for black students. Gooden's report included a description of different "styles of being black" among students, which helps clarify how black students interacted with the school. For some, it proved to be an empowering experience; for others, it proved to be irrelevant. To quote Gooden (1978):

> The students that I observed at H.S.C. have various ways of being and interacting: what I shall call styles of being black. There are many . . . personality differences among the black students at HSC but there are styles that seem to be shared by various subgroups . . . the style refers to ways of dress, use of slang and characteristic modes of interactions shared by a particular subgroup . . . the term 'style' seems appropriate because it refers to a way of being that is adopted and worn rather than one intrinsic to a person's development (pp. 10-11).

Gooden outlined three contrasting groups; the "hip," those "just making it," and the "regulars." The "hip" students were from poor families, and had poor class attendance with about average school attendance. They spent a lot of time in the hallways "rapping," and were described by other students as "cool," "slick," "hip," or "fast." They came to school "clean"; i.e. well dressed with fairly expensive clothes.

> Most of these kids had hustles. . . Their hustles included gambling, selling reefers, panhandling, etc. The hustle is not only an act of getting money; it is also a way of dealing with people to get an unfair advantage. This style of interaction is used both inside and outside the classroom. Very often one such student would try to run a game on a teacher to escape responsibility for his work. For example, a student complained to the teacher that his mother was seriously ill so he was unable to do the homework. By this story he gained the white teacher's sympathetic understanding. Later on in the hallway the student prided himself on his ability to 'cop'; i.e. to get the teacher's sympathy and not do the work . . . Being hip is important not just because one is able to hustle but because of the positive feeling that one gets when one's clothes are admired, when one is accepted by a subgroup and one feels capable of dealing with other people on one's own terms (p. 11-12).

The subgroup of students "just making it" came from the poorest families, many of whom had recently arrived from the south. Home difficulties and trouble with the law were frequent. Attendance at school was poor, often because these students either lacked the money for bus fare or had to babysit younger siblings.

> This subgroup stands out not so much because of its style in dress or language but because of the social and psychological problems that they have . . . If the style of the first group is active, positive, and aggressive, the style of the second group is passive, accepting, and withdrawing. Instead of confrontation they would tend to avoid conflict (pp. 11-12).

The "regulars" were those students with good attendance and academic achievement. Their parents were likely to be lower middle or middle class, and

> their style of being black was more in tune with the current ideas of blackness . . . They were not super militants but were conscious of their history. They tried to maintain their sense of self through a combination of academic performance and black consciousness. In comparison to the hip group, they were more stable and felt more positively about being black (p. 13).

Each of these subgroups engaged the school in different ways in terms of its structure, norms, and school staff. The "hip" subgroup took advantage of the lack of rules and ambivalence over disciplining students to use the school as a place to *be* more than a place to *learn*. "Being good manipulators, they got teachers to excuse much of their behavior. Their distinct 'street' aggressive and assertive style enabled them to dominate the hallways" (p. 18). Both the school structure and the sentiments of the white teachers allowed them the latitude to remain "hip" at school.

On the other hand, for those students just making it, the close personal attention HSC teachers provided was of great benefit. Many of these students took advantage of this attention to deal with both academic and personal problems. The "regulars" were able to cope effectively with the structure of the school and took advantage of its opportunities, but felt the greatest need for more black teachers and additional courses on issues that concerned them.

Gooden stressed that even in the face of these varied styles of adaptation, most blacks enjoyed HSC and preferred it to other local high schools. "They felt that at HSC they were treated as people, they were respected and listened to. . . . The students felt much more in touch with the teachers and felt that the teachers had an interest in their learning." However, blacks felt less support than whites, a reaction Gooden attributed primarily to the black/white teacher ratio.

The different adaptive styles of black students seem to have affected their involvement with the school. For some, both the loose structure and concerned teachers at the school provided the kind of enriching environment which had been lacking. For others, the lack of structure allowed an avoidance of engaging the school as an academic setting. And the general lack of minority presence among teachers added to a more marginal investment in the ongoing school life.

OVERVIEW

The complexities involved in HSC's efforts to confront and combat racism as an empowerment goal are clear. Defined in terms of *individual attitudes*, HSC demonstrated an ongoing commitment through teacher workshops, staff meetings, and informal discussions. In addition, HSC was successful at changing the interracial attitudes of its students (see Chapter 7), although more so for whites than blacks. Defined in terms of *interpersonal contact*, HSC was less successful on both a student and teacher level than it had hoped to be. The differing sociocultural histories brought by black and white teachers and students to the school inhibited significant interracial interaction. The power of these differences underscores the importance of conceptualizing empowerment within a sociopolitical context which influences both its definition and expression.

In the area of *school structure*, HSC's efforts at empowerment interacted with cultural and/or social class differences, yielding ambivalent results. While some black students were able to take full advantage of HSC's structures, others fared less well than whites. It is unclear whether or not this outcome was primarily race-related or social class-related. At HSC blacks tended to be poorer than whites. Nonetheless, there are indications that the "white concepts" underlying the structure of the school had a somewhat less beneficial effect on blacks. Thus, if empowerment is *defined in terms of outcomes or consequences*, HSC's efforts yielded mixed results.

THE COMMUNITY ORIENTATION PROGRAM (COP) AND THE POLICY COUNCIL: A TALE OF TWO EMPOWERMENT STRUCTURES[1]

In creating an empowering environment, HSC developed specific structures to increase the power of students and parents in shaping the educational process. The remainder of this chapter focuses on two such structures: the COP and The Policy Council. These different structures proceeded in different ways during the 1971-74 years, allowing further insight into the complexities involved in designing and carrying out social experiments designed to empower.

THE COMMUNITY ORIENTATION PROGRAM: 1971-72

The COP program was designed to allow students to use the community as a learning laboratory. During its first year, the COP struggled. "We didn't have a whole lot of discussion then about the COP," recalled Foote. "We did it for ideological reasons. It made sense, Parkway was involved with it, but we never had time to make it central."

With the awarding of a federal grant for HSC's second year, funding for a full-time COP coordinator was available. The position was filled by Tom Nelson, who brought ideas, energy, and organization to the program. Nelson used the summer of 1971 to work on substantive and structural changes which had been recommended in the first year evaluation of the COP. Substantively, it was recommended that community placements be diversified as well as multiplied, particularly for students not planning on post-high school education. A "fact sheet," distributed before the opening of school by the Facilitator, summarized progress on this issue:

> As a result of this summer work we now have commitments from the media of New Haven (newspapers and radios), civic departments (such as the police department, the Better Business Bureau), Yale (Computer Center), business (Junior Achievement, printing presses, photography), elementary school teachers, from hospitals, child care centers, the Hamden-New Haven Cooperative Educational Center and business schools . . . . We are presently prepared to offer community learning situations to 130 of our students. This number will hopefully reach 200.

Structural changes recommended by the evaluation included the need to: (a) clarify the intent of the program and communicate it clearly to students and community teachers; (b) develop guidelines of accountability and processes of communication; and (c) create ongoing systems for feedback on how the COP was doing. Nelson made extensive efforts in all those directions. In a letter to the evaluators on Sept. 5, 1971, he said "from my visits with last year's community teachers and from talking to this year's new ones, I think it's a good idea to coordinate any evaluation visits through me. The way it's going now, they feel quite solid about having one person to communicate with regarding their students—I'm acting as a kind of 'hub' for communication."

A week later he sent the following statement to students about the program.

> The Community Orientation Program is one of the ways that High School in the Community (HSC) tries to live up to its

name of 'being in the community'. . . . One of the key concepts behind the COP is 'community utilization.' Involved in this is a redefinition of what there is to learn, how it can be learned, and who is qualified to teach it. . . . I think the program should be providing learning experiences which are in some way useful to you. In terms of the future, we all come to a point where we want to, or have to, decide on a job or a career. The COP can help in this decision by giving you an inside glance at some of the careers available in the world. In terms of the present, there are things which we confront every day that a curriculum in the community can help us understand . . . politics, sex, drugs, law enforcement, alcohol, race, purchasing and selling. . . . It is with learning experiences like these that you can learn the games, rules, and skills needed in 'the world.'

Now the reason I'm giving you this discussion now instead of a 'catalogue' is that an effort like I've described . . . requires good timing. Last year we tried to start everything at once and it was really confusing. This year I want to take all the first quarter (nine weeks) and talk with you about the sorts of things you're interested in doing, the sorts of things I and others can arrange, the sorts of things you need to know, and the ways to find them out. In other words, the curriculum for the first quarter of the COP is mostly choosing . . . taking advantage of the freedom you have to design your own curriculum and *choosing* the things most useful and interesting to you" (pp. 1-2).

About 120 students participated in the COP during the first quarter of the 1971-72 year, and 80 added COP to their schedule during the second quarter. Here, more than in any other area of the curriculum, structuring, defining, and regulating were being undertaken.

In addition to developing placements, setting a thoughtful tone for students contemplating the COP, and creating regularized relationships with community teachers, Nelson wrote two lengthy reports during the 1971-72 year. These reports provide candid and insightful glimpses of the struggles encountered in carrying out this kind of empowering structure. The first was a winter 1972, report to the Policy Council; the second was a "Report to The Community" at the end of the 1971-72 school year.

REPORT TO THE POLICY COUNCIL

Nelson approached the Policy Council both to promote its legitimacy as *the* governing body of HSC and to promote the norm of teacher accountability by "making our work and thoughts open to evaluation by colleagues." His report began by describing the philosophy behind the COP and the level of student interest in it. He then added a number of thoughts useful in understanding both the culture of the school and the development of COP as a viable educational vehicle.

> A few things should be clear to all who read this report. One is that it is exhausting to work at HSC. Long hours coupled with these hours being difficult ones; lead to physical and emotional havoc. This comes, to my mind, primarily from the fact that we are at last 'doing our own school,' and feel that we alone are responsible for it . . . So we work with intensity. Often not with enjoyment, but certainly with intensity. Another thing to bear in mind is the temptation most of us have (because of the above) to evaluate our work with extraordinarily high standards. We often feel (too quickly) since some things ought to be, they can be immediately . . . We are not working in a social/cultural/ historical vacuum. We should be careful of the temptation to compare our school to some educational heaven. It creates an anxiety, and it shows that sometimes we forget where we have come from—our past and the students' pasts. Another (thing to bear in mind) is that we have a temptation to see failures or shortcomings at the school as *our* failures and shortcomings. We've shied away from the assertion that the students are not picking up their end of the stick . . . I've been disappointed by students as well as excited and pleased by them.

Nelson spoke of his optimism about the COP as a potentially major educational idea. He outlined the steps he had already taken or was planning to take to further the COP. These steps included working on its future with a small group of HSC students and developing small groups of community people representing different sectors to help in planning and finding placements. He mentioned upcoming efforts to coordinate the COP with the work of the guidance counselor who, like himself, had been hired at the beginning of the school year. There were other topics, however, which signalled more difficult issues.

> One of the frustrations to date has been the problem of the community teachers encountering the same difficulties with students as does the staff. I must first say that this is beneficial in one way; the community at large must begin to realize concretely the 'educational problems of today' . . . the form that these problems usually take is this: I'll go to someone in the community to see if they would be interested in teaching and working with our students. The person will say something like 'Sure, I'll be glad to as long as the students are prompt, civil,

responsible, and interested.' I will then go back to school and realize that this is exactly the point to which we are trying to *get* students and to which many have not gotten. In fact, if all of our students *had* gotten to this point, HSC may not need to exist at all. The community is willing to accept the 'successful products of the educational process,' but is often not so willing to take on the process of getting to that end.

In designing the COP, HSC had taken on a complex series of issues based on unexamined assumptions about what the COP would demand of students, teachers, and the community.

The importance of broader organizational issues at the school was also evident in the Nelson memo. Difficulties were cited in having clear and dependable ways of communicating with students whose classes ranged across different locations in the city. "There is no flow pattern for messages to students other than personal evening phone calls to students at home. Staff is no more likely to run into specific students within two days than I am. Seminars (as a structure where, in principle, students could be found regularly during the week) have substantially fallen apart in terms of my making use of them."

Behind these specific concerns was the same need for organizational and pedagogical coherence which was beginning to be discussed more broadly.

> Uncontrolled or incomprehensive diversity is of no advantage to students who have not had a past of evaluating and choosing from limitless options in freedom. . . . I would generally characterize the COP catalogue as fragmented, as would I the HSC core catalogue. . . . Such a vast and fragmented learning scene as currently exists seems to come from (or lead to) fragmented working styles to the point that we work as fragmented and isolated 'colleagues,' neither pushing nor congratulating one another, or knowing enough about the work each other is doing to be able to do either.

Nelson's report highlights a paradox of empowerment broadly reflected at HSC during this time. The very ideology which was intended to build a sense of connectedness and community was simultaneously undermining it. Nelson's description of his own adaptive style under these circumstances is telling.

> Although partially due to individual idiosyncracies, there is a certain tendency for HSC to operate along the lines of 'overcrowded solitude' . . . the way I've felt is: in the beginning of the

school year I was anxious to facilitate shared work/credit/ responsibility for the COP. Quickly I saw that everyone was extraordinarily busy (knowing only vaguely with what, which was mutual) and that overtures of dividing my work amongst people would likely be either avoided or resented and surely inefficient. I pulled in to a rather efficient hierarchy (me) and proceeded to do a job. Recently, there have been indications at both units that folks may be more interested in sharing the load now that the year is in process. This is really exciting to me, and I am anxious to begin ways of solid cooperation.

REPORT TO THE COMMUNITY

At the end of the year, Nelson completed a "Report to the Community" which was distributed internally and sent to the community teachers. It was intended as both an educational and informational document, outlining the idea of the COP, its brief history, a list of organizations which had participated that year, and including sections on "Irritations and Difficulties" "Strengths and Encouragements" and "Lessons."

> An important conversation for me this year included the comment, 'If you're trying a good new idea, it probably will not be successful the first year. In fact, if it is successful the first year, the idea is probably not that good and certainly it is not that new . . . The Community Orientation Program is a good idea within the good idea of the school. But they are new ideas — troubling ideas — and ideas lacking precedents. People often do not know how to behave appropriately and responsibly in these ideas, which is another way of saying that people often do not know how to best make use of the ideas. It is for this reason that the year for this writer has been frustrating, exhausting, and depressing while at the same time challenging, educational, and occasionally even enjoyable.

"Difficulties" included not only those related to student apprehension about working with adults in the "real world" and adult apprehension about dealing directly with high school students, but with issues such as transportation. Issues of attendance and promptness were related partly to student inadequacies ("too often students said they could do something they couldn't, said they would be responsible for something but weren't"), and partly to structural issues such as transportation and communication problems within the school.

Nelson publicly appreciated the risks taken by the community teachers and their willingness to continue their efforts on behalf of HSC students. In promising a better future, Nelson wrote that "the COP has been defined, attempted, and validated to the extent that it can now be taken seriously as an integral part of contemporary high school education." Tightening up, collaboration, acknowledgment of problems, and hope were the themes Nelson brought to the COP.

COP: 1972-74

During the next two years, the COP continued to provide education for HSC students in the community. Clarity of mission increased, structuring energy remained high, and efforts to integrate the COP into the "in-house" HSC curriculum were undertaken. In June 1973, during a series of staff meetings, one meeting involved a discussion of the COP. Concern was expressed that the COP students were still too much on their own and that the experiences were too specialized to generate broad student interest. Out of this meeting came the decision to develop a "placement seminar" for students in the two most popular areas: Health Care and Education. The intent was to link COP experiences with academic content and provide a place for COP students to share experiences and reduce their feelings of isolation.

The mandate for these changes fell to Ed Linehan, who became COP Coordinator in January 1973, when Nelson ascended to the role of Unit Head at Unit I. Building on Nelson's efforts, Linehan continued to tighten up the program internally and develop more collaborative relationships with community teachers. Indeed, the 1973-74 evaluation called the COP "one of the most innovative aspects of the structure of High School in the Community." It commented very favorably on the performance of Linehan as COP coordinator, and concluded that "it is basically succeeding as an integral part of HSC and deserves support."

Data for these conclusions came from questionnaires sent to community teachers and COP students. These showed that successful efforts had been made to clarify student expectations about the COP and to improve attendance. Further, before beginning a community placement, joint meetings were held with individual students, the COP coordinator, and the community teacher to discuss expectations and requirements. In a significant change from earlier years, essentially all COP students reported that they understood the purpose and expectations of the COP.

Other evaluation data support the positive evolution of the COP from its meager beginnings. While applicants to COP decreased slightly from the previous year (172 from 198), about 60 percent were successfully placed each year and 87 percent of these students said that their educational goals had been met. Over 80 percent of the community teachers who participated during the 1973-74 year said they would be interested in continuing to work with the school the following year. In contrast to an earlier period, 77 percent of the community teachers rated student attendance as "good" or "excellent." Over 90 percent of the community teachers stated that the COP coordinator was "available."

The evolution of the COP during these years saw an increasing effort to forge partnerships with community resources. Clarifying the philosophy and structure of the program, increasing the demands on students for accountability, and integrating the more practical community experiences with seminars were all steps in developing a more coherent COP. Yet this process also greatly increased the demands placed on the COP coordinator. Indeed, the group auditing the evaluation[2] asserted that the COP "is a task that became too great for a single individual to run," and concurred with the idea that the COP coordinator should work more intensively with fewer students in the upcoming year.

Overall, then, the COP seemed to be an empowerment structure which was successfully implemented. While it is difficult to gauge the specific contribution of the COP to students' educational development, data show that the COP became a program which earned the praise of students, community teachers, and the outside evaluators. At a time when HSC was concerned about its internal structure, it served as a model for how such structuring might be undertaken. Why this is so, probably reflects a number of factors, not the least of which was the involvement of two energetic and organized COP coordinators who cared deeply about HSC and its innovative potential.

The COP also stands as testimony to the positive aspects of role differentiation and tempers the case for viewing empowerment as "participation in everything." It was only after the COP was removed from the teacher role and placed in the hands of a single individual that it could receive the attention necessary for it to develop. This individual may have lamented the relative lack of community input—and at times teachers themselves questioned the autonomy granted the COP coordinator—but, in assessing his role, Nelson articulated the conditions that allowed the COP to develop: "I pulled into a rather efficient hierarchy (me) and proceeded to do a job."

For a variety of reasons—some involving teacher trust of who the COP coordinators were, and some involving the fact that everyone else was busy with their own job demands—the COP was allowed to remain under the control of an individual. While the COP may have floundered under less able leaders, both Nelson and Linehan were sanctioned to lead. The Policy Council faced different structural constraints than did the COP and had significantly more complex issues to resolve.

THE POLICY COUNCIL: 1971-74

Begun at Unit I midway through the HSC's first year, the Policy Council was a structure designed to empower students and parents by giving them representation in school governance. The intent was to develop a governing body comprised of equal numbers of students, parents, and teachers. With the creation of Unit II, two councils were formed, one at each unit. These two councils continued for two years, at which time they merged into one as part of HSC's broader consolidation.

The Policy Council was granted formal authority over a wide range of decisions which in most other schools were not even made by teachers, let alone students and parents. These decisions included hiring and firing of teachers, allocation of discretionary funds, and a variety of educational policies, such as issues of attendance and discipline. The wide range of issues which surfaced on the Council's agenda is evidence that the Council's mandate was a broad one. Indeed, during one early meeting a parent asked what the scope of the Council's powers were. "They are whatever we decide they are," said a teacher.

During these years, the Council debated a variety of significant school-wide issues. When the play *Lysistrada* caused concern downtown, the Policy Council discussed how the school should respond. When survival of the school became a recurrent theme, the Policy Council discussed and debated alternative strategies. When students developed a proposal to better the quality of instruction in mathematics, the Council reviewed the proposal because it had policy implications. The Policy Council covered important decision-making territory.

The Policy Council also operated with a spirit of openness which led to provocative and energized discussions. They displayed both candor and compassion around such issues as criteria for hiring new teachers, how student credit should be dealt with if a teacher strike occurred, and discussions with a teacher they had agreed to fire. To be sure, they sometimes argued about issues, occasionally around personalities, and predictably across generational lines. ("Students don't think parents should be part of the Policy Council," said one student, "kids don't want to share their business with parents.")

More than once humor lightened the atmosphere. One memorable moment involved a discussion of how the school could improve its public image to gain support for its survival. "We should go to the newspaper," suggested a parent, "and get them to write a story about the school." "Be realistic," said a somewhat disheveled student, "can you see pictures of us in the society section?" Another such moment arose in a discussion of the evaluation plans for the school. One student expressed disdain for the whole idea. "It's stupid," she said, "they ask questions like 'is despair thicker than tomato juice.'"

Still, over time, the Policy Council did not fulfill its aspirations to be the structure through which students and parents exerted strong influence in school decision-making. A brief analysis of this effort at political empowerment is presented here. It is based on notes taken during Council meetings during this period, interviews with parents, students and teachers who sat on the Council, and data collected for the yearly evaluations of the school. First, recurrent themes which occupied Council time are presented, followed by assessments by parents, students, and teachers of how they viewed the Council. Finally, an analysis of why the Council experienced such difficulty is provided, both to understand how difficult this kind of empowerment effort was and to contrast the structural differences between the Policy Council and the COP.

POLICY COUNCIL: THEMES AND ISSUES

The Policy Council began as many other aspects of HSC began, as an idea lacking precedent. The first organized effort at articulating its structure and mission is found in a 1971 student-faculty committee report.

> *High School in The Community*
> The committee of Student Representatives and Faculty is making the following proposal for setting up a SCHOOL POLICY COUNCIL. We are submitting it to the three groups involved—faculty, students, and parents—for their discussion and decision.
>
> It is proposed that:
>
> 1) The School Policy Council will have equal representation from each of the three groups; faculty, students, and parents.
>
> 2) The Council will have 15 members: 5 students, 5 teachers, 5 parents.
>
> 3) Each group will decide for itself how it wants to choose its representatives on the Council.
>
> 4) The School Policy Council will have the following powers:
>
> I. The Policy Council will propose and designate *courses* to be offered by the HSC; the Council will *not*, however, have the power to veto courses or to prevent courses from being offered.
>
> (Note: The specific content of courses will be determined

only by the faculty and the students in a given class. The faculty as a group will determine teacher assignments, i.e. which teachers will teach specific courses. The Policy Council will not determine that a specific teacher *must* teach a certain course.)

II. The Policy Council will approve and administer the *budget request* for the HSC.

III. The Policy Council will work to maintain an orderly learning environment and will have jurisdiction over *discipline*.

(Although suspension or expulsion of students is considered incompatible with the philosophy of HSC, in *very extreme* circumstances it may be considered by the School Policy Council.)

IV. The Policy Council will approve the selection of *new personnel*.

V. The Policy Council will have the final say on the *use of the building*.

VI. The Policy Council will identify and re-evaluate the *goals* of the HSC, within the limits set by the Board of Education.

5) It will be up to the Policy Council itself — once it is in existence — to decide how often it will meet, whether its meetings will be open, what its voting procedures will be, etc. etc.

These guidelines had not been formalized during the brief period of time the Council met during the school's initial year. Creating bylaws became a primary task for the Councils at both Units during 1971-72. In March 1972, the bylaws were approved. They included issues of voting and membership, areas of jurisdiction, specification of officers, quorum requirements, and a "committee structure based on anticipated needs of the Council."

GROPING FOR A CLEAR MANDATE

While the bylaws guided the processes of the Council and delineated its sphere of influence, they did not aid in developing priorities. Indeed, the potential opportunity to "exert power in whatever areas it wanted" brought with it the potential paralysis of "having so many choices that nothing gets done." Given that students, parents, and teachers brought different agendas, and that the ideology of the school required equal respect for each of them, it is not surprising that a recurrent theme was groping for a clear mandate about what the Council should deal with.

DECISION-MAKING PROCESSES

In addition to the need to develop a coherent overall mandate for the Council, it was necessary to develop processes for arriving at decisions. The *structure* of decision-making — in terms of votes required to pass resolutions, etc. — was spelled out in the bylaws. Still, the processes used to reach decisions were slow in evolving. The school-wide norm that decisions should be made by consensus penetrated the processes of the Policy Council, leading to lengthy discussions. Typically, issues were referred to committee for further study. Since Council meetings were held every two weeks, decision-making was protracted.

Notes from a November 1972 Council meeting show the concrete manifestation of the ambiguities around decision-making processes. The discussion involves the decision to hire an outreach worker. The situation was complicated by the fact that the position required working with both Units of HSC, thus requiring the approval of each Policy Council. A screening committee involving teachers from both units was set up.

Teacher 1:   (on screening committee): There were 6 candidates for outreach worker — the committee recommends W.H. from Unit I — already has good credentials at Unit I.

Student 1:   Can you explain what an outreach worker does?

Parent 1:   Troubleshooter — a student ombudsman.

Teacher 2:   A person who's not a teacher with responsibilities to students — personal visits in the homes of non-attenders, working with kids with problems.

Teacher 3:   I've heard from staff he couldn't do a good job. Are you convinced he's the right person?

Teacher 1:   He knows what the school is all about — last year's outreach worker is high on him — also, he's a black male, and that's important since Unit I is largely black; it's easier for a black male to work there than for a white female.

Teacher 4:   We should set up a mechanism for evaluation of the outreach worker's effectiveness.

Teacher 5:   Yes, that's very important for all staff.

Parent 1:   It's very important for student evaluation of staff.

(General discussion of various ways of thinking about evaluation of staff in general.)

Teacher 4: Was a recommendation made about the outreach worker?

Teacher 5: No vote yet.

Teacher 3: We've never voted on what power the screening committee has.

Teacher 5: Does the Policy Council or the screening committee decide? Does the steering committee feel strongly about W. and what do you recommend?

Teacher 1: We recommend we hire W.

Parent 1: Yes, with the proviso that we have a 3-month evaluation before a final contract.

Student 1: Why is this different from the way teachers are hired? They have to come before the Policy Council.

Teacher 5: The screening committee didn't agree on a top person — we rated the top candidate and the Policy Council talked to them.

Student 2: We understood our job as just to screen — to give the Policy Council a choice.

Teacher 5: If a committee of 6 from the two units agreed, maybe we should go ahead.

Parent 1: Let's add on something about evaluation.

Teacher 2: That's two distinct issues — evaluation will take longer to talk about — we can't vote on that tonight.

(Further discussion of evaluation of staff as a general issue.)

Teacher 5: Let's vote on W.

(They vote, there is confusion over what the vote means. The bylaws state that "a simple majority, one more than half of the voting members present, is needed on all proposals. Any voting member can ask for a 2/3 vote. The request needs to be approved by a majority vote.")

Teacher 5: (in response to a question about 2/3 vs. majority vote) If you don't read the rules, you lose the game. You can request a 2/3 vote, which we would have to vote on. If someone thinks we should have a 2/3 vote on hiring, move now.

Teacher 2: There are clearly questions in peoples' minds;

we're unclear what our decision means. I'm un-happy — I've never seen this guy. I'm willing to accept the screening committee to a point, but he should come to the Policy Council.

Parent 1:   You should have made this clear to the screening committee in advance.

Teacher 5:   I move we should have a 2/3 vote [seconded].

Parent 2:   As long as Unit I has to vote too, why don't we vote together.

Teacher 4:   I move we hire W.

Student 2:   The question now is on the 2/3 vote.

(They vote it passes by a 9-5 margin.)

Teacher 1:   I move we vote on hiring W. [seconded].

(They vote. W. fails to get a 2/3 vote.)

Teacher 5:   Why the 'no' votes and abstentions?

Student 3:   We should be allowed to meet candidates. Also, there should be an evaluation.

Teacher 1:   We should have a joint meeting with Unit I.

Teacher 5:   This issue is complicated. Unit I invested author-ity in the screening committee. The only reason for a joint meeting is if there is a difference of opinion.

Teacher 1:   Does he need the vote of the Policy Council to get the job?

Teacher 5:   The power of the screening committee or Unit is to select, so Unit I has already decided — we now have to decide.

Teacher 6:   I propose we have an emergency meeting next week and we invite W. and the Unit I screening committee.

Parent 1:   Next week we have a parents meeting. We could call an emergency meeting the half hour before.

Student 2:   A half hour's not enough.

Teacher 5:   I think we need to discuss the proposal on the floor.

Teacher: 1:   We should defeat [the motion to call an emergency meeting] and reconsider our earlier vote.

Student 3:   I'd like to reconsider my vote — things have been cleared up for me.

Teacher 5: I move that we have a revote on the screening committee's proposal [seconded and passed].

Teacher 5: I move we accept the committee's recommendation [seconded and passed, 12 in favor, none against, Teacher 1 abstaining].

Teacher 5: So W. is accepted.

While not necessarily representative of the majority of decision-related discussions, the preceding does highlight a number of issues which intruded into the functioning of the group. Multiple agendas, lack of understanding about the implications of prior decisions, and ambiguity about how various issues were to be resolved hindered the ability of the Council to focus their efforts and their goals. A further complication, leadership, requires separate mention.

LEADERSHIP

In an insightful book, *Organization Without Authority: Dilemmas of Social Control in Free Schools,* Swidler argues that "it is the torment of alternative organizations that they both need and abhor leadership" (1979, p. 81). The ideological tension between autonomy and structure in the school, and the difficulties this tension caused the Facilitator as leader, have already been described. It should thus not be surprising that the same issues should manifest themselves in the Policy Council.

An excerpt from an early meeting concretizes how the ideology affected the prospects for effective leadership. The topic of discussion involved a proposal to establish regular Council officers.

Parent 1: Are we thinking of the purpose of the council? Is it a training group or here to get the school running? If the latter, we need the best leader.

Student 1: There shouldn't be a permanent chairman and vice chairman. They should rotate. A permanent person will have too much power.

Parent 2: We need an organizer.

Teacher 1: The chairman should have an overview of all Policy Council operations. We need a permanent person for this to make sure committees are functioning properly.

Student 1: The chairman would wind up being a parent or teacher. One person shouldn't have that power. All should be equal.

Teacher 2: I support a rotating chairman. It gives people experience. A chairman can have a lot of power.

Parent 2: It's not a question of power but of coordination.

Teacher 3: The Policy Council is a training area for all in it. It's unfair for adults who've had experience in other organizations to deprive students of the opportunity to learn. The Policy Council is an essential part of education.

Student 2: We're wasting time. We're not dealing with the school's problems, we're wasting time with mechanics.

The situation around leadership involved a paradox regarding empowerment efforts. On the one hand, teachers reported being willing to assume leadership roles but felt that this would undermine the empowerment intent behind the Council. Parents and students were often reluctant to assume leadership roles because they lacked the resources of time and knowledge to be able to keep on top of the organizing tasks. On the other hand, students did not want teachers in charge, while parents often did, stating that teachers were really in the best position because they knew what was going on in the school and were trained as professional educators. The chair role rotated considerably during the early years of the Council and was subject to resignations at other times. On one occasion a number of people declined the nomination, and finally a reluctant teacher was persuaded to assume the position.

CONSTITUENCY ISSUES AND THE PROBLEM OF RESOURCES

One of the key assumptions behind the inclusion of parents and students on the Policy Council was the belief that they would represent the larger constituencies, thereby providing a vehicle for widespread input. However, the Policy Council did not have the requisite resources for parents and students to communicate with their constituents. With both parents and students scattered throughout the community, it became difficult to view either group as representatives of a particular constituency. Efforts were made at the Council to rectify the situation, such as electing parents from different parts of the city and recruiting both black and white students to be on the Council. However, during the years from 1971-74, it was difficult to recruit representative students and parents. Black students and parents in particular participated only occasionally on the Policy Council.

Parents often voiced concerns about their inability to actually represent other parents. In their wish to serve as intended, they lamented both the lack of structures for them to communicate with other parents and the lack of interest they felt that many parents had. "It's a shame more parents don't get involved," said one staunch parent supporter of the Council, "but we've tried about everything we know how to. We just don't have the resources — the secretarial help, stamps, organization, to really represent. So we do what we can."

ATTENDANCE

It was evident early on that attendance at meetings would be an ongoing issue. Shortly after the Unit II Council was organized, for example, Unit Head Ed Linehan sent the following letter to Policy Council Members:

> February 22, 1972
> Dear Policy Council Members,
>
> Greetings! This letter is being sent in place of the minutes of the last P.C. meeting Thursday, February 17th. The reason for this is simple — the meeting never happened! At 7:30 two of us were there, then 3, 4, 5 all the way up to 8. Unfortunately 8 members doesn't make a quorum (12 is the magic number). At about 8:05 we decided it didn't look like we'd make it so we all went home.
>
> Right now we are going through perhaps the most boring part of a working Policy Council. Hopefully in one more meeting we will finish establishing the bylaws. It's most important that we begin to consider some of the more substantial matters, for instance: How can we best affect the Board of Education in terms of next year? How should next year's budget be allotted? How many teachers are leaving and who will take their place? Where will the school be located next year? etc.
>
> We must be responsible to each other and to the school. It may have been coincidental that so many could not attend or find an alternate. I hope so. *The next meeting is Monday Feb. 28th at 7:30 at H.S.C. See you There!*
>
> Ed Linehan

The issue of attendance continued throughout the history of the Council, with student and parent representatives most often absent. By the 1973-74 year, only three students and two parents regularly attended Council meetings. Poor attendance carried serious consequences for the ability of the Council to conduct business, as quorum requirements were frequently not met. For two of the three years, a quorum was attained approximately two-thirds of the time, while it reached 80 percent for the 1973-74 year.

THE IMPACT OF THE POLICY COUNCIL: PERSPECTIVES OF COUNCIL MEMBERS AND TEACHERS

The Policy Council was plagued with ongoing problems which, in contrast to the COP, did not get resolved over time. Teachers, students, and parents who participated on the Council were interviewed each year. While all shared a belief in the promise of the Council and supported its continued existence, each constituency emphasized somewhat different themes in summing up their experience.

Teachers viewed parent and student involvement as minimal and saw the Council as teacher dominated in spite of their wish that it be otherwise. Many students viewed the Council as a "waste of time," and believed that parents should not be represented at all. Still, a majority of students supported the concept. Parents, on the other hand, saw the potential for parent influence as positive, though basically unrealized. "We thought at first it was just a courtesy," said one, "but we're learning different now."

The Policy Council's decision-making role decreased over time. Instead, teachers increasingly assumed the role of decision-makers and placed the role of the Council as one of ratifying decisions. In spring 1972, for example, teachers asked the Council to approve an attendance policy which had already been put into effect. In early 1973, teachers undertook an administrative reorganization without informing the Council beforehand. Such patterns eventually became accepted as the respective roles for teachers and the Council. In fact, a January 1973 memo from a teacher offered for consideration the question, "Shall the Policy Council initiate as well as respond and approve?"

HSC's faculty also became suspicious of any potential Council action which they felt might jeopardize the distinctive nature of the school. While committed to a goal of empowerment as embodied in the Council, they saw themselves as the ultimate guardians of the school's ideology. Thus, when issues arose that seemed to challenge the assumptions on which HSC was based, the faculty questioned the legitimacy of the Council's powers. For example, faculty resisted granting the Council anything more than power over the general nature of the curriculum, not specific courses. One teacher warned that the Council must "be on guard against rejecting innovative ideas . . . this is an experimental program which should tolerate experimental programs. We need some restrictions on Council power to protect the right of the individual to experiment."

Teacher commitment to, and concern about, the Policy Council was the topic of one of the June 1973 joint staff meetings. Notes from that meeting confirm what the teacher, parent, and student interviews had suggested. "At this point in history," the Statement of Purpose began, "HSC, like other schools, does not involve parents, students, and teachers working together effectively. It is the specific purpose of the Policy Council to make the school responsible to students and parents, and to nurture the real involvement by these groups in the HSC experience."

The discussion which followed focused on the need to structure the Council more effectively. Teachers acknowledged that policy setting was a less central goal at this point than the development of strong parent and student organizations to provide input. Several teachers volunteered to work on creating strategies to increase the viability of parent and student input. Still, there was concern that increased teacher involvement not be seen by the Council as an effort to take it over. "This proposal . . . comes after three years of waiting for things to happen spontaneously."

THE COP AND THE POLICY COUNCIL: DIFFERENT STRUCTURAL ARRANGEMENTS FOR PROMOTING DIFFERENT ASPECTS OF EMPOWERMENT

In assessing the different paths taken by the COP and the Policy Council, it is useful to look at the goals and structures of each. The COP empowerment was defined primarily in terms of increasing the learning options of students. The idea of using the community as a learning laboratory might have taken other forms. Sarason (1984), for example, has promoted a vision of school-community interaction in which the resources of the community would be fully integrated into the ongoing academic curriculum of the school. Nelson's notes show that this was *one* long-term idea he had about the COP, but one which was not realized.

What was realized, however, was an increasingly organized COP which did promote students working with a wide range of community resources. While there were problems with the program, structurally it was one which could be run by a particular individual and which had a definable mandate and limited goal. Though the processes of the COP were influenced by the broader school environment, through strong and sanctioned leadership the COP became a viable structure.

The Policy Council, on the other hand, became, in the words of one teacher, an "unconscious last priority." There were many kinds of constraints on the Council involving the same kinds of school-wide issues facing the COP. Unlike the COP, however, its original mandate was both broad and ambiguous ("We can be whatever we want to be"). Most importantly, its structure was designed to reflect varied constituencies whose perspectives on the school varied greatly. Gruber and

Trickett (1987) provide one perspective on why the Policy Council was unable to fulfill its hopes for empowerment:

> At the heart of the issues facing the Policy Council lay profound inequalities of role, responsibility, knowledge, expertise, and ability to implement decisions. . . . Within the confines of the Policy Council, parents, students, and teachers were voting equals . . . Political power [however] is derived not merely from the formal properties of an organization but also from the resources participants bring to that organization. Participants derive these resources from their positions in other institutions and from their positions in society as a whole. As a result, the mere creation of a structurally egalitarian organization is not enough to insure that power is in fact equally distributed among participants if, as is almost always the case, the distribution of resources outside the organization is unequal . . .
>
> Power at HSC naturally resided in its faculty who had disproportionate access to formal levels of authority and to the potent resources of information, expertise, deference, and control over implementation. . . Because the institutional context of the school gave so much power to the faculty, the initial grant of power to the Council was not enough. If the empowerment was to be meaningful, the faculty had to bring relevant issues to the Council, provide the information necessary to develop and evaluate alternatives, facilitate the participation of their council members, and then put council decisions into effect. . . . The amount of thoughtful planning and the expenditure of resources necessary to accomplish all these necessities would have been, and was, prohibitive (p. 359).

These same authors describe what they call the "paradox of empowerment" around the structure of the Policy Council.

> The Council was created by the already powerful faculty, but its creation did not change the basic institutional forces that gave them power. As a result, their act of empowerment was inevitably incomplete. To make it meaningful, the faculty would have had to commit considerable resources to overcome the effects of the institutional context. If there had been few other claims on the school's resources, this might have occurred. As it was, the demands of running the school were more insistent than the demands of the Policy Council.
>
> Such a situation, of course, is far from unusual. Few organizations exist solely for the purpose of empowering their members. In those that do, empowerment must seem like a hollow prize since the power so gained cannot be used for other

ends. But the very existence of other ends will almost always dictate an institutional division of labor that will informally undercut an egalitarian governance structure. Thus we conclude that there is a fundamental paradox in the idea of people empowering people because the very institutional structure that puts one group in a position to empower others will also work to undermine the act of empowerment.

EMPOWERMENT AS THE FEELING OF BEING HEARD: A CLOSING NOTE

A rich, though complex, picture emerges in reviewing HSC's empowerment efforts in terms of the broad issue of race relations and the more specific structures of the COP and the Policy Council. This picture suggests that empowerment takes on multiple and sometimes contrasting meanings, depending on the sociocultural context of the individuals involved and the different kinds of structures developed to further empowerment goals. HSC's efforts in the different spheres of empowerment have been described as mixed successes. There is one general area, however, where data clearly show that HSC created a responsive and empowering environment. Students, parents, and teachers all felt that they had the power to influence the school if they so desired.

Teachers consistently felt that they had sufficient influence in policy making, although the creation of the Facilitating Unit caused some concern that teachers would have less input than before. As described in the next chapter, student perceptions of the school consistently showed greater satisfaction and perceived ability to influence school policy than did the perceptions of students in the other high schools. Data from parent interviews conducted from 1971-74 show that parents, too, viewed HSC as more responsive than they viewed the other high schools.

It thus appears that HSC's efforts at creating a school where various groups felt their concerns would be listened to was quite successful. While different empowerment themes and structures — such as race relations, the COP, and the Policy Council — took different paths with differing degrees of success, the overall impact of the school suggests that empowerment, defined as feelings of influence, was real.

CHAPTER 7

The Student Experience: 1971-74

Previous chapters have described the four-year evolution of HSC as an organization. During these years, many shifts and changes occurred as the school confronted new internal and external realities. New roles evolved, and old roles took on different directions as the school worked through the implications of its basic ideas. The portrait is one of high energy, struggle over processes and leadership, the increasing focus of some structures, such as the COP, and the recurrent problems with others, such as the Policy Council. Throughout these changes was a strong underlying commitment to the egalitarian philosophy of education which formed the core of HSC's ideology.

The purpose of this chapter is to assess the impact of HSC on students, for the school wanted to create a student experience consistent with its educational ideology. Empowering conditions for students included significant choice in crafting their own education, influence over school policy, and a more personal relationship with teachers. This meant having teachers who were accessible, classrooms that were both organized and personal, and a feeling by students that their concerns about the school were taken seriously, regardless of whether teachers agreed with them. Further, the school wanted to foster positive interracial attitudes and relationships. It wanted students to view school as a connecting rather than alienating experience. And, of course, HSC wanted students to learn as much or more than students in the other local high schools.

How closely *did* the school come to meeting its aspirations? What kind of environment *was* created for students? What effects did this environment have on students? During years 2-4 of the school (1971-74), extensive evaluations were done on these issues, involving data gathered from students and from archival sources as well (e.g. attendance, post-high school education). Four general areas of the student experience were covered in these evaluations: student perception of the school environment; student attendance, achievement, and college admissions; student attitudes, satisfactions, and involvement in the school; and who the school served best — the effects of HSC on different groups of students.

THE EVALUATION DESIGN: 1971-1974

In assessing the HSC environment and its effects on students, contrasts were made between two different groups of students. The first involved comparisons between HSC students and randomly sampled students in the other high schools. For example, in assessing classrooms at HSC and the other schools, HSC classrooms are compared to random samples of classrooms in the other high schools. This answers the question of whether HSC, as a school, created a different classroom atmosphere than was found in the other schools.

When assessing the impact of HSC on students, a different comparison is made. Here, the contrast is between HSC students and those who wished to attend HSC, but were not selected in the lottery. As previously mentioned, in the service of the egalitarian commitment HSC admitted students by lottery. Further, to avoid the possibility that HSC might be used to further "white flight" from the other inner-city schools, HSC`s racial composition intentionally reflected that found in the other New Haven high schools. Taken together, these processes served the social science goal of creating two groups of students stratified by race and matched by random selection for academic ability, personal characteristics, and motivation to attend HSC (see Campbell and Stanley, 1963).[1]

The lottery was used during the 1971-72 and 1972-73 years, when more students applied to HSC than the school could accept. In the third year, not enough students applied to form an adequate control group. A sample of students from the regular high school matched for gender, race, grade in school, and academic performance was selected as a comparison group. Most frequently, then, when differences between HSC students and other students are reported, they refer to the sample of students who wanted to attend HSC but were not selected in the lottery.

STUDENT PERCEPTION OF THE HSC ENVIRONMENT

In assessing HSC's environment, the evaluation focused on the classroom, teachers, and the school more generally.

Student Perceptions of Their Classroom Experience: Within schools, the classroom is a primary vehicle for the expression of the broader school ideology. While what goes on in classrooms only partially represents the overall high school experience, the classroom is still central. The evaluation team put considerable energy into understanding what HSC classrooms were like, how satisfying they were, and how they compared to classrooms in the other schools.

The primary vehicle for assessing the student classroom experience was the Classroom Environment Scale (Trickett and Moos, 1973), an instrument which assesses the social climate of the classroom *as perceived by students*. It was given to HSC classes during each of the three years covered here and, during the last two years, was given to a random sample of classes in the feeder schools as well.

The CES assesses three broad domains of the classroom environment: the *Relationship* domain, the *System Maintenance and Change* domain, and the *Goal Orientation* domain. The Relationship domain involves the quality of interpersonal relationships among students and between students and the teacher. The System Maintenance domain covers the authority structure of the classroom — its rules and regulations — and System Change concerns the degree to which the classroom experience is similar or varied from day to day. The Goal Orientation domain highlights those aspects of the classroom which are related specifically to the learning goals of the classroom, such as sticking to the subject matter and not getting sidetracked.

The CES includes nine specific dimensions of the classroom which fold into the three broad classroom domains. Table 7-1 outlines these nine dimensions. To arrive at a classroom score for each dimension, student perceptions for each dimension are averaged within each classroom. To derive a school score for each dimension, each classroom score on each dimension is averaged.

The CES was chosen because its specific dimensions are relevant to the kind of environment HSC wanted to establish. The school was designed to emphasize the importance of personal relationships between teachers and students and to promote positive student-student interactions. HSC's anti-bureaucratic origins and philosophy suggested that rules should be minimized and innovation in classrooms high. Further, the egalitarian commitment was intended to minimize competition — written evaluations rather than grades were given, for example. All these aspects of the school are assessed by CES dimensions.

During the 1971-74 school years, an average of 80 persent of the HSC teachers gave the CES in their classrooms, while randomly selected teachers at the feeder schools did the same from 1972-74. Overall, this included 51 HSC classes (N=334 students) and 49 feeder school classes (N=487 students).

Table 7-2 presents these data relative to a normative sample of 314 public school classrooms from various parts of the United States. The data are aggregated across years because no overall statistically significant differences were found across years for any of the schools, although there were small fluctuations in one subscale or another. All the schools remained remarkably stable in terms of average classroom environ-

Table 7-1: CES Subscale Descriptions

I. Relationship Dimensions

1. Involvement — measures the extent to which students have attentive interest in class activities and participate in discussions. The extent to which students do additional work on their own and enjoy the class is considered.

2. Affiliation — assesses the level of friendship students feel for each other, i.e., the extent to which they help each other with homework, get to know each other easily, and enjoy working together.

3. Teacher Support — measures the amount of help, concern, and friendship the teacher directs towards the students. The extent to which the teacher talks openly with students, trusts them, and is interested in their ideas is considered.

II. Goal Orientation Dimensions

4. Task Orientation — measures the extent to which it is important to complete the activities that have been planned. The emphasis the teacher places on staying on the subject matter is assessed.

5. Competition — assesses the emphasis placed on student's competing with each other for grades and recognition. An assessment of the difficulty of achieving good grades is included.

IIIa. System Maintenance Dimensions

6. Order and Organization — assesses the emphasis on students behaving in an orderly and polite manner and on the overall organization of assignments and classroom activities. The degree to which students tend to remain calm and quiet is considered.

7. Rule Clarity — assesses the emphasis on establishing and following a clear set of rules, and on students knowing what the consequences will be if they do not follow them. An important focus of this subscale is the extent to which the teacher is consistent in dealing with students who break rules.

8. Teacher Control — measures how strict the teacher is in enforcing the rules, and the severity of the punishment for rule infractions. The number of rules and the ease of students getting in trouble is considered.

IIIb. System Change Dimension

9. Innovation — measures how much students contribute to planning classroom activities, and the amount of unusual and varying activities and assignments planned by the teacher. The extent to which the teacher attempts to use new techniques and encourages creative thinking in the students is considered.

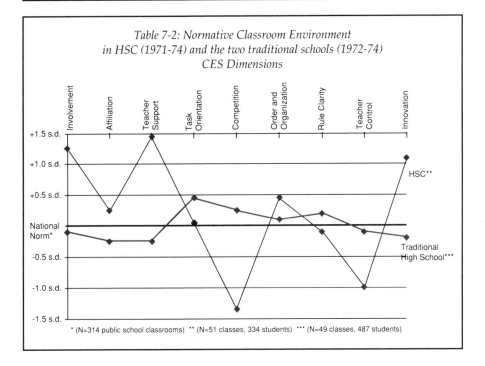

Table 7-2: Normative Classroom Environment in HSC (1971-74) and the two traditional schools (1972-74) CES Dimensions

* (N=314 public school classrooms) ** (N=51 classes, 334 students) *** (N=49 classes, 487 students)

ment.

Table 2 clarifies that student perception of HSC classrooms is consistent with its ideology and consistently different from classrooms in the other high schools. The first three dimensions of Table 2 present the Relationship domain of the classroom. Here, HSC students report their classes as significantly more involving than do students in the feeder schools, with teachers being more supportive and affiliation among students being higher.[2] HSC's emphasis on interpersonal relationships was consistently reflected in its classrooms during the 1971-74 years.

Task Orientation and Competition represent the Goal Orientation domain of the classroom. Here, HSC classrooms are comparable in task orientation to the feeder schools, while being much less competitive. This suggests that HSC's noncompetitive ideology was carried out in classes, but that classes were not seen as aimless or lacking a focus on learning.

Order and Organization, Rule Clarity, Teacher Control and Innovation represent the System Maintenance and System Change domain. Once again, HSC classrooms were seen in ways which supported its basic philosophy. They were as organized as those in the feeder schools, with equally clear rules governing student behavior. Teacher Control, which assesses how strict the classroom rules are, was much less in HSC classes, a finding consistent with the egalitarian ethic which permeated the school. In similar fashion, HSC classes were seen as significantly more innovative and varied than classes in the feeder schools, reflecting both the freedom of HSC teachers to teach as they wished and their interest in creating distinctive educational experiences for students.

Taken across three years, the CES data represent many classrooms and hundreds of students. Its consistency and pattern over time leave little doubt that *within the realm of classrooms taught by full-time HSC teachers*, the HSC student experience was congruent with its basic philosophy and greatly different from that of students in the feeder schools. The options for other kinds of courses taught by volunteers and community people through the COP program suggests that, if anything, the CES data *understates* the differences between HSC and the feeder schools in terms of overall educational environments and options.

Perceptions of school and teachers: HSC and control group students in the feeder schools were also asked about their school and teachers. Student perceptions support the general picture painted by the CES data. Across the three years, students at HSC viewed the school as consistently less tense and more cooperative than did control group students. In response to the question "Do other students interfere with your learning?," HSC students reported less interference each year than did students in the other schools. While there were organizational hassles and, on occasion, outside intrusions into HSC's shared space during this time, this did not overwhelm its more comfortable and cooperative atmosphere.

With respect to perception of teachers, HSC students stated that a higher percentage of their teachers were "really good," a lower percentage were "really bad," and that teachers at HSC were "more likely to ask students how they might improve their classes." Further, HSC teachers had more contact with parents or guardians through home visits and were "easier to find if you want to express a gripe." Finally, students at HSC were consistently more likely to agree that they could "bring up personal opinions in class" if they wanted to. Students' responses corroborate the CES data in affirming that HSC was creating a congenial, informal, and caring learning environment for students.

Student Achievement, Attendance, and Admission to Post-High School Education

Certain kinds of outcomes in educational research are considered "hard" in that they represent important, definable, and *measurable* criteria which in some ways are better than "soft" criteria. Within educational research, *achievement, attendance,* and *percentage of high school students who continue their education after high school* are generally seen in the "hard" category. While such outcomes are of obvious relevance, the experience of evaluating HSC helped clarify both their limitations and their underlying value assumptions. Indeed, it raised the possibility that they are not as *"hard"* as they appear at first blush.

The definition of *student achievement*, for example, has traditionally posed problems for those schools whose ideologies define achievement in nonstandardized ways. HSC was concerned about the potential cultural biases in standardized achievement tests. Teachers further believed that personal development was as important an outcome as reading or math achievement. The protest was not against having adolescents read and write; rather, it was with the primacy of those goals over all others *and* the specific ways in which those goals were measured. For HSC, such "hard" data implied both a narrow and a discriminatory conception of the goals of education.

Attendance was also problematic as an evaluation goal for HSC. During its first year, HSC had no attendance policy, and some of the teachers refused, on principle, to keep attendance records. Policies involving student attendance were reluctantly developed over time. However, HSC's criteria for defining attendance differed from those at the other high schools. During these three years, the other high schools took attendance during "homeroom" at the beginning of the school day. This approach allowed students to show up for homeroom in the morning, leave the school for part or all of the day, and still be counted as present. HSC initially took attendance on a daily basis as well, though the process was more informal since, after the demise of the seminar, HSC had nothing comparable to a homeroom. Later, HSC adopted a class by class attendance record-keeping process which was more precise, but administratively more cumbersome and more likely to increase teacher resistance and distortion. Attendance remained a complex and slippery variable to assess meaningfully in all the schools.

The issue of *post-high school education* proved to reflect another complex set of factors. As a new alternative school which relied on written evaluations rather than grades, HSC struggled with how to place their graduates in colleges, vocational programs, and so forth. In the process, it expended great effort not only on guidance, but in visiting technical schools and colleges, explaining the school and its program. Data show that HSC was quite successful in placing its graduates in post-high school educational settings. It also suggests, however, that their success rate was probably less related to students' academic credentials than to the efforts made by HSC to promote itself as an educational institution. While post-high school placements may be seen as a sign of school quality, it is important to distinguish the quality of the education from the quality of the efforts and services designed to place students. Once again, an objective, "hard" outcome can be complex in its specifics, and this complexity may lend a different meaning to the outcome.

The preceding is not intended to discount the importance of achievement, attendance, and post-high school education as important criteria for assessing the impact of school on adolescents. Rather, it is to clarify that for HSC some of these criteria had different meanings than for the feeder schools, and that these different meanings affected how one evaluates their success. With this in mind, let us turn to the data.

Student Achievement: An overview of the 1971-74 data on student achievement shows both HSC's ideological struggles and its intent to use data to improve its educational impact. Initially, HSC attempted to create its own instruments to assess the achievement of its students. To quote the evaluation report of that year:

> "The evaluation team worked with HSC teachers in an effort to devise tests of verbal and quantitative skills that related directly to the specific material being taught in HSC classes. The design of such tests is time-consuming; the HSC faculty was not in a position to develop a test in verbal skills which was found acceptable. A diagnostic math test was developed, but the number of students who took the test in both the fall and spring is too small to allow any conclusions" (Hawley et al., 1973, p. 30).

Teachers had neither the time nor the expertise to add test construction to their lengthy list of responsibilities.

Data do exist, however, on the impact of HSC compared to control group students on standardized tests of achievement. During the 1971-74 years, each of these groups of students was given portions of standardized tests of reading, writing, and mathematics.[3] Achievement was assessed for three different groups: (a) students in general; (b) graduating seniors; and (c) students with unusually low levels of performance in reading and math.[4]

HSC's hopes for these different groups differed somewhat. With respect to students in general, HSC hoped to do as well as the feeder schools, not necessarily better. This reflected the belief that if standardized achievement was equal to that of other schools and HSC was superior in other areas, the school would be fulfilling its mission without sacrificing traditional criteria of school success.

Overall, data from the evaluations show that HSC students performed at a level comparable to students in the control and comparison groups during the 1971-74 years. While race differences were often found, with blacks scoring lower than whites, these differences occurred both at HSC and in the feeder schools. Thus, HSC achieved its goal of having its students achieve as well as a comparable group of students in the regular high schools.

HSC wanted to show that graduating seniors improved from year to year. Such improvements were not found. Graduating seniors at HSC did show gains in reading and math from the end of their junior year to the end of their senior year, but these gains were not statistically significant. In addition, each year HSC seniors scored slightly higher than seniors in the control and comparison groups at the feeder schools. However, these differences were also not significant. Using this criterion of achievement, then, HSC did not measure up to its goal.

Considerable effort was devoted to poor readers and math students. All reading and math teachers learned the Gattegno "Words in Color" method to use with these students. In addition, a consultant well versed in the Gattegno approach was hired. Tests were developed to screen students in reading and math, and class sizes of 10 or less were established for remedial math and reading. Students with these difficulties were thus identified and provided special help, both tutorial and in classes. Indeed, in response to the evaluation question, "Did you receive any special help with reading or mathematics (e.g. special classes, tutoring, conferences with your teacher)," 95 percent of poor readers and math students at HSC responded "yes," compared to less than 40 percent of the comparable groups at the feeder school. In terms of effort, HSC was very active in identifying and providing special help for students needing it most.

The overall impact of these efforts, then, was somewhat mixed over the two years these programs were in place. Poor readers significantly improved the first year but not the second. Neither poor writers nor those poor in math significantly improved either year, though gains on standardized achievement scores were made. Despite significant effort, HSC was not particularly successful in improving the standardized test scores of poor readers and math students.

Student Attendance: Comparison of attendance data from HSC and the feeder schools suffered from different definitions of attendance and forms of record keeping. The evaluation report for the 1971-72 year was candid in stating the difficulties these differences caused.

> We have found it difficult to obtain accurate records on student attendance at either HSC or at Hillhouse and Cross High Schools. Official school records seem most precise with respect

to whether a student is in school on a given day; however, as students tell us, establishing one's presence in school is one thing and going to class is another. We will not, for these reasons, compare student attendance rates from school to school (Hawley et al., 1973, pp. 56-57).

Comparative data were gathered during the other two years (1972-74) at both HSC and the feeder schools. For the 72-73 year, HSC average daily attendance was 89.6 percent compared to 85.7 percent at the feeder schools. The following year, the figures were 77.5 percent at HSC and 84.4percent at the feeder schools. If one considers only those HSC students in residence for the entire year (excluding dropouts, late arrival, etc.), the percentage rises to 82 percent. In general, however, the attendance rates at HSC and the feeder schools seem quite comparable, though fluctuating over time.

Data were also gathered on whether students with prior attendance problems at HSC improved from year to year. Poor attenders were defined as those who had attended less than 60 percent of their classes the previous year. During the 1972-73 year, this group increased in attendance to 85 percent. The following year poor attenders increased to 72 percent The first year represents a significant increase, the second does not. Still, put together, HSC was reasonably successful in its efforts to pull poor attenders into school over time. Further, as the evaluation report suggests: "There were dramatic instances in the behavior of individual students which are not reflected in the analysis here. For example, one student missed more than eighty percent of his classes during 1969-70 while at another city high school. In 1971-72 at HSC, he attended more than eighty percent of his classes" (Hawley et al., 1973, p. 59).

Post-high school plans: To an unusual degree, teachers at HSC shared responsibility with the guidance counselor for advice around post-high school plans. The guidance counselor had responsibility for insuring that records and recommendations were sent on time and for collecting and making available information about colleges and vocational programs. Teachers played a more personal role with students around guidance. And, as the school evolved, a small group of four teachers was created specifically to deliver guidance services to seniors. These efforts, plus the previously mentioned outreach of the Facilitator and COP coordination to promote the school more generally, seemed to work well for students.

The post-high school goal was stated in the 1971-72 evaluation as follows: "All students who seriously desire college or technical school admission will be accepted for such further education." To quote the evaluation:

It appears that this very ambitious objective has been attained. Of the graduating seniors who completed one or both of the questionnaires we administered during 1971-72, all of those who indicated that they were hoping to attend college, art, or trade school were accepted by one or more of the colleges or schools to which they applied. A small minority of students whose academic performance would have assured their entry to college did not seek admission . . . Overall, eighty percent of the graduating seniors planned to further their formal education in the immediate future (Hawley et al., 1973, p. 90).

The report continues in the ideological spirit of HSC:

Of course, going to college may be no more a measure of personal accomplishments than pursuit of a job after high school graduation. While we do not mean to imply that a school's success can be measured by the proportion of its graduating class that undertakes higher education, it may be reassuring to many HSC parents, and to many parents considering the possibility of HSC for their children, that HSC graduates have experienced substantial success when seeking college admission. Indeed, some admissions officers apparently felt that students who could perform reasonably well in a relatively open and unstructured environment like that at HSC were also good prospects for the comparatively undisciplined learning situations that students find in college (op. cit, pp. 97-98).

For the two following years, HSC sent 72 percent and 65 percent of its graduates to post-high school education, a significantly higher percentage than the comparison groups in the feeder schools. These consistent differences strongly suggest that HSC had a positive influence on its students' pursuit of education beyond high school, even though HSC was no more successful in improving standardized test scores than the other schools. HSC's efforts at providing guidance and their work at selling themselves and their ideas were pivotal in creating this important difference.

School Attitudes, Social Attitudes, and Personal Qualities

Both because of origins and ideology, HSC placed great importance on the quality of school life for students and the impact the school could have on student attitudes: the so-called affective side of education. As a revolt against bureaucracy, HSC wanted to create a satisfying learning environment responsive to student concerns and needs. As a reaction to social tensions, HSC wanted to improve race relations, lower the incidence of racial conflicts, and foster positive interracial attitudes. As a socializing institution, it wished to develop students' sense of control over their lives and provide structure and personal support to promote this goal. During the 1971-74 years, the evaluation dealt with each of these areas.

School Attitudes: School attitudes covered a range of different areas of student opinion, including: perceived ability to influence school policy, mutual affection and respect between students and teachers, the importance of assuming personal responsibility for one's own education, and general school satisfaction. Each of these four areas represented specific goals that HSC teachers had articulated to the evaluation team.[5]

Perceived ability to influence school policy at HSC was assessed by student response to a six-item scale measuring student influence (e.g. "I feel I have a real influence on the way my school is run," or "The members of the administration are likely to consider the wishes of students whenever they make a decision"). For each of the three years (1971-74), HSC students scored higher on this measure than did control and comparison group students from the feeder schools. HSC successfully increased the sense of perceived student influence in the school.

The assessment of mutual affection and respect between students and teachers consisted of two short scales, one measuring affection, and the other, respect. These scales were given during two of the three years. The affection scale measured mutual liking among students and teachers, as well as teacher approachability and success at their work (e.g. "Teachers are easily available to talk to or get help from," and "The teachers in my school are generally doing a good job"). HSC students rated mutual affection significantly higher than did control students for both years.

The mutual respect scale included such items as "Most students at my school have respect for the teachers as people," and "Most teachers at my school have respect for the students as people." HSC students rated mutual respect significantly lower than did control students. The specific explanation for this finding is by no means clear. That students generally liked their teachers and found them approachable is consistent with all we know about the school. Lack of respect may imply that liking a teacher and respecting a teacher are opposite ends of the same continuum (and indeed the negative correlation of these two scales was significant). It could also refer to the behavior of a small subset of teachers who did not take the job seriously and sometimes missed class without notifying students. Regardless, the data do suggest that one possible negative consequence of HSC's informal and congenial atmosphere was in the area of mutual respect.

The importance of assuming personal responsibility for one's education was assessed by a scale measuring the degree to which HSC fostered the development of personal initiative (e.g. "Having a chance to work on my own on some subject I want to learn about is important to me" or "If things don't go the way I want them to in this school, I should try to change the things that are wrong"). On this scale, HSC students did not differ from those in the control groups.

General school satisfaction was assessed by a scale given to HSC students and control/comparison group students and by questions given to students who completed the Classroom Environment Scale each year. The former compares HSC student satisfaction with the school satisfaction of those students who wanted to attend HSC but were unsuccessful in the lottery. The latter deals with how satisfied HSC students were compared to feeder school students in general.

A seven-item satisfaction scale was developed, including such items as "Most of the time I'm proud that I go to my school" and "The courses I'm taking are generally suited to my needs." This scale was used during two of the three years (1971-72, 1972-73) and each year showed that HSC students reported higher general school satisfaction than did students in the control groups.

Classroom satisfaction data focused more on how satisfied students were with various aspects of their classroom experience. Data gathered in classrooms during the 1972-73 and 1973-74 years revealed the following: across both years, HSC students reported their classrooms as more satisfying, easier places to get academic help if they wanted it, and easier places to talk about personal matters. For the 1972-73 year they also reported learning more actual material, but this significant difference disappeared during the 1973-1974 year.

Thus, in the broad area of school attitudes, the HSC student experience was one of strong satisfaction with school in general and classes in particular. The students expressed a clear sense that teachers were accessible for academic and personal help and that the school was responsive to student concerns. In addition, for one of the years, HSC students reported learning more material in their classes than did feeder school students. On the other hand, respect between students and teachers was not as high at HSC as among control group students in the feeder schools.

SOCIAL ATTITUDES AND PERSONAL QUALITIES

The social attitudes of concern to HSC faculty focused on the promotion of tolerance for social and political diversity and more positive interracial attitudes. The personal qualities they wished to encourage in students included self-esteem and a sense of control over one's life.

Social Attitudes: Three different scales were developed to measure social attitudes. The *Social and Political Diversity Scale* assessed student tolerance for the expression of communist, black militant, atheist, and feminist philosophies in high school and public settings.[6] (e.g. "Should a communist be allowed to teach in your high school?" "Should books by people in Women's Liberation be available in the libraries of the city?"). In each of the 1971-74 years, HSC students showed more tolerance for social and political diversity than did students in the control/ comparison group.

The other two scales were more directly related to interracial attitudes. The *Social Distance Scale* assessed student tolerance for being involved with whites or blacks in a variety of situations which differed in terms of "social distance." Being willing to share a locker at school would involve more social distance than being willing to marry someone of the other race. Blacks responded in terms of social distance toward whites, and whites in terms of social distance toward blacks. Only during the 1973-74 year did HSC students report preferring less social distance than their counterparts in the feeder schools. Race differences, however, were consistent across years. Each year, whites across all schools favored less social distance between themselves and blacks than did blacks between themselves and whites.

The final interracial attitude scale was the *Black Fault for Discrimination Scale*, tapping student opinions of the extent to which blacks should be held responsible for discrimination (e.g. "The best opportunities always go to whites" vs."Blacks have not prepared themselves to take advantage of the opportunities which come their way" or "Even when blacks make an attempt to 'fit in' they still meet with serious discrimination" vs."Any black who is educated and does what is proper will be accepted"). This scale consistently showed that HSC students blamed blacks less for discrimination than did students in the control/comparison groups.

Personal Qualities: To assess the impact of the school on more basic aspects of personality, *measures of self-esteem and locus of control* were also given. The measure of self-esteem, adapted from the California Psychological Inventory (Gough, 1957), assessed student self-confidence and assertiveness in social situations, while the Rotter (1966) Internal-External Locus of Control Scale assessed students' general sense of personal control over and responsibility for events. No significant school differences emerged on either of these measures, leaving two possible interpretations. First, HSC may have had no effect on these personal qualities, despite its intensive efforts to provide a school environment which promoted choice and student influence. Second, the time period between school entry and testing (approximately eight months) was not sufficient to allow changes in these basic personality dimensions to emerge. If the evaluators had been able to follow a large enough number of HSC students over a greater period of time, this possibility could have been further studied. This was not possible, however, given the shifting population in the various schools and the resources of the evaluation team.

SUMMARY

To summarize, HSC was consistently able to influence attitudes toward tolerance for political and social diversity and reduce attitudes which blamed blacks for the discrimination they face. HSC had no consistent effect on reducing social distance between blacks and whites, a somewhat more specific aspect of interracial relationships. This specific finding fits with other data previously reported suggesting HSC was excellent in reducing negative indices of interracial contact (e.g. hardly any fights or discipline issues related to interracial problems), but not particularly successful in promoting more positive interracial contact (e.g. blacks mostly socializing with blacks and whites with whites).

Finally, though HSC provided a school environment where students felt empowered and influential, this immediate sense of control at school did not affect their overall sense of personal control over their lives. This broader goal may have been unrealistic, given that school is only one of the influences on inner-city adolescents. In many other spheres they may not indeed have much control.

Different Strokes for Different Folks: Applicants, Transfers, and Individual Differences in the School Experience

The preceding has outlined how students in general perceived HSC and what some of HSC's effects were across a wide variety of cognitive and affective domains. As an alternative school, however, the question "who does best at such a school" was constantly on the minds of teachers. Over time, teachers formed several opinions about what kinds of students were most likely to succeed, including self-starting students, students committed to completing high school, and students interested in crafting their own education. Teachers also began to articulate a concern about those students who could too easily slip through the cracks. In particular, there was some concern, especially on the part of black teachers, that the structure of the school discriminated against blacks, albeit unintentionally.

The evaluation data, plus other research conducted in the school during this time, add to this picture. The first source of pertinent data involves who chose to apply to HSC compared to those who chose to stay in their current school. The second involves students who transferred in and out of HSC. Finally, data exist on how different groups of HSC students perceived various aspects of the school. Taken together, these kinds of data add richness to the teacher impressions of teachers about the kinds of students best suited for HSC.

Who Applied. According to teachers, the nature of the HSC student body changed over time. When school opened, a greater percentage of students were attracted to the school for positive reasons; e.g. wanting and being able to take advantage of the kind of learning environment HSC offered. Several students who began HSC in its initial year were in leadership roles in the Black Student Union at Hillhouse, for example. Over time, however, an increasing number of students entered HSC as a "school of last resort." These students tended to be more poorly prepared academically, had less positive images of school, and were more prone to attendance problems. The following data refer to that time period before the major change in the student body.

Information was available for the 1973-74 year on who applied to the school. During September 1973, data were gathered on a sample of students first entering HSC and a sample of students in the feeder schools who had not applied to HSC. The two samples were comparable in terms of grade level and included both black and white students. Students not only responded to the various achievement, satisfaction, and attitude measures previously discussed; they answered a number of other specific questions about their school experience and attitudes.

With respect to achievement level, several differences emerged. On the standardized tests of reading and writing, entering HSC students scored significantly higher than feeder school students who did not apply. No overall school differences were found for math achievement. However, school by race interactions were found on each of these three measures of achievement. In the area of reading and writing, black students at HSC scored slightly (but not significantly) higher than blacks in the feeder schools, but whites entering HSC scored significantly higher than feeder school whites. In mathematics, HSC whites scored significantly higher than feeder school whites, but blacks scored significantly lower.

These data suggest that HSC had a different kind of pull for blacks and whites. Whites who applied were, overall, more academically successful, while blacks who applied tended to be more representative of feeder school blacks in terms of reading and writing achievement, though less successful in math. As groups, blacks and whites may have opted to attend HSC for somewhat different reasons. In response to a question about what course of study students were taking, blacks at HSC reported more interest in "business/vocational" than did blacks at the feeder schools, who were more likely to report "college prep." The reverse was true for whites.

Students who applied to HSC also differed from non-applicants in their attitudes. HSC applicants reported more tolerance for social and political diversity and blamed blacks less for discrimination. These overall differences were mostly attributable to differences in white attitudes, however. Blacks who applied to HSC had the same attitudes about social and political diversity as non-applicant blacks. Whites who applied to HSC, however, held much more positive attitudes about this diversity than whites who did not.

On the social distance scale, which assessed how close blacks prefer to be to whites and vice versa, there was no overall difference between students who had applied to HSC and those who did not. However, blacks at HSC preferred greater social distance from whites than did blacks at the feeder schools, while whites at HSC preferred less social distance from blacks at HSC than they did at the feeder schools.

These different patterns of black and white attitudes at HSC may have reflected a stronger ideological commitment to race issues than was present in the feeder school students. Black students preferred a more separatist stance while whites viewed positive race relations as involving less social distance between blacks and whites. Regardless, the data suggest that blacks and whites at HSC did have attitudes about interracial issues which differed from each other in their behavioral implications.

The data also suggested that applicants differed from nonapplicants in terms of their orientation toward staying in school. Asked if they had "*ever* thought of dropping out of school," HSC students were more likely than nonapplicants to say "yes." When asked whether or not they had thought about it recently, there was no difference between applicants and nonapplicants. In addition, no differences were found between these groups in level of self-esteem or general sense of control over their life. The overall differences, then, focused on the areas of achievement, interracial attitudes, and general attitude toward school.

Who transferred out of and into HSC. While everyone at HSC was a transfer student from another high school, this section refers to two groups of students: (a) those who initially applied to HSC, were accepted into the school, and subsequently transferred back to their original school, and (b) those who initially did *not* to apply to HSC but who later decided to apply. Both groups provide information on which students found HSC a positive alternative and which did not. Students in these samples responded to the same sets of questions as did those in the preceding section on "who applied."

Those transferring out of HSC back to their original school: In contrast to the students who decided not to apply to HSC, this group had actual experience at HSC ranging from several weeks to over a year. It included 37 students — 23 black and 14 white — who returned to their original school after attending HSC.

Differences between students who stayed at HSC and those who transferred back were not evident in the area of achievement; the differences were evident in social attitudes and attitudes toward school. HSC students who transferred back were significantly less tolerant of social and political diversity and preferred increased social distance in interracial contact than did HSC students who did not transfer. Transfer students professed less interest and affection for the school and were less generally satisfied with HSC, even though they had been at the school only a month when the data were gathered. They were also less likely to endorse the notion that students should take responsibility for their own education, reported less participation in classes, and were less likely to agree that HSC was achieving its purpose. They thought that a lower percentage of teachers at HSC were "really good," and a higher percentage "really bad," than HSC students who stayed in the school.

Data further suggest that these transfer students were responding to HSC in particular rather than school in general. While they reported caring less about HSC, there was no difference between transfer students and nontransfer students in whether they thought about dropping out of school entirely or whether they "ever cared about school."

Those transferring out of the feeder schools after initially not applying to HSC: The pattern of results for those 20 students (9 black, 11 white) who were originally in a sample of nonapplicants, but later decided to apply to HSC, is essentially the reverse of those who transferred from HSC back to the feeder schools. This group did not differ in academic achievement, but were more tolerant of social and political diversity and blamed blacks less for discrimination than did students who stayed at the feeder schools. These students were less satisfied with their school in general, participated less in class, and agreed less that their school was achieving its purpose.

In sum, both groups of transferring students suggest that attitudinal variables and satisfaction with the current school were the primary factors influencing the decision to transfer. Level of academic achievement did not differentiate either group, nor were differences found in such personality variables as locus of perceived control over one's life or self-esteem.

An Examination of Person-Environment Fit. One other source of data is available which bears on the question of how HSC was experienced by different groups of students. It comes from a study conducted during 1974-75. The study was designed to see how the coping style of social exploration (see Edwards, 1971) affected student satisfaction in HSC and the feeder schools. High social explorers prefer novelty and seek out new situations, while low social explorers prefer routine and similarity of experience. The initial logic was straightforward. Students high in social exploration would be more satisfied in HSC because HSC fostered, indeed demanded, social exploration from its students (see Gooden, 1975; Schreck, 1976).

The study involved 315 juniors in high school; 84 from HSC and 231 from the feeder schools. All students were given a measure of social exploration and asked to respond to a 27-item satisfaction questionnaire dealing with four different kinds of satisfaction with the school: (1) general satisfaction, (2) satisfaction with rules, (3) amount of school-related discussion with parents and friends, and (4) degree of active class involvement. The total sample was divided at the median according to their scores on the social exploration scale. High and low social explorers in each type of school were compared on each of the four areas of satisfaction. The analyses included level of social exploration (high/low), race, gender, and type of school.

The data provided a complex picture. First, a number of school differences emerged. HSC was seen as more generally satisfying, with rules being emphasized the right amount (e.g. not too much), and classes being more involving. This primarily confirms and extends what was found during earlier years at the school. Across all schools, high explorers were more generally satisfied with school and were more active in their classes. Only one race difference was found across all schools: blacks thought that rules should be more strict and students should have more discipline than did whites. There were no gender effects.

Level of social exploration did not, as predicted, affect the school experience across a wide variety of areas. The only area where the student coping style significantly interacted with the different schools involved rules. High and low social explorers were equally satisfied with the emphasis on rules in the feeder schools, but high social explorers at HSC wanted much less emphasis on rules than did low social explorers. More important in school satisfaction was the race of the student. Significant school by race interactions were found on three of the four areas of satisfaction. With respect to satisfaction with class involvement, blacks at HSC were *somewhat* more active in classes than blacks at the feeder schools, while whites were *much* more active. The same pattern occurred in the area of satisfaction with rule emphasis, where blacks were slightly (not significantly) more satisfied at HSC than at the feeder school, and whites *much* more satisfied at HSC. Finally, in the area of school-related discussion with parents and friends, blacks at HSC discussed school less than blacks at the feeder schools, while whites at HSC discussed school more than whites at the feeder schools.

CONCLUSION

Data on the student experience suggest that the overall HSC environment was consistent with its ideological commitments. Classes were seen as personal, noncompetitive, and involving. Teachers were described as friendly, caring, and innovative. With respect to HSC's impact on students, standardized measures of achievement showed HSC students to be comparable to their feeder school counterparts and to attend school at the same rate. A higher percentage, however, pursued post-high school education. HSC student attitudes toward school were positive and interracial attitudes, particularly for whites, were changed. No change was found in such basic areas as self-esteem and sense of control over one's life. The school attracted and retained students who held attitudes congruent with HSC's ideology and goals. Finally, some evidence exists that HSC attracted blacks and whites for different reasons, and that whites at HSC differed more from their feeder school counterparts than did blacks. While the overall pattern of findings on the student experience is complex, there can be no doubt that HSC created a distinctive environment which affected its students in many different ways.

CHAPTER 8

Whatever Happened to the School Where They Tried All the New Ideas?

During the 1983-84 school year, the author returned to New Haven to discover what had become of HSC during the intervening 10 years. HSC had been founded as a teacher-run school whose policies and structures were intended to educate and empower. The fate of that vision is the subject of the present chapter. During its first four years, HSC engaged in an ongoing debate about how to maintain its basic ideology in the face of limited resources and the unanticipated consequences of its initial vision. As we have seen, HSC did indeed undergo significant internal changes, while still maintaining its basic ideology. Whatever happened to the school where they tried all the new ideas?

Once again, the school was cooperative about providing information on its history and current status. Several teachers whose experience with HSC spanned at least 10 years were interviewed on numerous occasions; records and documents of the preceding 10 years were made available, and students were given short questionnaires. From these sources emerged a picture of how HSC evolved between 1974 to 1984, providing a 14-year period over which to assess the creation and evolution of the school. Condensing a decade into a chapter unfortunately required both oversimplifications and omissions. Four topics have been selected to link HSC's later development with its early history: critical events in the chronology of the school; changes in the structure and organization of the school; student perceptions of HSC in 1984; and reflections on the development of the school by teachers who had spent at least a decade with HSC, a few of whom had been there since its earliest years.

Critical Events in Survival and Consolidation

At least three critical events occurred during the mid-1970's which held important implications for how HSC evolved: the change from being housed in the community to acquiring their own centralized location, the shift from being primarily externally funded to full support by the New Haven Public School System, and the successful application for a federal grant to disseminate knowledge based on the HSC experience to other school systems. Each of these events carried different implications for HSC's further development.

FROM "IN THE COMMUNITY" TO "IN THE SCHOOL BUILDING"

In January 1975, HSC moved for the last time — its eighth move (counting both units of the school) since it opened five years before. The site was a deserted elementary school which was the oldest school building in the city at over 50 years old. "We all helped move," recalled a teacher, "students, teachers, everyone. It didn't take too long and was an exhilarating experience — moving into our own building."

The school itself was in need of paint, had one leaky spot in the roof, and was furnished with chairs appropriate for elementary school students. Few school system resources available to other schools came with the building. It had no custodian, so teachers had to perform that role; there was no bus service to and from school for the students, and there was no cafeteria to serve hot lunches. Still, it was theirs.

Acquiring a building represented a compromise between the perception of how to survive as a school and how to maintain the autonomy to experiment and innovate. On the one hand, the push for a building was one aspect of HSC's strategy for survival. The argument to the Superintendent was that a building would help HSC consolidate its strengths and allow a more efficient use of resources. Further, it would provide a tangible symbol of its credibility and commitment from the school system.

Internally, moving into a single building raised the specter of becoming more like every other school in the city. Teachers did not unanimously support the move, and at least one teacher, in retrospect, felt that the move to the building signalled the beginning of teacher cynicism about what HSC could accomplish as an alternative. Students were concerned about how the move might affect their autonomy. Indeed, one rumor which spread around the school was that HSC might institute hall passes now that it had its own building.

The move into a school building also set in motion processes which, over time, significantly affected the school's internal workings and its relationship to the school system. "We had to learn to live together for the first time," said one teacher. "There was really no time for planning — anticipating what the move might mean to us in terms of how *we* would get along with each other. It brought together departments from the two units with different perspectives — each with a strong tradition of doing things their own way." "It also increased our visibility to each other and meant that accountability was higher," said another. "When the teachers were all over the place, we never really thought about it, and when we did, we couldn't figure out what to do. Now, we knew about each other every day."

Externally, the building signalled a significant increase in the amount of contact HSC had with the broader school system. In clarifying its building-related needs, HSC discovered a variety of resources available to other schools of which it had not previously been aware. Monies for science equipment, books, and other educational supplies became accessible. Negotiations over renovations to the building began.

In short, the move to a single building increased the interdependence among teachers in the school and between the school and the school system. These changes incurred both costs and benefits. Teachers were more obviously accountable to each other, a potential threat to autonomy, yet were more accessible to each other for support, consultation, and collegiality. Further, HSC learned how to obtain needed resources from the school system. The cost of this was the increased ability of the school system to influence the school. Though there was ambivalence over the move, the most dominant perspective was voiced by a teacher. "Moving into the building played a strong role in changing the character of the school," said one teacher. "A school without walls made sense in 1970, a building made sense in 1975."

THE SHIFT TO LOCAL FUNDING

HSC began as a school funded by external sources. These origins had several initial advantages. First, it allowed experimentation and some space to breathe without being under high surveillance from the broader school system. Second, because it required few resources from the local system, HSC's existence did not force a confrontation with the school system about how to allocate its finite resources. External funding gave HSC a grace period to make the case for its viability as an alternative school. From the beginning, however, it was clear that HSC could not ultimately survive unless it was incorporated into the public school budget like any other public school.

As external funding neared it conclusion, HSC's Facilitating Unit put extensive energy into deciding how to incorporate the school into the system in a way that preserved its ideology and structure. To this end, HSC initiated ongoing meetings with the Superintendent which began in spring 1974 and continued during the following year.

HSC had cause to be concerned about the Superintendent's support, for he had expressed skepticism about the school and had himself heard rumors of organizational confusion at the school. One specific issue of concern was the Superintendent's decision to replace the Yale evaluators for the 1974-75 year with evaluators whom he knew personally. HSC was unclear about the motivation for this change, and worried that the Superintendent was hiring his own team to gather data detrimental to the school. The group auditing the evaluation, however, suggested a more open-minded agenda.

> According to local administrators, the primary reason for employing a new evaluation team relates to the fact that the local program may attempt to replicate itself throughout the New Haven School System and in other locations during the 75-76 school year. As preparation for this replication effort, HSC is attempting to determine the degree to which another group of outside evaluators will obtain results as favorable as those obtained by ERS (the Yale-based group) (Cohen, Claussen, & Hurst, 1974, p. 2).

HSC did have several points in its favor, however. It had shown a responsiveness to the Superintendent's concerns, made proactive plans around its consolidation which it put in writing, and had internal support within the administration itself, most noticeably from Sam Nash, who helped stimulate and shape the original HSC concept. Further, HSC had shown that it could attract a meaningful number of students each year, had developed some national visibility, and had a few local success stories of students who were in serious trouble in their prior schools but who flourished at HSC.

HSC also had in its favor a series of positive evaluations conducted over the previous few years by Yale-based researchers. These reports showed that HSC was equal to the other high schools in promoting academic achievement, while creating more positive school attitudes and sending more of its students to post-high school education. The 1974-75 evaluation, conducted by the Superintendent's own team and using essentially the same measures and evaluation design, found the same positive results.

In fall 1975, HSC achieved its goal of being fully funded by the New Haven Public Schools. Because of budget cuts within the system, full-time staff was reduced from 20 to 15 teachers, but funding for the teachers and the building was secure. Reflecting on the various factors influencing the decision, teachers and administrators cited several factors mentioned above. But Sam Nash had additional ideas about forces that supported HSC's survival.

> When something is around long enough, it generates its own momentum. Doing away with it would require more system energy than keeping it, particularly when it seems to be doing

well and not causing problems. This worked in HSC's favor. In addition, by this time there were other alternatives that had sprung up either in New Haven or with other local school systems. The fact that they were around and were successful created a momentum of legitimacy which supported HSC as an *idea* and as an institution.

The switch to local funding ended the central importance that survival had played in the school's early history. It validated the teachers' belief that their ideas were viable and their struggles worthwhile. It also freed up the Facilitator and the Facilitating Unit to focus on other issues, such as the push for internal coherence. Most importantly, it allowed HSC to look forward to planning a future it could count on. The immediate vehicle for this was their successful application to the U.S. Office of Education for a Dissemination grant. This grant provided a further impetus to crystallize HSC's own identity and increase its national visibility.

THE DISSEMINATION GRANT

Discussion about applying for funding to disseminate the HSC experience had been ongoing since 1974, as evidenced in the earlier quoted audit report for the 74-75 evaluation. Such a grant would validate the success of the school, provide external resources in carrying out school-related objectives, and involve HSC in a National Diffusion Network with educational alternatives throughout the country. Further, the preparation of such a proposal would aid in clarifying the organizational structure and processes of the school, for HSC had to convince the funding source that it could not only articulate its philosophy but show concretely how was implemented.

The application was prepared during the 1975-76 year, and outlined the five core elements of HSC which the staff deemed critical for other potential alternative schools:

1) A target audience of disaffected students at the secondary educational level.

2) Small size, no more than 300 students.

3) School of choice, students may not be forcibly placed in the program.

4) Shared decision-making, at a minimum, staff members as a group must be actively involved in decisions about curriculum and guidance.

5) A significantly different school experience for students

through either curriculum and/or guidance structures. It is important that the emphasis be on the process of education, not just on the product; i.e. both affective and cognitive goals need to be stressed.

The proposal was approved to begin in fall 1976, and for three years HSC was funded to carry out demonstration and dissemination activities. These activities included both external and internal tasks, each of which aided the school in different ways. For example, the grant supported the travel of HSC staff, particularly Ed Linehan, Dissemination Project Director, to many school districts across the country to discuss educational alternatives. Linehan and other staff participated in regional and national meetings of the National Diffusion Network. These activities provided HSC staff with new ideas and forums for discussion. Further, they brought national attention to the school system.

Internally, carrying out of the grant required developing materials to describe HSC's philosophy and structure. These materials not only provided an update on how the school was changing during the late 1970's, but the need to create them supported the ongoing efforts of the school to articulate its internal structure.

Changes in the Organizational Structure of the School: 1974-1984

By 1974, momentum was growing at HSC to attend to its internal processes and structures. The consolidated location, secure funding, and dissemination grant increased HSC's freedom and resources for looking inward. The importance of attending to this internal evolution came not only from staff concern about how the school was working; it was augmented by two external forces which impacted on HSC.

First, during the mid-1970's, HSC attracted fewer and fewer academically oriented students. "Our 'we can work with anybody' fantasies got us in trouble," said one teacher. "We would admit anyone who wanted in. After a while, we became a kind of dumping ground for students who couldn't make it in the other schools. Actually, one year we had *no one* with reading scores above grade level. We also began to get special education kids with learning disabilities and we didn't have the resources to deal with them." The second external force was an increase in required credits which the New Haven School System instituted during the later 1970's. These additional requirements, reflecting the national reaction against permissiveness in schools, decreased HSC's freedom to run its educational program as it wished.

Out of the various internal and external forces came a number of changes between 1974 and 1984. Changes carried across roles, structures, policies, and norms governing the ongoing organizational life of the school.

ROLE SHIFTS: LEADERSHIP CHANGES AND THE ROLE OF TEACHER

Historically, the roles of leader and teacher had been sources of controversy and conflict. During the 1974-84 years, these roles altered somewhat to reflect HSC's evolution as a more coherent and differentiated setting.

Leadership Changes: Both the leaders themselves and their primary organizational tasks changed from 1974 to 1984. During the early years of the school, George Foote occupied the role of Facilitator, and the group called the Facilitating Unit was formed to serve a global leadership function. In the words of Foote, the Facilitating Unit "allowed the leader to lead by developing support for various positions." As a basic organizational structure, the FU has continued to function effectively to the present time.

In 1977, George Foote, after serving 8 years as Facilitator, decided not to seek re-election for the following year. While a variety of factors were involved, the changing demands placed on the leader and the general frustrations of trying to lead a participatory democracy had taken their toll. "The external stuff was the most fun," recalled Foote, "hustling funds for a good idea, being in on the ground floor, negotiating with people. I was often 'on the road' looking for sites. Once the school became secure, it was a different ball game. And moving into the building ended the 'in the community image' — things became more school-like. But inside the school, I often felt incompetent because I couldn't do what I was supposed to do. I was authorized to worry about everything but I didn't have the authority to do anything."

"Foote was the key," recalled Nash. "He was steadfast in his commitment to getting the school started and seeing that it survived. He had a knack for being in the right place at the right time and knowing when the right time was." Foote stayed at the school two more years before leaving to start another alternative school in New Haven.

Ed Linehan succeeded Foote in the Facilitator position in 1978. "Ed was very active in moving the school to look at itself," said a teacher. "The student population was changing, we now worried more about inside threats than outside threats. The student changes required more structure and there was less internal support for the original vision of the school. Ed was the right person for the job because he was very interested in internal issues and was organized." "It was a logical progression," said Alice Mick. "Ed helped get the school together as an organization so we could be more focused about the educational agenda, not the survival agenda but the organizational agenda."

Linehan, however, reported that the staff was not at all meek in response to his leadership efforts. "They wanted a more aggressive disciplinarian," he reported, "and they didn't want to be as responsible for everything any more. I was willing to put my ideas out there, but there was still real resistance and some anger about my leading. 'Kill the leader' didn't go away as a dynamic just because the leader changed." "Ed got the bureaucracy of the school organized," recalled Alice Mick, "though the school still looked somewhat permissive in general." After three years, Ed voluntarily stepped down and was replaced by Alice Mick.

"Ed was into structuring," recalled one teacher, "while Alice was into process, what our norms were, our definition of ourselves as a school." "I didn't think the school could last unless there was more order, norms about control, and general rules," Alice recalled. "In many ways I was building on the structuring process which started when George was Facilitator and got more focused with Ed. I began to push for the importance of having the staff authorize the leader to enforce boundaries and the value of developing shared norms about how the school would operate. Still, some teachers still feel that a strong leader equals the disenfranchisement of teachers, and they fight it."

Under Mick's leadership, HSC furthered its efforts at increasing its organizational coherence, not only in terms of the development of shared norms, but of policies as well. These developments will be briefly discussed in a following section.

In sum, the leadership issues at HSC showed both continuity and change during the 1974-84 years. The Facilitating Unit remained the central leadership group, while remaining highly accountable to the staff as a whole. The role of Facilitator changed hands as the demands for differing kinds of leadership in the school changed and as the personal agenda of the leaders changed. "I don't think that you can define the stages in the school in terms of who the leader was," said Linehan. "Rather, the school itself needed different things at different times and we had people who could do what was needed. That's always been a strength of the school — having people around who can do what's necessary."

CHANGES IN THE TEACHER ROLE

In the planning stages, teachers carved out a very expansive role for themselves as classroom teachers, guidance counselors, links to the community, and participants in the governance of the school. Even in the early years of the school, teachers began pulling back from their initial vision of what their role could be. As was evident in the previous discussions of the COP and Policy Council, teachers had been asking too much of themselves and were stretched too thin.

During the years following 1974, this trend to consolidate the teacher role continued. Over time, for example, teachers taught the same classes more regularly as student influence over the content of courses waned. The number of outside volunteers decreased to a trickle, relieving teachers of what was once a major supervisory responsibility. Two particular aspects of the teacher role require more specific comment because of their historical salience: the seminar and guidance.

The seminar: The original intent of the seminar was for each teacher to meet with 15 students daily to share student experiences and concerns about themselves and the school. It never fulfilled its promise as a school-wide mechanism. While the seminar initially worked for some teachers, within the first few years of the school it ceased to function.

"It was revived around 1977 as the 'Family Group'," recalled one teacher. "We got the idea from the National Diffusion Network, and it served a variety of purposes." According to the 1978-79 HSC course catalogue:

> Family groups are a new approach to counseling. Students participating in Family groups will have an opportunity to share and discuss their opinions and feelings about their school experiences, growing up, friends, and their future. The purpose of the group is for members to gain a better understanding of themselves and others and to help make their school experience more successful.

Unlike previous times, Family group was offered as an elective course and was taught only by those teachers interested in teaching it. Later, during the early 1980's, Family group became a *required* course for all incoming students as a way of introducing them to the school. "It's now part of the definition of the school," said a teacher. "It represents the way we've tried to keep alive the humanistic concern for students and their school experience."

While the original conception of the seminar failed in its specifics, the concept of having a setting for students and teachers to interact on a personal level thus remained as a metaphor for HSC's values. "The family group was a very important resurgence of the old seminar idea," said Alice Mick. "It served a critical role in holding the school and its identity together."

Guidance: In like manner, the guidance aspect of the teacher role has remained part of the job description for HSC teachers. To quote Alice Mick:

> Teachers are still assigned a group of guidance students. They help students figure out their schedules, call parents if there is a problem. Their actual involvement with students in school has changed somewhat over the last four years [1980-84]. Teachers used to be called out of class when one of their guidance students got in some difficulty — we used to see the guidance function as *so* important. Now guidance issues are responded to less immediately in favor of a classwork emphasis. In this sense, guidance teachers are less involved with students than they had been. Teachers, of course, are now required to teach more because credit requirements for students have gone up and our staff hasn't increased in proportion. So there really is no free time for our staff.

Thus, over time, the teacher role at HSC became increasingly consolidated. Role boundaries became sharper and more consensus was achieved on how teachers defined their job. While structural changes are evident — particularly the switch in the seminar from a school-wide requirement to an elective course to a kind of introduction to the school — the teacher role still emphasizes a personalized and humane education for students.

The Fate of Empowerment Structures: The COP and the Policy Council

Earlier chapters have discussed the first four years of the COP and the Policy Council, concluding that the former was far more successful than the latter in achieving stated goals. The longer-range fate of these structures follows.

THE COMMUNITY ORIENTATION PROGRAM (COP)

During its early years, the COP struggled from a somewhat disorganized beginning to a program with increasing cohesion and purpose. The evaluations conducted on the COP through the 1973-74 year thus showed a positive trajectory in terms of student attendance at the community placement and enthusiasm from a meaningful number of community teachers about the program. It was hailed as a clear success.

During the years immediately following, however, many of the community placements decided not to continue working with HSC. The primary reasons were those issues discussed by Tom Nelson in his 1973 COP report: students needed to be responsible for commitments made to community teachers and community teachers needed to understand the issues that their adolescent students would pose. Both the program's broad scope—it was open to any student who had any interest—and the changing student population exacerbated these long-standing issues.

In 1974, Tom Nelson left HSC to attend law school, and Ed Linehan took over as Director of the COP. The following year he initiated a series of teacher discussions about the future of the COP, and a decision was made to reduce its size and sharpen its focus. After a year as COP Director, Linehan became director of the dissemination grant activities, and Dee Speece assumed the COP role. She related the following about the program under her leadership:

> When I started there were 150 kids placed in the community, but a good portion only stayed a few days on a placement. Too many kids weren't ready for community placement. We decided to name the program the *Career* Orientation Program and focus it mostly on kids who were not planning on going on to college. I also advocated that a career class be put in to provide support and education for students taking COP. So we'd start with a smaller group, have a class to prepare them for COP, and not send them out at the beginning but later on when they were more ready.

This idea was described as follows in the 1978-79 Dissemination documents: "The program involves students in classes and work experience placements designed to help them make more informed choices about their future. A new aspect of the program is the *Career*, which involves job placements (four hours each day) combined with classes at HSC to develop specific job and career skills."

Later, the COP program was combined with other work-study programs and was carried on by another staff member, Barbara Greenwood. Over time, however, the COP coordinator position included more administrative work related to work-study programs, and placements became more focused around job options than community learning experiences related to career decision-making. "We calculated two or three times when we would have to terminate the COP position because it essentially relied on outside money," recalled Linehan. "When the city reduced our number of staff (in the early 80's), we as a staff decided not to continue the COP." "It just didn't seem so central to the school and wasn't *that* successful," said another teacher.

Thus, the COP, HSC's primary structure through which to relate to the community as a learning laboratory, did not survive as the school evolved. Linehan reflected on its structure, its goals, and its assumptions as contributing factors:

> If I were to do it over, I'd want more goal clarity, not go in too many directions at once, figure out what you want to accomplish and for whom. *Then* I'd test it out to see if the goal was achievable *in that community.* I'd be clearer about what kids need to be able to do it. We made some wrong assumptions about how kids could handle it. And you'd need support and structure to help the community teachers cope with these experiences; they had their own set of assumptions about kids. Finally, I'd give the staff person in charge a reasonable amount of time to do it. We tried to do too much without enough resources. And it really lived on soft money.

Sam Nash, the originator of the COP idea, said "the original intent was that the COP teachers would be more connected to the school, but that never really happened. The COP became a fanning-out process, an adjunct to, not an integral part of, the school. Its conceptualization was not fully developed. We just didn't anticipate all that would be required to pull it off."

The Policy Council: The Policy Council was originally intended to provide an empowerment vehicle for parents and students to influence school policy. Even in its early days, however, it became clear that teachers wielded the most power on the Council, even though many of them wanted to see the Council succeed as a participatory governance structure. It was shifting from a policy-making group to an advisory group, even though it still theoretically had policy-making power. Alice Mick recalls:

> The Policy Council has continued to kind of stagger along. We still have both a theoretical and genuine commitment to parent participation in the school, and we maintain a lot of parent contact. The council, now, however, is mostly a parent-teacher group, although students are always invited. There's no real ongoing student involvement, however. As it was in the earlier days of the school, the council has been most active when the school is threatened — parents have *always* been very supportive. But, you know, we've never been good at *ongoing* parent involvement, the staff always does the organizing. Some programs, of course, hire a person to coordinate parent involvement in school decision-making, and we've never had the resources to do that. It's hard to describe. It's not really a policy-making group, it's more advisory. It's not really a PTA — it has

bylaws that give it power but which aren't clearly appropriate anymore. But it's still going, still very active around the hiring of teachers in particular, and we've recently decided to put more energy into recruiting parents for next year."

The preceding comments suggest that the paradoxes of empowerment which plagued the Council's early history remained over time. On the other hand, HSC's commitment to student and parent influence has also remained. "We were — and are — very responsive to both students and parents," said Alice Mick in 1984. "All the evaluation reports showed that. In a sense, by being so responsive to them we made the Policy Council less important, less critical. They could get their individual concerns met elsewhere, on a more personal basis. They knew they'd be listened to."

Such a perspective was confirmed by data gathered from students at HSC and the traditional New Haven high schools in spring 1984. On the "Perceived Ability to Influence School Policy" scale, HSC students still scored significantly higher than did students in the traditional schools. While the Policy Council itself had a checkered history over the first 14 years of the school, the school's responsiveness to its constituents had remained.

Toward Organizational Coherence: Policy Changes and the Begrudging Development of Shared Norms

As can be inferred from the above, the 1974-84 years included a variety of efforts to develop a manageable and coherent internal organization for HSC. These efforts included an examination of the curriculum and policy changes around admission, attendance, suspension, and discipline — those areas that historically had symbolized HSC's aversion to bureaucratic rules and hierarchical relationships. Behind these changes was the ongoing tension between the unusual autonomy which characterized HSC's early history and the value of developing shared norms about how the school should run.

Curriculum Revision: While efforts to develop a more shared curriculum were evident in the earlier years of the school (particularly in the June 1973 summer planning meetings), the 1975-79 years brought about a number of changes made possible by being in a single building and made necessary by the changing school population. Students' basic skill level was decreasing, absenteeism and turnover were increasing, and teacher morale was suffering. A major effort was made to screen students to aid class placement and to devote more staff time to basic skill development.

Perhaps the largest single change in the structure of the curriculum, however, involved the introduction of *Block Classes*. In prior years, classes were taught in different locations and for differing numbers of times during the week; further, students not having a class at a particular time during the day were free to go where they pleased. The document on Curriculum prepared in 1978 as part of the Dissemination grant paints a very different picture as it describes the class schedule in general and Block Class in particular.

> "Regular classes at the High School in the Community are scheduled between 8 A.M. and 1 P.M. as follows:
>
> | A Period | 8:10-9:00 |
> | B Period | 9:10-12:00 |
> | C Period | 12:10-1:00 |
>
> The B Period Block Class represents the core of the student's curriculum at HSC. After four weeks in a Block Class, a student can earn half year's credit in a subject. This three-hour class allows students to have an intensive learning experience. They can see more clearly the goals of a particular cause and can have clear accomplishments over a short period of time. The Block Class also offers teachers the opportunity to experiment with several learning environments. Block Classes are generally taught by a team of two teachers.

Thus, HSC's curriculum became tighter and more focused on the changing educational needs of its incoming students, but remained innovative in designing structures and courses congruent with its educational philosophy. Its "looking inward" included a greater concern with issues of attendance, accountability for students, and a generally greater sense of shared teacher control over the curriculum.

Admissions: Initially, HSC had no admissions policy to guide the recruitment and selection of students. When there were more applicants than openings, students were admitted by lottery. If openings were available, any applicant was welcomed without regard to educational history or learning style. The belief was that HSC could deal with any student and that any student had the right to attend.

In the late 1970's, criteria for admission became an area of focused debate. On the one hand, the traditions and values of the school supported its historical stance as a school for everyone. On the other, experience was mounting in favor of making discriminations previously unthinkable. Teachers were increasingly aware that HSC was not for everyone, and that more and more students seeking admission were seriously educationally disadvantaged and/or learning disabled. Further, some students at the school were endangering the school's reputation and credibility. "It came to a head in the late 70's," said one teacher, "when we had several kids in school who were known criminals — drug dealers — who were allowed to come to HSC."

As a result of these forces, placement screening for students was instituted routinely, additional efforts were made to recruit more academically oriented students, and a more careful examination of the history of applicants was undertaken. As one teacher said:

> We've now decided we simply can't take special education students unless the city gives us the resources to deal with them. Our own time and energy is limited. And now — and this is a big change — we at least *question* the admission of students with bad attendance records at other schools. And we won't take students in mid-year anymore — it's too disruptive of the program. We want to make a student actively choose to come to HSC for some positive reasons. That was the case in the early years of the school.

Attendance: HSC had long struggled with the issue of attendance in its ideology and policy. Initially, HSC had no policy on attendance. Indeed, when the school system imposed a general attendance policy in the early 1970's, HSC responded negatively, viewing it as a threat to the school's autonomy. Then, teachers were required to keep attendance records, but could define and report them as they wished. The move into a single school building, however, increased the awareness of attendance problems, since students could be accounted for more readily. In addition, as the student body became more marginal, attendance dropped.

These changes once again forced on HSC the issue of attendance policies. As we have seen, the adoption of policy implies a decrease in individual autonomy over how to cope with specific circumstances. This was traditionally a difficult step for HSC teachers to take. Nonetheless, during the mid and late 1970's, they took it. During these years, individual policies of teachers gave way to school policies which teachers gradually grew to support. Indeed, by the 1978-79 year, the Teacher Orientation Handbook included a section on "Academic Attendance Agreements," including signed attendance contracts between the school and students who were not earning sufficient credits toward graduation. While the credit requirements were not very strict, they represented shared school commitments and policies where, originally, none had existed.

Suspension and Discipline: The same kinds of shifts occurred in the areas of suspension and discipline. "We didn't have a discipline policy till the merger [into one building]," recalled Matt Borenstein, "now its 'any fighting and you go home.' We used to meet all the time about what to do with students who caused trouble or were upset or whatever — call their guidance teacher out of class and try to resolve the situation immediately. We had an implicit policy designed to avoid discipline. And we would never suspend a kid."

The 1978-79 Teacher Orientation Handbook includes a section on "Suspensions" in which it states: "In general, sending a student home is always with the intent of having the student return the following day to discuss what happened. In most instances, parents are called and frequently they are asked to return with their child on the following day." "Now," said Alice Mick in 1984, "it's 'if you get in trouble, come back with your parents.'"

Still, the forms these evolving policies took always reflected the long-standing HSC concern with giving students every chance to succeed at HSC. For example, the school adopted an "Advocacy Policy" to protect the interests of students threatened with disciplinary action. This policy, invoked only when serious or repeated school violations occurred, allowed the accused student to solicit a teacher to serve as his or her advocate. The Teacher Orientation Handbook (1978-79) outlines the policy, and its wording shows the concern over equity which lay beneath the larger HSC struggles to create boundaries and limits.

> "The advocate should not be considered as a lawyer who will argue the student's case and defend him/her at the meeting (concerning the alleged offense). The role of the advocate is that of a supporter who will assist the student to present his/her own case. The idea of the advocate is to help the student realize that he/she is not being railroaded or shafted by people out to get him/her. The advocate should be a person with good relations with the student."

Policy Changes and Shared Norms

These policy changes pushed consistently for a clearer set of shared expectations for student behavior and attendance. However, they were constantly fought over in the context of HSC's basic ideological commitments. Said Matt Borenstein:

> "We had internal struggles for years — sometimes over a decade — about these issues. We have had an increasing belief in policy — there *will* be a policy — even if teachers feel free to

> bend it a little. Our old ideas of each teacher having their own
> policy just didn't work. Kids don't understand what having a
> variable policy is, and over time we really didn't either. We
> have a consistent policy for attendance, and a minimum pen-
> alty for lateness to class, although individual teachers can
> adopt a stricter policy if they want. But discussions about these
> have gone on for a long time, and they're still going on. We now
> understand that these policies protect teachers as well as stu-
> dents. Last year, there was a fight in another teacher's class. I
> said, 'the parents have to come in' to the teacher. She said, 'what
> a relief that I don't have to handle all this myself.'

While begrudging in their acceptance of the individual constraints
which school-wide policy entails, teachers also experienced the support
that such broader norms provide.

In addition to policy changes involving student attendance and
behavior, shared norms around teacher behavior also developed during
these years. The Teacher Orientation Handbook included a short section
on a "Teacher Attendance Policy," which included both expectations
about meeting classes and spelling out procedures for dealing with
illness. Failure to notify the Facilitator would result in loss of part or all
of a day's pay. In addition, "the Facilitating Unit will make spot checks
of faculty attendance." These steps represented significant changes over
the earlier years, when such intrusions into teacher autonomy would
not have been tolerated.

In addition to these concrete manifestations of increased teacher
accountability, during the latter part of the 1974-84 years many more
teacher discussions occurred about what norms *should* be developed to
aid the growth of the school. "Alice [Facilitator from 1981-1984] paid a
lot of attention to process" said Borenstein. "She was concerned about
the norms we operated under, what was behind some of the issues we
had discussed for so long."

"I didn't think the school could last unless there was more order,"
recalled Alice. "We still didn't really have clear norms about control —
sometimes it felt like what we mostly had was a policy of exceptions to
our policies. I thought they needed to authorize the leader to enforce
boundaries and develop shared norms. But we *are* changing. Last year
I suggested that staff lesson plans be turned in to me for review. The staff
went crazy, but they decided in 10 minutes on a way to deal with their
accountability on their own. It was a good way, too."

STUDENT PERCEPTIONS OF THE SCHOOL: 1984

These previously discussed changes in the organization of HSC carried implications for the student experience. In the spring of 1984 two of the questionnaires given in the earlier evaluations were readministered — the Classroom Environment Scale (CES) and the *Perceived Ability to Influence School Policy* scale. The intent was to discover how HSC's organizational changes were reflected in students' classroom experience, and whether students still felt they were empowered to influence their school.

As before, we sought to gather data from a random sample of classrooms and students at HSC and at the high schools from which most HSC students had come. We were successful in accomplishing this at HSC but not in the other two high schools. In one of the schools, teachers in the English Department participated, while in the other, volunteer social studies teachers agreed to give the instruments in their classrooms.

In all, nine classes at HSC (112 students) and 19 classes in the traditional schools (203 students) were sampled. While the HSC sample is representative of the school, the traditional school sample is not, either in class content or class size (an average of less than 11 students per class). Because of these selection factors in the traditional schools, it is possible that the traditional school data may be somewhat more positive in terms of the classroom environment than the average classes in those schools.

Two kinds of comparisons are available through these data: (1) how HSC classes have changed from the early 1970's to 1984; and (2) whether or not HSC classes and perceived student influence in 1984 still differentiate HSC from the traditional high schools. Table 8-1 presents HSC data on the first of these issues: how HSC classrooms were different in 1984 from the early 1970's. It shows that HSC classes have indeed changed over time.

In the *Relationship domain* of the classroom (Involvement in class, Affiliation among students, and Teacher Support for students as individuals), HSC classes in 1984 were still well above the national norm (represented by the 50th percentile). The school has retained its emphasis on a more personal and supportive classroom environment. However, its current classes are significantly lower in both Involvement and Teacher Support than they were 10 years previously. On the Goal Orientation dimensions (Task Orientation and Competition), HSC's current classes are higher than 10 years before, with a very large difference in the emphasis placed on competition in the classroom. The classrooms are more focused around learning and are much more competitive than they had been. This tightening up of the classroom evident in the Task Orientation and Competition dimensions extends to classroom rules as well. Compared to 10 years before, HSC classes

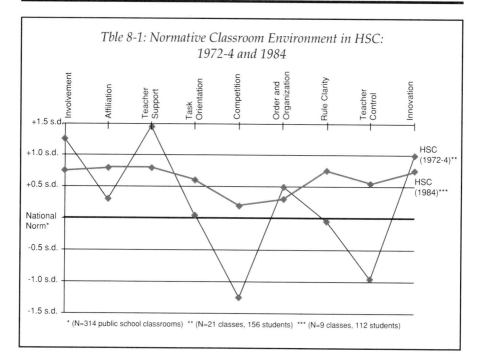

Tble 8-1: *Normative Classroom Environment in HSC: 1972-4 and 1984*

* (N=314 public school classrooms) ** (N=21 classes, 156 students) *** (N=9 classes, 112 students)

currently have rules that are more clear and more strict (Rule Clarity and Teacher Control). The general levels of Order and Organization in the classroom are comparable across time periods, as is the generally high emphasis on Innovation in teaching practices.

Overall, then, HSC classroom environments are perceived by students in the ways teachers described the school as having changed. Classes remain easygoing and personal places for students in terms of interpersonal relationships, and the teaching remains innovative. Classes have, however, become more businesslike in terms of learning, and the rules governing student behavior have become significantly more strict. The CES data support the consistent perception of teachers that, over time, the school had increasingly developed boundaries, limits, and clearer rules governing behavior inside the school.

A second kind of comparison involves whether HSC classes and perceived student influence differentiates HSC from the traditional schools as it did 10 years previously. Table 8-2 compares the 1984 HSC classes to those assessed in the traditional high schools.

As 10 years before, HSC classes are still higher on Teacher Support and Innovation, and lower on Competition than classes in the two regular public schools. In addition, the schools placed equal emphasis on Rule Clarity, Order and Organization, and Task Orientation, as they did in the early 1970's. However, on the classroom dimensions of Involvement, Affiliation, and Teacher Control, the schools are now

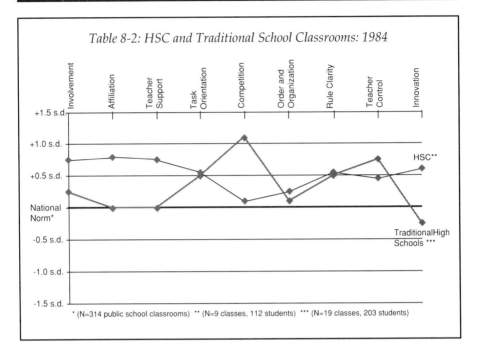

Table 8-2: HSC and Traditional School Classrooms: 1984

* (N=314 public school classrooms) ** (N=9 classes, 112 students) *** (N=19 classes, 203 students)

similar in emphasis, while 10 years previously HSC was higher on Involvement and Affiliation and lower on Teacher Control.

While the traditional school data may not be truly representative, it does appear that HSC classes have changed over time (i.e. become more competitive) and, in some areas, are more comparable to regular public school classrooms. They have also, however, retained a distinctiveness in areas consistent with their educational philosophy. Thus, a more personal teacher-student relationship is found at HSC. Classes remain more innovative, and, in spite of the increased emphasis on competition from 10 years before, HSC classes are still less competitive than those found in the traditional high schools.

A final comment on HSC's distinctiveness involves the data from the *Perceived Ability to Influence School Policy* scale. Here, as in the early 1970's, HSC students reported a greater degree of perceived influence than did students in the other schools.

"HOW WE'VE CHANGED": TEACHER REFLECTIONS IN 1979 AND 1984

A final set of comments on the evolution of HSC as an organization comes from teachers themselves. In spring 1979, toward the end of HSC's tenth year, the HSC staff sat down to discuss the history of the school and how it had changed. Geoff Smith, an HSC teacher, taped the discussion. Five years later, in 1984, the author interviewed a number of HSC teachers about the same issue of how HSC had changed and why.

The spring 1979 meeting included several teachers who had been at HSC since it began or shortly thereafter. All five quoted below had been with the school since Unit II opened in 1971 and had been key figures in its early history. Their own words provide not only substance, but a flavor of the candor and reflectiveness which they brought to the school.

> *Matt Borenstein:* I think that [one reason we're still an alternative] is that we're much better at sitting down and rethinking and replanning what we do with kids. Each year we sit down at the end of the year — and sometimes much earlier — and say "What's wrong with what we're doing? What's working? What isn't working?" Maybe by being able to maintain that kind of flavor in the school ever since I've been here — and I've been here ever since the first year that we had two units (1971) — that ability has increased. We do it a lot more efficiently, a lot faster, and make changes more easily. In the beginning making changes seemed very difficult, and the process was very confusing... What we're doing to change the students, to change the environment, to change society, to change ourselves has been increased. Our ability to handle conflict and recognize our limitations has increased. Some people might say that our recognition of our limitations has made us more institutionalized, but I think it has made us more rational human beings. To realize we're not going to solve the problems of racism, we're not going to solve the problems of poverty...We can deal with them openly, and talk about them, and work on them. You know when I first came here teachers... and some of the students were going to change the world. I don't think that was a bad kind of alternative spirit...

> *Alice Mick:* I think that one of the strengths of the school from the very beginning was that there was a lot of room for individuals to make changes in their teaching habits, in their growth as teachers. We were very free to do that. I think what Matt said has really been a solidifying of our strengths as a school, now that it's an institution. I think it's those two things together which make it such a good place to teach in.

> *Ed Linehan:* I think the core thing that has continued to be important is that kids, especially when they first come in, sense that we treat them more like people. We still do that on an important level, both individually and institutionally, but in ways that are very different from 8 years ago. Then that was utmost in our minds. One of the things that's happened over

the 8 years... is that we've gotten better at doing things as a team. That meant, to the extent that we did things together, we lost the flexibility of doing them alone as teachers, so that we gave up some of our individual things. The first years at HSC, both at Units I and II, the kids had a much greater sense of mission. This was a place that's going to be different, so they tolerated all our craziness organizationally, and they exercised a lot more self-direction, and I think that had to do with being new. That's surely changed. I think we're still an alternative, although we're a better organized school than we were, because the kids who come in, the first time they see it, say we're different. But I don't think we're the same as we were. It's not that we're just better organized.

I don't think we have the energy that we had. I know I don't. Just the sheer time. We're all 8 years older.

Charlotte Hilton: That's part of our strength, that we deal with people as people. I remember how I was treated at [a previous school]. I was hassled and harassed as a staff person, and that was minor in comparison to what they did to kids. I'm still reacting against that. I met a bunch of people this summer who said to me, "are you still at HSC?" I said "yes..." Some would say "good," and some would say, "why?" I responded, "I wouldn't know where else to be." That's pretty close to the truth...

Karen Wolfe: I agree with Charlotte a lot... Personally, I think the biggest change is that... the staff really feels comfortable in the school, with the job, and with the students... Just sort of not expecting kids to lie to us, so we don't get lied to very often... there is less tension and hostility in the school as a whole, among the kids, and the staff...

Ed Linehan: One of the things I've been thinking about recently ... is that the name of the school is now more of a contradiction than it was 8 years ago... We don't use buildings all over this city anymore... We were going to try to get New Haven to respond differently to high school kids. We responded differently. We've succeeded in controlling ourselves, and directing ourselves. What we haven't done very much is to make that name a reality. It's hard, but we haven't. The community, that community out there doesn't seem to be a central part of our school, but it's a central part of our name. So there's a contradiction...

(Later in the conversation, discussing the origins and implications of team teaching):

I think we all owe Matt, Ed Lichtenstein, and Jim Pepe a repeated thank you for 4 or 5 years ago deciding to do a "Transportation-end-of-the-year-help-kids-get-credit-last-week thing when everybody else stopped teaching. The idea was to have this intensive learning experience where teachers will work together, it will be interdisciplinary, and we'll see how it goes. Well, how it went was, the curriculum that you see this year, and for the first time it's both thematic and planned half a year in advance, is a result. And I think, if nothing else, the in-service, interpersonal support structure that resulted from team teaching, is umpteen times more important than all the ... in-service meetings that we're going to go to this year as a school system — people work together and learn from each other, and when people are in trouble, they have to get help from the other person and have to be supportive. And that dynamic, that structure, is very important to all of us, but not dependent on any of us. But it makes us work together and support each other.

George Foote: When we were early in the business, really not at all clear about what we wanted to do, little practice in working together, we had a very high staff attrition. People who came in, got disillusioned and went out. I can think of half a dozen people who were good at creating a lot of enthusiasm and just got very disillusioned quickly and left after a year. The holding power for those with a little patience was that the structure kept on delivering opportunities for people. People hang in there because they get a lot out of it. I suggest that alternatives that fold have something wrong with them structurally; that the folks don't get enough out of it, don't get enough rewards, and leave. I think this staff is special, but I don't think we've a staff of super-people at all; and that we happen to be lucky to know what was here and grab it. But that comparable groups have failed because they didn't come up with a structure that paid dividends for them.

In 1984, the author interviewed teachers about the further evolution of the school. How was the school different now and what were the main changes? Were there discernible stages in the school's history and what characterized those stages? And, from the three people who had been Facilitators at HSC, how had the leadership issues changed as the school confronted the paradoxes of empowerment? Everyone agreed that the general tightening of policy and rules captured the more general tone of the school in 1984. "The missionary phase has been over for a while now," said one. "Discipline really has changed," said another. There's still a healthy dose of individuality, and teachers still feel free to make exceptions, to not comply, but it's nothing like it used to be. We've worked it out, written up attendance rules. Teachers have less autonomy now, but they have less total responsibility too, and more support."

"The staff now fully understands that it's not fair to provide kids with no clear structure to work in," said a third. "As time passed and our student body changed, we had to learn that. In the late 70's, our increased absenteeism and turnover rate made it impossible to teach. We had to deal with who got in and what rules we needed to make." "We're still a very humanistic place," said a teacher who had been there since 1972. "We spend a lot of time with kids, get to know them and deal with them as individuals. But we do have some structure, that's for sure."

Teachers with the school since its early years characterized the stages of the school in somewhat different ways. "In the early years," said one, "survival was the name of the game. All our decisions about the school were made in the context of survival. Part of the legacy of the early years was accommodating, not really fighting, downtown. Internal politics became very low key at those times, very adaptive I think. But the turning point in the school came with the move into the new building and, of course, getting school system money so that we knew we'd survive. And they happened about the same time, so it's hard to say what caused what." "It [the building] was a symbol of permanence," recalled George Foote, "and it was an important symbol. At the same time, it was the end of the 'in the community' symbol."

Every teacher agreed that the move into a single building changed the character of the school and that the move, plus knowing the school would survive, changed the demands on the leader. Further, they did see the different facilitators as presiding over different kinds of organizational tasks at different times in HSC's history. However, they tended to view that history of the school as a gradual set of transitions rather than a discrete series of stages, with the exceptions of the move to a single building and knowing the school would survive.

The evolution of the facilitator role was also discussed with the three individuals who served as Facilitator for the school's first 14 years. They were in accord about the difficulties of being in that role. "Until we started the Facilitating Unit in 1973, it was impossible to lead," said Foote. "Then it became only improbable." "Both Alice and I vowed not to repeat the problems we saw in earlier Facilitators," recalled Linehan, "and we all left the job saying we'd never again accept a position that has responsibility but no power."

Still, as in other areas of the school, HSC changed in terms of its relationship to the Facilitator. "Originally," recalled Mick, "the Facilitator was seen as a slave; everyone wanted the leader to have authority but only when they agreed with the leader. Now there is more acceptance of the idea of having a leader, but some staff still fear that a strong leader means the disenfranchisement of staff. And it's hard because the position is not an official administrative position. The Facilitator gets paid as a teacher. There's still a belief that 'The Facilitator's job is just like everybody else's; it's not harder, it's not more responsibility.'" "We all really cared about the school," recalled Linehan, "otherwise we wouldn't have done it. But after all, why take all that grief for the same pay? It became very hard, and as time passed there were fewer and fewer volunteers for the Facilitator job."

The strength of the teacher belief in its egalitarian origins, while a source of frustration to the leadership, also remains a source of strength for the school. "We're still a teacher-run school," said Matt Borenstein. "That much hasn't changed. And many of us are and have been very active in the Union. Whenever this Union calls for a picket, you'll find a lot of HSC teachers there, even though we have much more control over our working conditions than other teachers in the city."

Asked about the future of the school, Alice Mick was reflective. "You know, we've been through a lot; many of us personally are at very different places than we were 14 years ago. We started with a bunch of ideas — we were so naive, but many of the basic values still give us energy. We're a small school, now there are other alternatives in New Haven, and we can't be everything to everybody. We need to be clearer within the school about who we can best teach, how the school wants to run itself, what's important to teach; generally, what kind of school HSC wants to be. We've done a lot, and we can do a lot. I think the real staying power of the school — what sustains it — involves the sense of empowerment each staff member has had — we all still believe that 'it's my school.' That sure causes problems, but it's what's kept us alive."

Epilogue: The more things change, the more they remain the same

In spring 1985, I returned to HSC for a visit. Alice Mick was in the process of resigning from HSC to pursue a career in law. Her resigning meant that the position of Facilitator was open, and, once again, the issue arose about whether that position should become an administrative one or remain a teaching position as it had been since the school opened. One of the prime candidates for the position stated she would accept the position only if it were changed to an administrative one. However, if such a change were made, the school system, not HSC, could hire and fire that person. The staff, after considerable discussion, decided *not* to

CHAPTER 9

The Creation and Evolution of Settings: The HSC Story in Context

Preceding chapters have documented the creation and fourteen-year evolution of an alternative public high school founded on an ideology of empowerment and dedicated to the development of a caring and humanized approach to education. By almost any criteria, HSC's story represents one of the most successful reports of an innovative educational alternative thus far documented. Evaluation data from its early years show that the school was able to create an institutional culture consistent with its ideology. Classrooms were interpersonally oriented, innovative, and deemphasized hierarchical teacher-student relationships and competition.

During its initial years, HSC students overcame many obstacles associated with inner-city schools when compared to control group students. They became more tolerant of individuals from diverse racial backgrounds and political perspectives; were more satisfied with school and their ability to influence policy; continued post-high school education more frequently; and performed as well on standardized achievement tests. While comparable data were not gathered after HSC's first four years, its beginnings were clearly positive in terms of its intended impact on students.

In addition, HSC demonstrated a capacity to cope with the organizational implications of its ideology, even though the process was long and laborious. Many efforts at creating alternative settings have succumbed to internal dynamics which eroded both morale and commitment. Tales told of other efforts at educational innovation (e.g. Gold and Miles, 1984; Smith and Keith, 1971) show how corrosive and negatively spiraling such processes can be. And, as has been amply documented, HSC confronted a number of unintended consequences of its empowerment ideology which caused serious and recurrent organizational problems.

Why was the school able to succeed in such a wide variety of areas? Any answer to such a question is necessarily complex. However, HSC's story does contain important lessons for those committed to creating alternative settings. These lessons include both individual and institutional factors.

Over the course of HSC's history, there were a number of individuals whose energy, ideas, and commitment were critical for the school at certain times. Sam Nash was credited with being an ongoing driving force; George Foote with being in the right place at the right time with the right skills; Ed Linehan and Alice Mick for having the necessary leadership strengths during the time they were Facilitators; and Tom Nelson, who used the Community Orientation Program as a model for how the school could get organized without giving up its ideology. Many other HSC teachers not visibly prominent in the preceding pages also played critical roles in the school's development. Overall, HSC attracted many talented individuals to its social experiment.

It may be tempting to attribute the success of the school to the unusual qualities and strong commitments of individuals attracted to the school. However, none of the many individuals the evaluation team interviewed, nor the hundreds of meetings attended or documents read, suggested that HSC attributed its success *primarily* to the qualities of key individuals. Rather, credit was given to the empowering structure they had created. This structure not only promoted the enduring commitment of core teachers, it allowed distinctive skills to be recognized when needed. "We were all in it together," said one teacher. "Sure, when the Facilitating Unit formed, there were issues of disenfranchisement, but basically we always knew that we, the school, needed the different skills of different people at different times to survive. We all contributed."

Foote, in particular, consistently maintained that the autonomy granted teachers provided them opportunities for growth and energized their commitment to struggle with ongoing organizational processes. He was particularly proud that HSC had avoided the "charismatic leader" approach so prominent in other alternative schools because he felt that few such schools remained vital when the charismatic leader left. "It was no fun trying to lead," he said, "but it certainly gave us all skills that came in useful over the long haul."

Two additional aspects of HSC's institutional character were critical in HSC's success. First was the strong shared belief in the ideology on which the school was founded. Even though its implications were not always clear, the overriding value of empowerment served, as does any deeply held faith, to carry the school through difficult times. It remained the consistent framework within which choices were made across a wide variety of spheres, from teacher hiring to policy making to the structuring of the curriculum. It provided a sense of shared continuity which bound teachers to each other and to the school.

Second was HSC's commitment to self-examination. From its origins, HSC was a school that sought out and processed data on its effectiveness. It held yearly meetings after the end of school to assess the past and plan for the future, and it consistently reflected upon and used data from the evaluations to change aspects of its program. This commitment to acknowledging its successes and learning from its mistakes kept the school responsive to its own internal workings.

In addition to its own personal and structural resources, however, were important supports in the school system and broader community. Within the school system itself, Sam Nash and Superintendent Gerald Barbaresi not only helped create the school through the development of resources but protected it in its early years. Parent support could always be counted on, particularly in times of crisis, and the evaluation team provided credibility and useful feedback to the school. These combined supports helped create and maintain a climate of opinion in the school system which buffered the school from its critics.

This internal commitment and external support allowed HSC to negotiate one of the historical problems of alternative schools initially supported by outside funding: becoming financially integrated into the ongoing public school system. Unlike many alternative schools begun in the early 1970's, HSC has survived to the present day. Internally, the school, and the Facilitating Unit in particular, showed political savvy in "reading the environment" around sensitive issues, accommodating to broader school system pressures in a way that preserved the school's integrity. Its backers in the school system, however, also played critical supporting roles.

HSC also succeeded in contributing to an innovative climate in the public school system, where it is now one of several alternative schools currently operating in New Haven. These schools, representing both elementary and secondary school options, have all come into existence after HSC became incorporated in the local public school budget. One of them, another alternative high school, was begun by George Foote after leaving HSC. While HSC was not itself instrumental in creating these other settings, its ability to survive and achieve a degree of national prominence surely lent a credibility to the system and a hope for innovative educators that they, too, could create new educational settings.

While HSC has succeeded in many ways, it also failed to realize some of its initial aspirations. For example, both of its most innovative and empowering structures—the COP and the Policy Council—fell short of their intended mark. In both instances, issues of resources and unexamined assumptions hampered the achievement of goals. "We had a good idea," recalled Nash about the COP," but we simply didn't realize at the time what it would take; what it would require of us, the students, and the community." The political empowerment of students and parents through the Policy Council was likewise undermined, even though HSC students still perceive greater influence over school policy than their peers in the other high schools. Thus, two of the school's boldest efforts did not survive the test of time in their original form.

In like manner, the original hopes for the multifaceted teacher role were increasingly scaled down as their implications became clear. The seminar, initially conceived of a pivotal aspect of the teacher role, was quickly abandoned and then restructured in the service of more limited and focused goals. The supervision of volunteer teachers diminished greatly over time, and the guidance aspect of the teacher role, while still an ongoing activity, has also receded in importance. Teachers found they could not spread themselves into these various roles without some sacrifice in their classroom teaching. Such pulling back need not be seen as a long-term adaptive failure. Rather, it more likely represents a realistic accommodation to the unanticipated consequences of trying to accomplish too much. Still, HSC failed to achieve its goals in some important areas.

In sum, the 14-year history of HSC allows some important lessons to be learned about how the school was able to survive and succeed. It should be emphasized, however, that HSC, like any institution, is always undergoing change internally and in relation to its external environment. In this sense, this story does not have a natural end. HSC has not stopped its evolution; it did not simply reach a steady state and cease to change. Rather, we have placed an artificial ending on a story still in progress. It is a story covering a considerably longer period of time than other stories describing the creation of settings, and for that reason may allow us to see processes and outcomes in a different light.

In the remainder of this chapter, three broad areas of inquiry stimulated by HSC's story receive comment. These topics provide additional ideas about why HSC succeeded and how its story can inform the creation of future alternative settings.

HSC:
AN ELABORATION ON THE CREATION OF SETTINGS

One goal of this narrative is to use the HSC story to extend our knowledge about how we create new settings. While Sarason's initial work stemmed primarily from a concern about the problems and pitfalls facing new settings, the focus on one that succeeded should provide a useful test of the validity of his early formulation. In general, HSC's early development provides a general correspondence with Sarason's early formulation, with some relevant refinements and, in a few areas, contradictions. In addition, however, it illuminates some of the non-obvious implications of Sarason's formulations of importance to the successful creation of settings.

The Zeitgeist and the range of alternatives. Sarason's superordinate framework began with the importance of the larger Zeitgeist, both in setting the stage for innovation and in framing what kind of innovations are conceivable. It is clear that HSC, in its initial formative stages, was a "creature of its time." Indeed, its origins closely reflected the national Zeitgeist of criticism of social structures in general and public schools in particular. This Zeitgeist created a climate of opinion which supported the ideas behind HSC and provided certain resources to test these ideas.

Yet more than an awareness of the national climate of opinion is necessary to understand how HSC came to be created, for the local ecology of New Haven funneled these larger forces in particular ways which differentiated New Haven from other cities of comparable demography and culture. The broader Zeitgeist needed local resources which, as we have seen, were able to link up with each other for mutually useful though different professional and institutional reasons. Yale University's reasons for supporting the school's first year were undoubtedly different than those behind Sam Nash's initiative to stimulate educational alternatives in the New Haven Public Schools. While the notion of Zeitgeist seems useful in framing the thinkable and do-able, its specific implications are always filtered through local mediating structures and networks.

One influence of the Zeitgeist, asserts Sarason, is that it restricts the thinking of setting creators to a small range of alternate problem solutions. Such was the case at HSC, both in terms of its guiding assumptions and in their implications for how the school would be structured. For example, the goal of racial integration was never questioned, nor was the empowering value of having a teacher-run school. In addition, there was no sustained initial discussion about how shared goals for the school might be pursued in different ways. Use of the community as a learning laboratory, for example, could in theory have been accomplished in numerous other ways than the form originally taken by the Community Orientation Program. Similar observations are applicable to each of HSC's other early decisions about how to implement its ideas.

Sarason's assertion that such unexamined premises often lead to unintended consequences was clearly confirmed. The school was unprepared for the tension and/or frustration which their participatory decision-making process entailed. They did not appreciate the implausibility of teachers adopting a wide variety of diverse roles. And they neglected to assess how much self-direction students would need to profit from the Community Orientation Program. Sarason's assertion that "the implications of the obvious are not always themselves obvious" is fully supported by the HSC experience.

Yet it is understandable that HSC's creators were often unable to consider alternatives and anticipate the long-range institutional consequences of their decisions. They had neither an articulated theory of organizational structure and process to work from, nor had they significant prior professional experience to draw on. "None of us had ever started a school before," recalled Foote," and we'd never been responsible for running a place either. It wasn't like there was a lot of information we could draw on. We were, in our own way, pioneers. We had all been classroom teachers. We knew what we didn't want to do — what we wanted to avoid. Actually, if we knew then what we know now, I'm not sure we would have done it in the first place."

Foote's last comment suggests something further; that it was potentially adaptive *not* to focus too extensively on the potential consequences of early formative decisions. There is paradox in this. For example, much current work in social skills training and interpersonal problem-solving (e.g. Spivak and Shure, 1980) begins with the premise that thinking through the consequences of one's actions is good. In this work, children and adolescents are taught to consider alternative problem-solving strategies, weigh the consequences of different possible solutions, and assess how likely their preferred means of behaving will lead to an adaptive solution.

The ecological conditions facing those creating such settings as HSC are quite different, however. Here, one might argue that, in order to sustain the energy and hope necessary to create a setting with an unknown future, the most fundamental assumptions and their implications *cannot* be the subject of scrutiny and measured debate. Such scrutiny may undermine the requisite sense of purpose and dilute commitment by provoking doubt.

Thus, Sarason's formulation that new settings quickly confront their own internal contradictions and unanticipated consequences is an accurate portrayal of HSC's story. What is important in the HSC story, however, is not that such consequences occurred — that phenomenon has now achieved the status of one of Murphy's laws. Rather, HSC's experience suggests that how such a confrontation is conceptualized and dealt with is critical. If processes and structures can be developed to cope with unanticipated consequences, these occurrences need not have long-range negative influence. Rather, they may provide the opportunity for self-analysis and self-renewal. The weight of evidence from HSC is that they served to deepen and enrich the school as a setting, even though the process was often a difficult one.

Superiority of Mission and the Myth of Unlimited Resources. Sarason postulates that two specific assumptions held by setting creators are the sense of superiority of mission and the myth of unlimited resources. Any recounting of the creation of HSC would have to start by agreeing that these two concepts were reflected from the planning stages on. As educational reformers, the teachers clearly believed that their reform was superior to the ongoing public schools. Notes from the spring 1970 planning meetings also provide irrefutable evidence that the teachers believed that resources — particularly the resource of time — were unlimited.

These myths provided both energy and liabilities during the early years of the school, "On the one hand," recalled Alice Mick, "we must have been crazy to think we could do all that, but it kept us working 18 hours a day to make sure we would." The liabilities revolved around the implications of the sense of superiority of mission for (a) a lack of questioning of basic premises, and (b) the way HSC chose to relate to external settings during its early years. The lack of questioning would, over time, become tempered by another HSC characteristic — its openness to self-examination. Its relation to external settings is discussed in a subsequent section. In sum, however, both the sense of superiority and the myth of unlimited resources characterized HSC's origins. In retrospect, they provided both benefits and costs to HSC's subsequent development.

Agreement on Values. Sarason also comments that agreement on fundamental values is assumed to be both necessary *and* sufficient by those who create settings. The general issue of shared and divergent values of setting creators becomes important because, over time, either differences in values emerge or differences in how the same values are implemented become apparent. This adds a dynamic tension to the evolving setting which interacts with the increasing awareness of other emerging unanticipated consequences. How settings manage this value differentiation and elaboration constitutes an important developmental task.

At HSC, agreement on the fundamental values of empowerment and egalitarianism was strong and pervasive. One can trace throughout HSC's history an institutional character or organizational culture anchored by these values. They provided a framework for decision-making, a perspective on leadership, a stance from which to process outside influence, and a set of implicit rules which shaped how students and parents were treated.

Sarason's point, however, is that agreement on fundamental values is not enough to insure agreement on what courses of action to take. At best they provide a framework for deciding what to do. This means that unanticipated conflicts around how values are enacted can be expected to occur.

HSC's experience confirms that shared values, while perhaps necessary, do not sufficiently promote a clear vision of how to proceed as time passes. From its earliest days, for example, the specific implications of empowerment differed from teacher to teacher. Some teachers felt that creating a discipline policy did not necessarily undermine the value of empowerment, while others felt it did. When the school was threatened because of the *Lysistrada* incident, teachers arrived at different opinions about what to do. These differing positions did not reflect disagreement about empowerment per se; rather, the value of empowerment competed with other values (e.g. survival) which circumstances had pushed to the fore. Thus, Sarason's point that settings begin with a sense of shared values that prove insufficient as a guide over time is apt in describing HSC.

There is a time dimension to this issue, however, which bears noting. It may be quite adaptive in the early stages of setting creation to act as if agreement on fundamental values *is* both necessary and sufficient to insure success. At such a time, emphasis on group similarities can serve as a catalyst for group energy and effort. In the early history of settings, fundamental agreement on values is often cast as shared opposition to the values embodied in previous settings. As Foote said, "whatever we wanted to be, it was *not* Hillhouse." It is easier initially to bind together against a common enemy than to plan a more proactive and evolutionary program. It is in these latter activities that differences are likely to surface and value conflicts increase.

Thus, at the early stages of setting creation, it may be both predictable and adaptive to adopt the myth that (1) individuals agree on fundamental values; (2) such agreement is both necessary and sufficient, with the implication that (3) agreement will last over time. Again, context is critical, for what may be an adaptive short-term myth may become a long-term nightmare if it persists beyond its usefulness to the setting.

Settings are created for clients, not service providers. Sarason's assertion that setting creators usually assume that the setting is for the client, not those who provide the service, needs revision in light of the HSC experience. While setting creators may often deny their needs in the service of providing for clients, HSC was always concerned about the kind of work environment it created for its teachers. HSC believed in the connection between positive working conditions and a positive student experience. By providing teachers with an unusual degree of autonomy over what and how to teach, HSC was self-conscious about the value of caring for its staff as well as its clients. It was a school where teachers could agree that it was not only legitimate, but desirable, to "have fun."

This idea was not meant frivolously, but was intended to convey the value of joy in one's work which occurs in a context that, as Foote described, "kept delivering opportunities to teachers." This self-consciousness about the nature of the work environment was critical in maintaining teacher commitment to the school.

Necessity and Denial of Leadership. As a reaction to the perceived evils of bureaucratization and hierarchical relationships, many alternative settings created during the late 1960's and early 1970's engaged in debates about how to avoid creating leader-follower hierarchies (see Reinharz, 1984; Riger, 1984; Swidler, 1978). Sarason highlights this in his assertion that new settings deny the necessity of leadership, setting the stage for future unanticipated issues of authority and direction. If the denial of leadership is intended to sharpen issues of power and authority in newly created settings, then HSC's experience epitomizes Sarason's thesis. These issues not only characterized the early history of the school; they were still being debated in 1984.

On the other hand, HSC's story may be more usefully portrayed as one which denied the necessity of leaders rather than leadership. Throughout the school's history, the concept of leadership resided in the teachers as a group, with continual ambivalence about the formal role of the Facilitator as leader. Over time, structures such as the Facilitating Unit and the Policy Council were developed to provide leadership. However, these efforts were always suspect, even when it was acknowledged that they were necessary. The initial denial of the necessity of leadership caused ongoing problems. However, it also strengthened the school's empowerment ideology and proved an important component of HSC's success over time.

Relation to Other Settings. It is reasonable to assume that such factors as a sense of superiority of mission and the perception of a common external enemy would affect a newly created setting's relationship to other settings. Basically, HSC's relationship to other *school system* settings conformed to the pattern described by Sarason and other writers on the alternative setting movement (e.g. Reinharz, 1984). In its origins, the teachers planning HSC were engaged in a surreptitious activity unknown both to their colleagues in other schools and to the broader administration of the school system. Such origins set an isolationist tone which was basically maintained over the early years of the school. Informal networks with teachers and administrators in other schools were maintained. With the exception of student recruitment and the guidance-related issues involving school records, however, HSC developed little functional interdependence with the rest of the school system. It was only over a period of years, accelerated by the move to a single building and to being supported by the local school system budget, that HSC became more integrated with the ongoing structure of the public schools. This involvement, as we have seen, included both increased resources and increased pressures and demands.

A retrospective look at this pattern of relating to existing settings again suggests adaptive behavior for HSC. In its earliest years, when it was supported by external funding, its primary organizational tasks were facilitated by its autonomy from the rest of the school system. Its early years included considerable floundering, and it needed the freedom to make mistakes and learn from them. It did not need the resources of other local settings as much as it needed to be given time to develop. What links to external settings it did make were for those resources it needed for its growth and evolution; the community for classroom space and its COP program, and Yale for its evaluation team.

Some of the dynamics behind the lack of involvement with existing settings in the school system may have stemmed from an arrogance related to superiority of mission. However, it was the insecurity of its own program that made HSC's early isolation adaptive. Importantly, however, HSC kept in close touch with the politics of the school system, particularly as they involved HSC's survival. They were keenly aware of the importance of remaining credible to downtown throughout their history. As their internal workings consolidated, however, and as issues of survival became less critical, relationships with other settings inside and outside of the school system became both politically functional and a resource for the school. Thus, both the earlier isolation and later rapprochement served adaptive functions for the school.

Concluding Comment: One can see the general usefulness of Sarason's effort to delineate relevant factors in the creation of settings. These factors, many of which were influential in HSC's early history, did indeed set the stage for issues and debates which HSC had to face later in its life history. However, two points seem important to emphasize. First, while sowing the seeds of potential later problems, attitudes like superiority of mission and myth of unlimited resources also served positive and adaptive functions. Thus, they should not necessarily be viewed only in terms of the problems they foreshadow.

Second, the rather lengthy time period covered in the present story clarifies how early assumptions affected HSC's later history. These assumptions exercised formative and enduring influence. However, their early impact was significantly moderated by the way in which HSC sought out information and created opportunities for self-scrutiny over time. Thus, early history, while setting the stage for later issues, did not determine HSC's future course. Rather, *how* unanticipated consequences were sought out, discussed, and dealt with became an important evolutionary aspect of the HSC story.

This, then, signals that Sarason's framework for the creation of settings is perhaps best viewed as a perspective on early pre-history and history which sets the stage for, though does not determine, the setting's future. Focusing as it does on the hopes and attitudes of setting creators, it highlights the potential for early assumptions and experiences to exercise formative influence over the challenges the setting may face over time. The HSC story affirms the importance of understanding this early history but underscores the later significance of various external and internal factors as critical in determining what happened to the school. We now look at this evolution, examining its development in terms of stages.

THE EVOLUTION OF HSC OVER TIME: STAGES OR CONTINUITIES?

The issue of organizational stages provides a longitudinal framework for following the development of HSC in terms of its internal dynamics and its relationship to its external environment. Two different emphases emerge from previous writings. The first is the relative emphasis on continuity versus change over time. Sarason, while underscoring the "inevitable" confrontation with the limitations of the setting's initial assumptions, was cautious about postulating distinct organizational stages. He feared that such an emphasis might minimize the focus on continuity of the basic values of the setting. In contrast, Perkins et al. (1983) outlined a five-stage theory of organizational evolution which emphasized change from stage to stage rather than continuity. The second involves the adequacy of the stage theory postulated by Perkins et al. in describing the HSC story. Here, the evolution of the school is cast in a perspective which focuses directly on change rather than the relationship of change to continuity.

Three related questions seem relevant: (1) Was HSC's early history decisive in understanding its later development? (2) How closely does HSC's history conform to the stages described by Perkins and his colleagues? (3) How were the different phases of the school defined by school participants, and what do these perceptions tell us about the idea of organizational stages? A discussion of these questions can add to our understanding of the evolution of alternative settings over time. This, in turn, may provide a useful roadmap for those creating new settings.

THE INFLUENCE OF EARLY HISTORY ON LATER DEVELOPMENT.

The first way of addressing continuity and change at HSC involves an examination of how its early history shaped its future. Early history, it should be recalled, includes not only the first few years of HSC, but its pre-history, the assumptions of its creators and the Zeitgeist in which it was planned. Sarason's general assertion about early history was not the "hard" determinist position that, in the imagery of psychoanalytic theory, "childhood is destiny." Rather, the notion was that the institutional character of settings emerges from their founding assumptions and that these founding assumptions frame the early experience of the setting. Continuity would then be defined in terms of the identifiable themes of the school's origins which guided later behavior.

To be sure, the story of HSC is, in part, a story of change and differentiation over time. As HSC developed, teacher roles became more specialized and new roles, such as guidance counselor, secretary, and COP coordinator, were added to accomplish overall school goals. Issues facing the school differed in emphasis, with survival occupying much early energy and organizational coherence becoming a later theme. Students were increasingly seen in differentiated terms, and eventually some grouping according to level of basic skills was undertaken. All these represented significant changes over time, involving teacher attitudes, roles, structures, and policies of the school.

In the face of these changes, however, was a continuity of working within an empowerment ideology that endured throughout HSC's history. From the 1970 discussion about whether to have a secretary, to the 1984 discussion about whether the facilitator should be a teacher or administrator, HSC's empowerment ideology and egalitarian commitment defined the parameters of the debate.

Decisions were not always consistent with ideological purity — ideology's expression is, and should be, tempered by an assessment of the contextual implications of decisions. Returning to the *Lysistrada* incident, when the school board expressed its concern, there is little doubt that the ideological instinct of HSC was to defend its right to operate the school as it wished, to maintain control over how it educated its students. Still, it could ignore the school board only at its own peril. Thus, it engaged in a lengthy debate about how best to preserve its core values without imperiling its survival. Political realities, however, were always confronted from the standpoint of a consistent ideology which formed the basis for school decision-making.

In this very important sense, Sarason's caution about focusing on change over continuity is well-taken. From the perspective of ideology or governing principles, HSC, for all its changes in personnel, structure, and policies, has had a continuous history of affirming the validity of its originating ideas. It has reacted in a way similar to Hackman's description of People Express Airlines, in which challenge to the organization always resulted in a reaffirmation of guiding principles. HSC's changes are real, but are surrounded by a context of values and history which has guided how these changes have been approached. The continuity provided by this shared and enduring ideology has been a source of strength for the school over time, even as its implications have often caused frustration and uncertainty.

ORGANIZATIONAL STAGES OF HSC

Though guided by an underlying continuity of institutional character, HSC's story shows that the school did focus on different issues at different points during its first 14 years. Because it represents one of the most articulated statements of the stages of organizational creation, we have drawn on the framework of Perkins et al. (1982) as an organizing perspective. HSC's history does not clearly conform to this perspective.

On a most general level, there is no evidence that HSC passed through the clearly demarcated stages evoked by the imagery of stage theories. Consistent with the formulations of both Sarason and Perkins, et al., HSC did begin with the stage of utopian fantasy, and even in its first few months of operation, had to begin confronting its limitations. However, these confrontations with the utopian fantasy came at different times and around different issues. The seminar as a fantasy structure for connecting the students to the school was almost immediately perceived as a problem, while the implications of not grouping students according to ability took many years to reach the level of being an agreed-upon school issue. Utopian fantasies then were not uniform in their elaboration.

It is true that a more general sense of worry occurred around Thanksgiving of the HSC's first year: Foote recalled the pervasive concern that they did not really know what they had gotten into. In this sense they confronted the ultimate fantasy of being able to create their own school, and took steps to cope with their early limitations. But the specific utopian fantasies about the kind of school they wanted were more complex and sequenced. Indeed, some of the teachers interviewed in 1984 see HSC as still dealing with how to operationalize its initial utopian fantasies. While present, the utopian fantasy seems more complex and differentiated than previous accounts have suggested.

Perkins et al. cite "Challenge to Authority" as a second stage in organizational creation, followed by "Resolution." "Failure to accomplish unrealistic goals, coupled with the difficulty in operationalizing the philosophy of the organization, will eventually lead to a breakdown in managerial control" (p. 24). Descriptively, this process captures one aspect of HSC's early history but not another. It is accurate to say that that difficulty in accomplishing goals and operationalizing the philosophy caused the previously mentioned crisis around Thanksgiving of the first year.

It is less clear that this crisis precipitated a "challenge to authority." The Perkins formulation may derive from a managerial structure found in industry but not present in similar form at HSC. At HSC, the concept of "managerial authority" rested with the teachers as a group. This aspect of empowerment diluted the impulse to confront managerial authority as embodied in George Foote. The teachers *were* managerial authority, even though Foote had a distinctive role in running the school. To be sure, Foote was blamed by some of the teachers at this time for the way he was enacting his role, but it was the teachers themselves who were empowered to sanction what he could and could not do. Thus, while the initial understanding that "it's not working" caused questioning on the part of HSC teachers, it was less funneled into a "Challenge to Authority" than a challenge to themselves to figure out what to do.[1] Further, as the narrative shows, this challenge was a continuous issue from the earliest planning meetings throughout the school's history.

Similar problems arise in applying Perkins' next stage — Resolution — to the HSC experience. "Resolution" refers to resolving the challenge to authority which characterized the preceding stage. This includes a redefinition of the relationship to the leader and is accompanied by tightening of organizational rules, regulations, and procedures.

Over a period of years, changes did indeed occur between the Facilitator and the other teachers, and after three years a Facilitating Unit was formed to resolve leadership issues. A gradual tightening of rules and regulations also occurred over the 14 years covered in the present narrative. But any resolution of these basic tensions around authority and rules was gradual and not specific to a particular period of time. Further, because teachers *were* the authority, "Resolution" had less to do with negotiations around power and authority with the leader than with resolving the difficulties teachers had around consensual decision-making.

Consonant with Perkins' formulation, however, HSC did shift its emphasis over time to focusing on the internal workings of the school. This shift occurred gradually and over an extended number of years rather than being a stage in a more time-limited sense. Teachers, reflecting on the history of the school, cited two factors which signalled this shift: the move into a single building and the tenure of Ed Linehan as Facilitator. Yet the move into the building took place five years after the school's creation and Linehan became facilitator after HSC's first eight years. Thus, a more gradual and piecemeal picture emerged than the imagery of stage theory suggests.

Further, it is not clear that the push toward internal coherence can be accounted for primarily in terms of internal forces activated by a previous stage of the teacher group. During this time, the students admitted to the school changed from a more self-directed group to a group whose academic skills and interest were more marginal. This change brought various issues of curriculum, policy, and discipline to the fore which required the school to reflect on its operations. It may be argued that the changing student population was as responsible for the school's turning inward as any other set of factors. While the present study cannot disentangle these influences, it does argue for a complex view of the determinants of HSC's changes over time which takes into account both internal forces and ecological influences in the broader environment.

Perkins et al.'s fourth stage likewise seems to reflect the embeddedness of their work in an industrial setting. "Intergroup Conflict" is seen to result in a heightened need for autonomy following the increased bureaucracy created during the Resolution stage, with individuals "thwarted by cumbersome procedures and a centralized hierarchy" (p. 27). Rather than being manifested in a specific stage, the empowerment ideology of HSC heightened the tension between autonomy and bureaucracy throughout its history. This instinct to preserve autonomy surfaced under the threat of any perceived constraint, bureaucratic or otherwise. Because of this, HSC never achieved the necessary degree of bureaucracy which is a prerequisite for this type of intergroup conflict.

The final stage — "Quasi-stationary equilibrium" — is difficult to define as it pertains to HSC. Certainly, over time the school developed more shared norms and procedures which served to increasingly standardize school life. On the other hand, some teachers view HSC as still needing to come to terms with its educational identity, particularly since New Haven now provides other alternatives for students in public high schools. Again, the image is more one of a constant and changing encounter of the school with its context, still guided by a history and a set of values, rather than the image of a "quasi-stationary equilibrium."

TEACHER PERSPECTIVES ON HSC'S STAGES

Interviews with teachers provided two additional perspectives on the issue of stages in the evolution of HSC. The first involves the issue of whether stages in the school could be linked to its three leaders. The second involves the role of external influences in defining possible stages. Included are the switch to secure funding and the shift to a single location.

There was some consensus that each of the three Facilitators emphasized different goals for HSC. "George was always involved in survival," said one, "and dealing with funding, the Superintendent, and external things. Ed was more involved in organizing the school, and Alice went on from where Ed left off." The three Facilitators were in basic agreement with the idea that each emphasized different aspects of the school. And they acknowledged that the school needed to confront somewhat different tasks at varying points in its history. However, each viewed the school's history more as a gradual evolution than a series of discrete stages.

Further, when asked to think about the biggest changes in the school over time, they and the other teachers were more likely to highlight two external issues, neither of which corresponded in time to leadership changes. The first involved secure funding for the school, a task accomplished three years before Linehan became Facilitator. "For the first five years, the name of the game was survival," recalled Linehan. "Everything we did revolved around that. After we were sure of funding, we could pay more attention to how the school was organized."

The second, commented on by most teachers, was the move to a single building. Not only did it represent a symbolic change ("we were not really in the community any more," recalled Foote), it forced HSC to confront a variety of new organizational tasks. Accountability of teachers and students to each other increased, opportunities for collaboration and conflict were enhanced, housekeeping chores became necessary, the development of sense of place became possible, and the idea of permanence became thinkable. Sam Nash likewise recalled the move into a single building as pivotal. "What New Haven needs now," he chided George Foote, "is a high school in the community."

CONCLUSION

Overall, then, HSC's story provides at best a complicating picture of the stages through which new settings pass. Three general emphases seem relevant to the concept of stage theories and the evolution of settings: (1) the importance of attending to both continuity and change in the development of settings; (2) the value of studying stages across different kinds of settings; and (3) the importance of attending to both internal and external factors as affecting the stages settings may go through.

Continuity and Change: The 14-year time period covered in the present narrative suggests the wisdom of Sarason's caution that stability as well as change may characterize the evolution of settings. At HSC, continuity of values and institutional culture seemed to be a significant and sustaining pattern, even though there were different tasks which HSC confronted at different times. Indeed, continuity seemed more fundamental, while change,though real, was protracted, piecemeal, and gradual.

Stage Theories Reflect the Characteristics of Organizations in Which They are Developed: A second learning from the present study is that stage theories are always developed with an implicit image of organizations in mind. In the present account, for example, Perkins et al.'s stage theory corresponded at several points with the present narrative. However, its stages were predicated on a different organizational structure than HSC began with or strove to achieve. HSC aspired to be a leaderless organization rather than a participatory hierarchy. Its definition of empowerment took a vastly different organizational form than was taken in the business studied by Perkins et al. Because of this, Perkins et al.'s stages did not capture well the themes and crises of HSC's organizational development. Organizational stages cannot be divorced from the types of organizations studied. Further, they are linked to the new setting's initial assumptions about what kind of Utopia it is seeking and what its mission is. Because of this, it is important to study the creation and evolution of settings across a wide variety of organizations with varied ideologies and missions.

The Stages of Settings Reflect both Internal and External Factors: The Perkins et al. stage theory implicitly stressed internal group dynamics as creating the conditions for successive stages. HSC's experience, however, highlights the impact of its external environment as an influence on its stages. The survival issue during HSC's early years forced it to direct energy and resources to its external relationships while simultaneously shielding itself from too close scrutiny. The shift to secure funding made this energy available for internal development, signaling a different stage in terms of primary organizational task. In like manner, the move to a single building signified a new stage by forcing a confrontation with HSC's "in the community" goals and increasing its internal interdependence. The changing student body over time likewise exerted influence on HSC's stages by creating new pedagogical and disciplinary issues. To a meaningful degree, then, HSC's changing *external* environment made meaningful contributions to its stages by forcing issues on the school which affected its internal functioning.

Overall, the HSC experience suggests that the issue of organizational stages is a complex one. It involves not only the degree to which organizations are characterized by a relative emphasis on stability vs. change, but the kinds of organizations they are and the kind of external environment in which they operate. The idea that organizations go through discrete, predictable stages should be tempered by an explicit acknowledgment of these complexities. The imagery appropriate to the HSC experience is not necessarily that of stage theories. Rather, it is more an image of ideological continuity which guided confrontations with both internal and external challenges. These challenges in turn were heavily influenced by the specific assumptions of HSC and its local Zeitgeist.

EMPOWERMENT AND THE HSC EXPERIENCE

The final aspect of HSC which informs setting creation and evolution involves the emphasis the school placed on empowerment. Empowerment was the binding commitment which held the school together. It was clearly articulated in the meetings planning the school; it was embedded in the decision to make decisions by consensus; to create structures like the Policy Council; to stress the importance of reducing racism and promoting interracial harmony; and to become an active force in the Teacher Union. Most fundamentally, it was the reason that teachers wanted HSC to be a school where they could control the conditions under which they worked. What role did it play in HSC's evolution, and what can be learned about empowerment more generally from HSC's experience?

Empowerment as a force in creation and evolution: The writing on the creation and evolution of settings is surprisingly sparse on how institutional ideology or values relate to the setting's creation and evolution. Far more emphasis is placed on process, perhaps under the assumption that while content may vary, processes are more basic and underlying. Both Sarason and Perkins et al., for example, stress the processes associated with setting creation and subsequent stages more so than the substantive goals around which processes are organized.

The present account strongly suggests that when thinking about the creation and evolution of settings, processes and substantive goals are interdependent. Indeed, the differences found in stages between the Perkins et al. report and the present story suggest that settings built on differing ideologies will have to cope with different process and content issues in their evolution. At HSC, for example, the empowerment ideology determined how debates about the school were framed. It constituted a primary assumption whose unexamined implications shaped the nature of subsequent crises and efforts to resolve them. It directly affected how leadership was conceptualized, what the definition of authority was, and how policy issues were resolved. In short, it interacted with all aspects of the creation and evolution of the school. The present story also suggests the importance for alternative settings of *having* a deeply shared and clearly articulated ideology. At HSC, faith in empowerment proved to be a central aspect of the school's institutional character and shaped its commitment to that character. HSC never lost sight of its shared assumptions, even when individual teachers believed that they should be operationalized in quite different ways. Any account of the creation and evolution of settings, particularly alternative settings that often exist at the margins of normative practice, is incomplete to the extent it minimizes or ignores the binding force of political and ideological commitments. The ways in which these commitments play themselves out over time determine whether and how alternative settings remain distinctive or "regress to the mean" and become like the settings they began as alternatives to.

Empowerment at HSC: Paradox and Potential. In addition to its particular importance for HSC, the school's experience is instructive about empowerment more generally. It suggests several implications. First, the concept of empowerment can be maintained over time and in the face of changing organizational and environmental conditions. Second, empowerment is not necessarily tied to the continued existence of specific structures — structures can be changed without necessarily undermining the underlying ideology. Third, empowerment can be conceived of as either a psychological or a political phenomenon, and enhancing one does not necessarily enhance the other. And fourth, different empowerment goals require different frameworks and structures for their successful implementation.

Finally, the present narrative clarifies that any effort at empowerment, however defined, must be conceptualized within a specific social context which affects its achievable goals, structure, and processes. To discuss empowerment without reference to context is to put the concept at risk for failure. Empowerment always takes places somewhere and involves specific individuals and groups who, to once again use Sarason's phrase, occupy a certain place in the social order. Knowledge of the ecological context is essential to the successful implementation of empowerment efforts.

A brief recounting of some of the history of the school provides supportive evidence for these assertions. First, HSC has been able, over time, to remain an empowered institution. By creating and maintaining a school where teachers rather than administrators decide on the educational program, HSC has succeeded in being essentially self-governing.

To be sure, the threats to this central aspect of the school have been many. In the early years, the presence of outside funding and the school's accompanying marginal status made this stance relatively uncontested. With incorporation into the school system budget came an increasing threat to HSC's autonomy. More recently, debate around redefining the Facilitator role as an administrative rather than teaching position serves as a reminder that local empowerment is always at some risk.

These risk factors, however, do not only arise from external threats. For example, the problems of leadership at HSC have, paradoxically, contributed to the debate over whether the Facilitator role should be defined as teacher or administrator. Because teachers are under more local control than administrators, who are primarily accountable to "downtown," this debate is linked closely with the power of the school to govern itself. Thus, the internal paradox of leading a participatory democracy has generated its own worries around empowerment. Still, HSC has been able to protect its autonomy for 14 years.

Further, it has maintained this stance as many of its initial empowering structures have undergone change or indeed dissolution. The seminar represents a useful example of how specific structures of empowerment can change while still serving the larger empowerment goal. It began during HSC's first year, stopped, and re-emerged as the family group almost 10 years later. The *idea* behind the seminar remained over time, even though the specific structure was altered in response to feedback about its effectiveness and the changing needs of the school over time.

The HSC story also, however, clarifies the important difference between empowerment as a psychological and political phenomenon. Psychological empowerment implies a personal sense of control or influence over events. Political empowerment is defined by participating directly in decision-making. There is a paradox within organizations in the idea of one group empowering another. Those who have the power to empower another group have the power to disempower them. It is, however, conceivable that a powerful group would willingly give up power in the service of an overriding ideology. And there are many indications that HSC wanted to grant political power to both students and parents.

But as the story of the Policy Council affirmed, HSC did not become a vehicle for the political empowerment of students and parents. In attempting to put this idea into practice, the school encountered many unanticipated obstacles, for the implications of attempting to run the school through a group of teachers, parents, and students were far from obvious.

If HSC failed in its goal of political empowerment, however, it clearly succeeded in creating a psychologically empowering setting. Through a variety of mechanisms other than the Policy Council, both students and parents experienced HSC as a *psychologically* empowering school. Interview data from parents and questionnaire data from students show unmistakably that both groups viewed HSC as a school that sought out their feedback and listened to their concerns. Even after 14 years, HSC students still reported greater perceived ability to influence school policy than did students in the regular high schools.

HSC's experience affirms that political empowerment at one level — the teachers — implied relative disenfranchisement at another level — the students and parents. However, within a psychological definition of empowerment — e.g. a sense of influence over one's life — HSC was clearly successful in promoting such a perspective in students and parents. Indeed, the political empowerment of teachers *supported* the psychological empowerment of students and parents. To the degree this assessment is correct, the HSC story may serve to moderate the expectations for direct political empowerment in such a participatory experiment, while heightening the possibility that a psychologically empowering setting is possible to create and sustain over a lengthy period of time.

Finally, HSC's experience with empowerment suggests that differing kinds of empowerment goals require somewhat different conceptualizations and strategies for success. Coping with the disenfranchising effect of racism, for example, was one deeply held value of the school. Evaluation data showed some positive effects in terms of reducing interracial prejudice among students. In addition, teachers reported very few perceived instances of racism on the teacher level. There is evidence of attitude change at HSC consistent with its empowerment goals.

But it also seems that the attitudes of whites were more affected than the attitudes of blacks, and that, in general, interracial contact was still quite minimal at HSC. Further, there is some evidence that blacks did not always fare as well as whites in coping with some of the structural aspects of HSC such as the COP, and that some of the black teachers felt that black students needed more structure than HSC provided. In addition, few, if any, black parents ever became actively involved in the Policy Council. Thus, at least some aspects of the structures of HSC seemed to have a differential impact on blacks and whites as groups, although, of course, many blacks did profit from such structures and many whites did not.

Implicit in this portrait is a complex set of issues involving assumptions about empowerment, racism, and criteria for its elimination. The HSC experience suggests the importance of conceptualizing these issues not only in terms of attitudes but in terms of the impact of social structures on individuals of different races. Further, it requires a distinction between the potentially conflicting empowerment goals of integration, separation, and choice. HSC's initial assumptions seem to have focused primarily on racism at an attitudinal and interpersonal level; that is, how one thinks about and relates to individuals of other races defines the term. Further, the goal of such nonracist attitudes and behavior was one of integration, hence the value of increasing interracial contact. Such emphases and goals were consistent with the white liberal politics of the day.

However, HSC's experience suggested that the structures one creates can negatively affect the empowerment goals one asserts on an attitudinal and interpersonal level. While the data are not compelling, there are indications that the autonomy provided by HSC allowed some students to fall between the cracks, and that, for a variety of reasons, the burden fell more on blacks than whites. Further, it is not clear why a greater level of interracial integration was not achieved. Conceptually, however, it is plausible that integration was more a "white" than "black" goal; that, for blacks, solidarity and access to resources were seen as more empowering than integration. Most generally, however, the point is that underlying the empowering goal of reducing racism was a complex and relatively unarticulated set of issues whose history runs deep and whose implications cut across different levels of analysis from the attitudinal to the structural.

The previous comparison in Chapter 6 of the Community Orientation Program and the Policy Council highlights the structural issues in empowerment from a somewhat different perspective. To be effective, such structures needed to be thought through in contrasting ways, for they were based on different assumptions. The COP, for example, initially assumed that (a) students were sufficiently self-directed and responsible to function as the program required; (b) community teachers would behave more like teachers than employees who needed to rely on the COP students' dependability; and (c) that HSC had enough resources to manage the program adequately. The Policy Council assumed that (a) equal power could be defined in terms of equal votes of different groups; (b) teachers would willingly give up the power they had worked so hard to achieve (i.e. control over their school); and (c) parents and students would have high investment in exerting influence over everyday school governance.

The COP was thus supported by assumptions about the personal qualities and work roles of students and community teachers while the Policy Council involved assumptions about political power and parent/student motivation for political involvement. Many of these assumptions, while critical in how these structures were designed and implemented, were never clearly articulated. Indeed, such a differentiated conception of how to translate values into social structures is neither internalized, nor executed easily.

In sum, the idea of empowerment, while attractive and, in many ways, achieved at HSC, contains a complex set of contradictions and assumptions about (a) definition; (b) processes/structures, and (c) goals. The HSC story highlights the distinction between political and psychological definitions of empowerment, the fact that different aspects of this larger goal are mediated in different ways through different kinds of structures and processes, and that the goals of empowerment may be differently defined by various groups. Its power for the teachers, however, allowed HSC to maintain its efforts in the face of the many problems described above.

THE CREATION OF SETTINGS AS AN ECOLOGICAL PROBLEM: A FINAL COMMENT

The preceding comments on the creation and evolution of HSC show clearly that its development was influenced not only by the internal assumptions and group dynamics created by those assumptions, but by the larger ecology in which HSC was embedded. Further, it suggests an interdependence between these two sets of forces. HSC's story is one of reciprocal influence between ideology, internal organizational structure, and external forces in the school system and ever-changing communities which provided HSC with students. A comparison of HSC's story with other accounts of the creation of settings suggests that many underplay the interdependence of internal and external forces in affecting the creation and development of settings. It is this combination of influences which defines the creation of settings as an ecological problem.

The intent of this book, then, is to contextualize how we think about the creation and evolution of settings. New settings, and alternative settings in particular, often operate under a variety of internal and external constraints in terms of resources, prior experience in beginning new organizations, and external support for the new setting. Success under such conditions requires an active and accurate assessment of the context within which the new setting emerges, a commitment to understand what the setting will require of its members, and an abiding faith that the setting will succeed. That such faith is blinding is perhaps inevitable in the short run, though not, as we have seen, over the long haul, since it enhanced a successful survival.

HSC was graced with competence, savvy, and dedication in its teachers whose professional lives have been described in the preceding pages. These individuals were bound together by an idea which allowed them to persevere in the face of great uncertainty and frustration. From this idea came a school that, to use George Foote's phrase, "kept delivering opportunities" to those who participated in it. The power of this idea, as well as the contradictions in enacting it, can teach much to those concerned about creating settings that empower and are humane.

An Appreciation — High School in the Community's Legacy to its Graduates: Thoughts for a Graduation[1]

In September 1984, HSC will begin its 15th year as a public alternative high school in New Haven. Today, at its 14th graduation, it is my privilege to speak with you on the occasion of this graduation. I do so from the perspective of one who, during HSC's early years, was one of a group of persons hired by the school system to see how HSC was doing as a new and experimental school. I returned to New Haven this year to find out what had happened to the school I first knew, if you will, as a child. How had it grown up, matured, as years passed and times changed? It is a different school now than it was then, but it is also the same school. Its values, its traditions — such as graduating to the sound of music selected by each student individually — go back to its first year, when it opened in a donated space that had previously been an automobile dealership.

And it is these values I want to address briefly today, for schools, just as people, are defined by what issues they choose to tackle, what causes they define as just, what struggles they are willing to involve themselves in, and how much they are committed to participating in the important issues of the times. I do not wish to underestimate the central importance of such basic skills as reading and writing as a primary purpose for schools, and HSC has worked hard and successfully to provide its students with these fundamental building blocks for future careers. It has embedded these substantial efforts, however, in what might appropriately be called a larger vision about what the educational process can be.

I would like to discuss — briefly — what I have come to believe several aspects of this vision are. But first, I should state why, on the occasion of your graduation, I think it appropriate to focus on the school from which you graduate. I have a friend and colleague, a psychologist named Robert Reiff, who likes to make the point that each of our personal biographies are history — that our own development as kids, adolescents, and adults reflects the historical times in which we grew up.

The values, beliefs, and hopes we develop are grounded in the historical issues of our day.

Schools, like individuals, reflect a confrontation with the issues of the day, and today you, the senior class of HSC, are graduating from a school which, more than any public school I know, has actively participated in the issues of its time. I cannot help but believe that some of the goals which HSC hopes you will achieve involve your struggling with, and coming to terms with, many of the issues HSC as a school has decided to confront. Your teachers will smile — perhaps inwardly, but smile nonetheless — when they see you, as you move from the world of high school to the worlds of work, family, and further education — better able to achieve *your* goals because HSC has become better at achieving its goals. Your life, like HSC's, is embedded in a larger vision. Thus, not only, as my friend Bob Reiff says, are our personal biographies also a slice of history, but the biographies of our schools are as well. Let me pursue this by briefly discussing the history of HSC and the values and vision on which that history was built.

HSC began as a reaction to social turmoil in New Haven and in the nation. There was in the nation at that time a widespread concern about the bureaucratic nature of the public schools, the lack of appreciation of the positive value of cultural pluralism, and the coercive nature of a public school system which did not offer its students a *choice* about where to go to school. Out of these historical circumstances came a number of values which are still salient today.

The first one I wish to mention is *the value of controlling — to the greatest degree possible — one's own destiny*. HSC has a long tradition of fighting for this kind of control so that it can be flexible, can innovate, and can respond to students in an individualized manner. And it has proved itself a responsible keeper of its own counsel. There was a time, early in the history of the school, when it was more an isolated part of the school system than it is today. If it was seen as unfriendly to "downtown" during those early times, it was only reflecting what persons in the civil rights movement had known for years; namely, that there is a stage in the development of movements when energy comes from separation — even from potential friends — and that such separation is necessary before a coming together can take place. My hunch is that some of you graduating today have had discussions with your teachers and parents when you wanted them to appreciate more fully your own desire for a similar kind of separation, even while wanting to make sure they still cared about you. There are many parallels between HSC's commitment to controlling its own destiny and the value of that struggle for those of you who are students in the school.

Supporting this initial value is a second one which has served the school and its students well over the years — the value of being guided by, and informed by, a belief system which is clearly laid out and which forms the basis for making decisions about the ongoing life of the school. One pervasive and unmistakable component of this belief system is what could be called the egalitarian commitment, a belief in equality of persons regardless of background, status, or role in the school. Traditionally, this belief has extended to a critical examination of the concept of authority for authority's sake, and HSC has tolerated bureaucracy only when absolutely necessary, and sometimes not even then.

Wisdom is perhaps found in the strangest places. I remember seeing a saying on a bathroom wall in Minneapolis, Minnesota which reminds me of HSC. "Remember," it said, "it's always easier to apologize than to get permission." This constructive level of irreverence is, I believe, another cornerstone on which HSC has been built. While they may never say it in public, my hunch is that — at one time or another — George Foote, Ed Linehan, and Alice Mick — the three persons who have served as Facilitators at HSC for its first 14 years — would have felt comfortable writing that saying.

HSC has also been a school which has taken seriously the value of actively participating in issues of social justice. Through its course offerings, its internal structure, and the political activities of its staff, it has taken on, as part of its educational agenda, the issues of racism, sexism, and power politics. No school takes on such issues without discomfort, and ambivalence, but in this area, as in others, HSC has retained a commitment to face and participate fully in the social issues of our times.

Three other qualities of HSC stand out as important to mention today. First is the value of looking at school as a humanizing experience for both teachers and students. The quality of life and the emphasis placed on personal relationships among students and teachers has been a long-standing characteristic of HSC life. The constant struggle has been to insure that rules and regulations do not take on an impersonal life of their own — that they are created and enforced in such a way as to *serve* a caring personal relationship rather than impede it. HSC has taken the position that "we control the bureaucracy, the rules; they don't control us." *That* has been the intent of the school. To be sure, there are more rules and regulations than there were 14 years ago. Indeed, during this early time it sometimes seemed difficult for the school faculty to agree on *any* particular rules and regulations.

But this brings me to my next point. One of the qualities I have grown to admire about this school is *the degree to which HSC can adapt to changing times, changing circumstances, and changing demands without copping out on what it believes in.* My hunch is that having a pretty clear idea about what is important, about what the goals are, is necessary for this to happen. And I'm sure that many debates — some in public, some in private — go on about whether or not this policy or that policy is or is not consistent with what the school wants to be for its students. But, when push comes to shove, HSC has not confused adapting to things with copping out on what it believes education ought to be.

One final quality of the school bears mention: *the commitment to learning from, rather than hiding or ignoring, mistakes.* It should come as no surprise — perhaps particularly to seniors — that HSC — like every other school — doesn't always get it right. It has tried programs that haven't worked, and has offered advice to students they could probably have done just as well without. What has been uplifting about this is not that errors have been made — we all have done that, and will continue to do that — but that these errors have served as a basis for self-examination and self-improvement. There are many examples of how HSC had been strengthened through this process, and time does not permit discussion of them. But the lesson is clear that — like the healthy person — HSC has a tradition of reflecting on its shortcomings, using its experience to improve its functioning as a school, and caring about its mission.

The times have changed since HSC began, and many of the issues of the day have either been recast into different forms or seem to have receded in importance. HSC as a school has changed its location several times; some of its original structures — such as the idea of a daily seminar — have changed; and it now has to compete with other alternative schools for students — schools whose very existence was made possible through the success of HSC. But throughout its history, the school has worked toward maintaining its core values in the face of these many changes. It has participated, with integrity, in the issues of its time.

I have discussed the history of HSC, particularly the things which the school has stood for since its creation in September 1970 for two main reasons. First, because it is important to understand and appreciate the roots of the cultures we grow up in — and school constitutes one important culture. The second reason is because the values and hopes underlying the creation of this school *as a school* are ones which I hope you consider in terms of your own lives once you leave this school.

Consider that list: working toward controlling one's own life choices and decisions, with all the personal struggle and effort that entails; developing a perspective about what is important in life to guide your decision-making; being involved with your friends and your community in causes you believe are just; stressing the value of people over the efficiency of rules and regulations; being able to change with the times without fundamentally compromising what you believe in; and learning from your mistakes, however you define them. As I have come to understand the origins of HSC and its development as a school over the past 14 years, I see these values about the educational process reflected time and time again. All of them are legacies from this school to those who have graduated, those of you graduating today, and future graduates. If you take away from the school as individuals an understanding about the importance of those values which have energized HSC as a school, you should be proud, HSC should be proud, and the educational experiment which has just completed its 14th year will be even further vindicated.

One of the people I have come to admire and appreciate is a musician and labor organizer named Si Kahn. His songs speak to the hopes of people — what they aspire to, who they can become. The images in his songs come from his commitment to, and belief in, the values of controlling one's own destiny, one's own choices and options. But he knows that, when it comes to building a life, there is no free lunch, no easy ride. I'd like to close with a short and, I believe, appropriate verse of his.

It's not just what you're born with, it's what you choose to bear,
It's not how large your share is, but how much you can share,
It's not the fights you dream of, but those you really fought,
It's not just what you've given, it's what you do with what you got.

Let me offer my best wishes to the graduating class of 1984, and once again express my appreciation for the honor of speaking to you today.

References

Alderfer, C. P. (1980). Consulting to underbounded systems. In C. P. Alderfer & C. L. Cooper (Eds.), *Advances in experiential social processes, volume 2*. New York: Wiley.

Argyris, C. (1982). How learning and reasoning processes affect organizational change. In P. S. Goodman & Associates, *Change in organizations*. San Francisco: Jossey-Bass.

Barker, R. G. (1968). *Ecological Psychology*. Stanford, CA: Stanford University Press.

Bartunek, J. M., & Betters-Reed, B. L. (1987). The stages of organizational creation. *American Journal of Community Psychology, 15*, 287-304.

Boguslaw, R. (1965). *The new utopians: A study of system design and social change*. Englewood Cliffs, NJ: Prentice Hall.

Boyer, E. (1983). *High school: A report on secondary education in America*. New York: Harper & Row.

Bremer, J. (1971). *School without walls*. New York: Holt, Rinehart, & Winston.

Bronfenbrenner, U. (1979). *The ecology of human development: Experiments by nature and design*. Cambridge, MA: Harvard University Press.

Campbell, D., & Stanley, J. (1963). Experimental and quasi-experimental designs for research on teaching. In N. L. Gage (ed.), *Handbook of research on teaching*. New York: Rand McNally.

Caplan, N., & Nelson, S. (1973). On being useful: The nature and consequences of psychological research on social problems. *American Psychologist, 28*, 199-211.

Cherniss, C. (1972). *New settings in the university*. Unpublished doctoral dissertation, Yale University.

Cherniss, C. & Deegan, G. (in press). The creation of alternative settings. In J. Rappaport, & E. Seidman (eds.), *Handbook of community Psychology*. New York: Plenum.

Edwards, D. W. (1971). The development of a questionnaire method of measuring exploration preference. In M. J. Feldman (ed.), *Studies in psychotherapy and behavioral change: No. 2. Theory and research in community mental health*. Buffalo, New York: State University of New York at Buffalo.

Ellison, T. A. (1974). *High school in the community: The creation of an educational environment*. Unpublished senior thesis, Yale University, New Haven, CT.

Gold, B. & Miles, M. (1981). *Whose school is it anyway?* New York: Praeger.

Goldenberg, I. (1971). *Build me a mountain: Youth, poverty, and the creation of new settings*. Cambridge, MA: Maple Press.

Gooden, W. (1975). *The relationship between race, personality, and satisfaction in an alternative high school*. Unpublished manuscript, Yale University, New Haven, CT.

Gooden, W. (1976). *Racial issues and consultation in schools: A case example*. Unpublished manuscript, Yale University, New Haven, CT.

Goodlad, J. (1984). *A place called school: Prospects for the future*. New York: McGraw Hill.

Greiner, L. E. (1972). Evolution and revolution as organizations grow. *Harvard Business Review, 50*, 37-46.

Gruber, J. & Trickett, E. J. (1987). Can we empower others? The paradox of empowerment in the governing of an alternative public school. *American Journal of Community Psychology, 15*, 353-371.

Hackman, J. R. (1984). The transition that hasn't happened. Working paper, Yale School of Organization and Management, Yale University, New Haven, CT.

Hampel, R. L. (1986). *The last little citadel: America's high schools since 1940*. Boston: Houghton Mifflin.

Hawley, W. (1974). The possibilities of non-bureaucratic organizations. In W. Hawley & D. Rogers (eds.), *Improving the quality of urban management: Urban Annual Review*. Beverley Hills, CA: Sage Publications.

Hawley, W. D., McConahay, J. B., Frey-McConahay, S. F., Nelson, K., &

Gruber, J. E. (1973). *What if there were a school where they tried all the new ideas?: An evaluation of New Haven's High School in the Community.* Working paper, Center for the Study of Education, Yale University, New Haven, CT.

Kelly, J. G. (1970). The quest for valid preventive interventions. In J. Carter (ed.), *Current topics in clinical and community psychology.* New York: Academic Press.

Kelly, J. G. (1979). 'Tain't what you do, it's the way you do it. *American Journal of Community Psychology, 7,* 244-261.

Kelly, J. G. (1986). An ecological paradigm: Defining mental health consultation as a preventive service. *Prevention in Human Services, 4,* 1-36.

Levine, M. & Levine, A. (1970). *A social history of the helping professions: Clinic, court, school and community.* New York: Appleton-Century-Crofts.

Moos, R. H. (1974). *Evaluating treatment environments: A social ecological approach.* New York: Wiley.

Moos, R. W. (1979). *Evaluating educational environments.* San Francisco: Jossey-Bass.

Nash, S. (1970). Can we learn to govern? Establishing schools of choice. *American Journal of Orthopsychiatry, 40,* 606-614.

Perkins, D., Nieva, V., & Lawler, E. (1983). *Managing creation: The challenge of building a new organization.* New York: Wiley & Sons.

Powell, A. G., Farrar, E., & Cohen, D. K. (1985). *The shopping mall high school: Winners and losers in the educational marketplace.* Boston: Houghton Mifflin.

Powledge, F. (1970). *Model City.* New York: Simon & Schuster.

Reinharz, S. (1984). Alternative settings and social change. In K. Heller, R. H. Price, S. Reinharz, S. Riger, & A. Wandersman (eds.), *Psychology and community change* (2nd ed.). Homewood, Illinois: Dorsey Press.

Riger, S. (1984). Vehicles for empowerment: The case of feminist movement organizations. *Prevention in Human Services, 3,* 99-118.

Ryan, W. (1971). *Blaming the victim.* New York: Random House.

Sarason, S. B. (1972). *The creation of settings and the future societies.* San Francisco: Jossey-Bass.

Sarason, S. B. (1983). *Schooling in America: Scapegoat and salvation.* New York: Free Press.

Schreck, R. (1976). *An investigation of the relationship of perceived classroom social climate, perceived school organizational climate, and student personality.* Unpublished doctoral dissertation, University of Connecticut, Storrs, CT.

Schultz, D. (1971). *Evaluation of the Community Orientation Program.* Unpublished manuscript, Yale University, New Haven, CT.

Sizer, T. R. (1984). *Horace's compromise: The dilemma of the American high school.* Boston: Houghton Mifflin.

Smith, K. K. & Corse, S. J. (1986). The process of consultation: Critical issues. In F. V. Mannino, E. J. Trickett, M. F. Shore, M. G. Kidder, & G. Levin (eds.), *Handbook of mental health consultation.* Washington, DC: U. S. Government Printing Office.

Smith, L. & Keith, P. (1971). *Anatomy of educational innovation: An organizational analysis of an elementary school.* New York: Wiley & Sons.

Swidler, A. (1979). *Organization without authority: Dilemmas of social control in free schools.* Cambridge, MA: Harvard University Press.

Trickett, E. J. (1984). Towards a distinctive community psychology: An ecological metaphor for the conduct of community research and the nature of training. *American Journal of Community Psychology, 12,* 261-279.

Trickett, E. J. & Moos, R. H. (1973). The social environment of junior high and high school classrooms. *Journal of Educational Psychology, 65,* 93-102.

Trickett, E. J., McConahay, J. B., Phillips, D., & Ginter, M. A. (1985). Natural experiments and the educational context: The environment and effects of an alternative inner-city public school on adolescents. *American Journal of Community Psychology, 13,* 617-643.

Trickett, E. J., Kelly, J. G., & Vincent, T. A. (1985). The spirit of ecological inquiry in community research. In E. Susskind & D. C. Klein (eds.), *Community Research*. New York: Praeger.

Trickett, E. J., Kelly, J. G., & Todd, D. M. (1972). The social environment of the high school: Guidelines for individual change and organizational development. In S. Golann & C. Eisdorfer (eds.), *Handbook of community mental health*. New York: Appleton-Century-Crofts.

Van der Ven, A. H., Hudson, R., & Schroeder, D. M. (1984). Designing new business startups: Entreprenurial, organizational, and ecological considerations. *Journal of management, 10,* 87-107.

Notes

CHAPTER 1

1. It is not clear whether the ultimate demise of People Express is in any way a consequence of this commitment.

CHAPTER 2

1. The essay which follows was based on archival data and interviews with key informants (see Ellison, 1974 for a more thorough discussion of method). Because some of the events happened several years preceding the interviews, there is some lack of clarity about specific details and, on occasion, conflicting stories. In the latter case, both perspectives are given. All direct quotations used in the essay and not attributed to a published source were transcribed from tape recordings of the interviews that were held with key actors in the story.

2. The riot appeared to be organized. The head of the Black Student Union, who stood to catch most of the blame for the disturbance, calmly walked into the faculty cafeteria and sat down among the teachers before the riot began, creating his alibi.

3. Much of the controversy centered around Fred Harris, who was the leader of the very vocal Hill Parents' Association (HPA), in 1967 the most influential black organization in the city. Harris was arrested on October 26, 1967 on charges of possession of heroin and possession of stolen goods. He claimed the heroin had been planted in order to discredit him and the Hill Parents' Association. (A typewriter which had been stolen from a Yale student was also found. Harris said it had been given to him as a gift.) In November, while Harris was serving thirty days for his participation in a Hartford demonstration, he was recommended by some members of the New Haven Board of Education for a post on a committee which was searching for a site for a community college. The recommendation brought a strong negative reaction from the white community, led by Congressman Robert Giamo who called for the removal of the board members who had recommended Harris (*New Haven Register*, December 1, 1967). Then on December 24, five men were arrested on charges of conspiring to blow up "an important public building"— police headquarters. Four of the men were black. One was the

assistant leader of the Hill Parents' Association and another was an official of Community Progress, Inc. (CPI), New Haven's anti-poverty agency. (Explosives were found in a truck registered to the Hill Parents' Association.) The white community jumped on the fact that the city was funding revolutionary activities through CPI and through the HPA which had received a $32,000 grant to run its own community recreation program.

4. The presence of outsiders in the school was perceived to be such a problem that later on in the school year, the so-called "blue card plan" was adopted by the school system on a trial basis. Under the plan, legitimate students would be issued a different colored card every day and were required to show the proper colored card to get into the school. The plan was not long in operation.

5. It was estimated by a parents' committee that one third of the students in the New Haven Public Schools were functionally illiterate. Reading scores of freshmen at Wilbur Cross High School were used to illustrate the problem in the 1971 Title III grant application for funding for High School in the Community: 74% of the total sample fell below the ninth grade level. But 92% of the blacks (roughly 40% of the sample) fell below the ninth grade level. Seventy percent of the blacks fell below the fifth grade level.

6. Ahern, on leaving the room, put his arm around Foote and said, "You sonuva bitch, you suckered me into it, didn't you?"

7. The New Haven Educational Improvement Center was founded in 1969 to coordinate the efforts of seven colleges and universities in support of the New Haven Public Schools. The main support for EIC came from Yale University. Also involved were Southern Connecticut State College, South Central Community College and the University of Connecticut.

CHAPTER 3

1. This and following quotes are found in Appendix C., "Planning Grant for Restructuring Secondary Schools," submitted January 19, 1970 to the Connecticut State Board of Education by the New Haven Public Schools, Gerald Barbaresi, Superintendent.

2. One of the white male teachers involved in the spring planning decided not to teach at the new school the following fall, and a black female teacher was recruited, making the faculty composition for the first year of the school six women — three of whom were black — and four men.

3. Over time teachers at HSC not only joined the teachers union but became more and more influential, helping organize and lead teacher strikes in the mid 1970's and being in positions of leadership for the past several years.

CHAPTER 4

1. Lest the reader project the possibility of paranoia on such an interpretation, it should be stated that interviews with each succeeding head of the school and with several teachers who had been with the school since its early years independently discovered that the dynamic of "kill the leader" was widely acknowledged as part of the HSC culture. Indeed, it was not viewed as a totally destructive process, but one which kept the leader in a potentially responsive state of vigilance.

2. The report was based on perusal of documents and interviews with 30 students who had participated in the COP, 15 field supervisors, and 13 HSC teachers and interns.

3. Some of these students were later categorized as formal dropouts. Thus, this percentage should not be seen as independent of the number of formal dropouts cited earlier.

4. While the selection process combined random and representative sampling techniques, "those surveyed appeared to be a reasonably accurate cross section of the student body in terms of racial composition, sex, and academic performance. On all of these measures the characteristics of the sample differed no more than 8 percent from the distribution of these traits in the student body. . ."

5. Here the sampling process involved the selection of English classes representing a cross section of students "with the goal of obtaining a racial and academic mix of students similar to that of the entire school" (Hawley, et al., 1971, p. 78).

CHAPTER 5

1. The 1971-72 evaluation design lists over 15 goals covering a wide range of responsibilities. Included in this lengthy list were all facets of the teacher role previously defined, including: "Students will demonstrate progress in their courses *as measured by teacher evaluations*"; "*Teachers* will develop courses of study both for students planning to go to work and for those aiming at post-high school programs, i.e. college, apprenticeships"; "*teachers* will *develop courses*

of study which meet the needs of students deficient *in the basic skills*"; "*teachers* will develop a variety of approaches for *dealing with* the needs of students who are seriously deficient in their verbal and quantitative skills"; "*faculty involvement* in the COP (Community Oriented Program) will increase"; "*teachers* will participate in the management of their units through membership on the policy council of each unit and through regular attendance at faculty meetings"; "*teachers* will work with the guidance counselor to develop skills necessary to the guidance function of the seminar"; "each *seminar teacher* will take responsibility for assuring that the students assigned to his seminar receive the proper counseling and guidance with respect to course choices"; "*teachers* will develop a procedure for evaluating student performance"; "*teachers* will, prior to the opening of school, talk with HSC students and parents in their homes and will develop a curriculum suited to the needs and interests expressed in these discussions"; "*teachers* will contact the parents of each student in their seminars at least twice during the academic year"; and "teachers will be provided with the time and resources to develop their professional skills and sensitivity."

CHAPTER 6

1. In selecting out the COP and the Policy Council for more lengthy scrutiny we do not wish to diminish the importance of other role-related expressions of the empowerment ideology, particularly the idea of the seminar, the use of teacher as guidance counselor, and their role in supervising volunteer teachers who came into the school. During the three years covered in the current chapter, HSC devoted considerable energy to making these aspects of the school work. In contrast to these aspects of the teacher *role* at HSC, however, the COP and the Policy Council were specific *structures* embodying central educational ideas of the school. For this reason, and because they had different kinds of histories during this three year period, we have selected them for closer examination.

2. At this time, evaluations of such Office of Education funded programs were audited annually by an independent auditing firm. It is their report to The New Haven Board of Education which is quoted here.

CHAPTER 7

1. Pre-tests on a sample of students showed that this random selection process had been successful in creating two groups of students —

one attending HSC, one not — who were equivalent on all measured academic and personal variables when school began.

2. In reporting these and all other findings, the terms "more likely" or "significant differences" will be used. These terms mean that the difference between groups could have occurred by chance less than five times in a hundred.

3. It is important to remember that for the 71-72 and 72-73 years, students in the feeder schools consisted of those students who wanted to attend HSC but were unsuccessful in the lottery, and that the 73-74 feeder school students represented a matched comparison group. Thus, the comparisons are not between HSC and this feeder school per se, but between HSC and a control group or matched comparison group, which may or may not represent students at the feeder schools more generally.

4. To assess achievement, sections of the Educational Testing Service, Sequential Tests of Educational Progress (STEP), Series II, Form 2A were used. Reading was evaluated by Part I of Reading STEP Form 2A (comprehension of words and sentences). Writing was measured by Part I of English Expression STEP Form 2A (detecting errors in Grammar and Usage). Mathematics was evaluated through problems selected from the computation form 2A (fundamental operations with reading reduced to a minimum).

5. A more complete description of these scales and their psychometric properties is found in Trickett, McConahay, Phillips, and Ginter, 1985. All were developed specifically for the evaluation of the school, and all have adequate reliability to be used with confidence.

6. In testimony to the time-bound nature of such matters, it is clear that during this period "diversity" stood for leftist diversity.

CHAPTER 9

1. One might infer that, if Perkins, et al. were correct, the inclination to "kill the leader," so prevalent in egalitarian organizations, would have been particularly pronounced at this time. However, Foote recalled no special emphasis in this direction during this time; rather, his experience, dating from before the time school opened, was a recurrent concern with this dynamic which moderated only slightly over time. Both Ed Linehan and Alice Mick, subsequent facilitators at HSC, concurred in the enduring nature of this dynamic, while also agreeing that time had moderated, but by no means erased, it.

CHAPTER 10

1. In June 1984, the author was asked to deliver the graduation address to HSC's class of '84.

Biography

Edison J. Trickett, Ph.D., is Professor of Clinical and Community Psychology at the University of Maryland, College Park. With an extensive background in consultation and evaluation activity in public schools, he is well-known for his innovations in ecological approaches to intervention and the assessment of school environments. His current work involves the ecology of cultural pluralism as it affects research processes, methods, and questions relating to the high school adaptation of international students in the United States.

Index